Fragments of Wilderness City

black dog
publishing
london uk

Preface

This book has been long coming. The first version appeared in 1996, but only fleetingly, as when the first five thousand copies were delivered, four thousand five hundred and fifty were either blank, upside down, or unreadable. However, for those few who did receive one and it is still in one piece (which effectively means unopened) they have in their possession now a very rare collector's item.

This second version is a much more robust undertaking. The publisher ensured that. It not only contains considerably more projects, but includes also the contributions of five highly distinguished writers and critics; Richard Weston, Joseph Rykwert, John Worthington, Matthew Teague and Eddie Heathcote. Their insights have not only added immeasurably to the book's richness and diversity, but have prompted the thought that something of the subject's voice should be heard here too. Most architectural monographs are mute on this but I came to the conclusion that this might well reveal some of the more singular aspects of the methods and processes I use to derive visual form.

The Roman architect Vitruvius evolved his work through the filter of six design criteria; Order, Arrangement, Eurythmy, Symmetry, Propriety and Economy —for some unaccountable reason popularly reduced to three, Commodity, Firmness and Delight. I find that I need at least seven —the seven Cs I call them.

The first of my seven design criteria is arguably the most complex; the *Constraints*. These I take to include not just the myriad technical, legislative and statutory constraints that impact profoundly upon the form of the project, but the pragmatic requirements of the client—without which there is no project—and beyond that, his/her 'ambition'. Ultimately it is only the presence or absence of a client's ambition that determines whether a constraint will become an opportunity and a client a patron.

The second of my design criteria is the *Contiguity*—the context in both time and place, closer in meaning to the Genius Loci in its widest sense as interpreted by Norberg Schultz. This gives the form its 'rootedness'.

The third of my criteria is the *Content*—that the building should evidence both its purpose and its character and be empathetic with its content and the particularities of the culture in which it is situated. This gives the form its 'meaning'.

The fourth is the *Climate*—all the ecological and macro and micro environmental issues that impact upon mankind's being in the natural world—an ever more pressing physical and expressive issue as architecture becomes more globalised and climate change takes effect.

The fifth is the *Construction*—in essence all the materials and structure that go together to make a building but as these all have their own formal languages they carry powerful meanings that will echo down through the ages.

The sixth I call the *Choreography* —the work of the person (the conductor/architect) who brings all these criteria together and, by giving them a balance unique to each project, makes of them a singular work of significance. Over time this can generate a large and very personal formal vocabulary with huge expressive potential.

The seventh and final of the Criteria I offer hesitantly here as it is a fraught issue with few proponents and yet it is for me, as it was for Vitruvius, crucially important. It is that our buildings should look good; in fact more than just good, they should as far as is possible attain to beauty. I readily admit that beauty may be in the eye of the beholder but there is a universal acceptance that across time and cultures some buildings are transcendentally beautiful.

I call this last criteria therefore *Concinnity*, not beauty, as to distance it from the sentimental. Concinnity is the harmony of the parts—the relationship of the things that together make up the whole. By putting Concinnity last I hope thereby to make it the first of the seven "Cs" to be remembered.

Thus there are two essays here by me, one called "Beauty is in the Eye of the Beholder"; and the other "Wilderness City". This latter is an ongoing study and its researches permeate every project. The book's title *Fragments of Wilderness City* alludes to the importance of this in my work.

The final part of the book is the Chronology. Originally conceived as a technical device whereby to include projects not analysed elsewhere, it subsequently developed a life of its own and is now almost autobiographical, chronicling all the many influences, lines of development, and the detours, that have led ultimately to a body of work like this.

Bryan Avery
Avery Associates Architects:
London: 2011

Contents

Chapter 1

An Introduction to the Work of Bryan Avery

by Richard Weston

Bryan Avery is a quintessentially English architect, but the innovative cladding and kit-of-parts structure of the Museum of the Moving Image (MOMI) that brought him to national attention was all too readily pigeon-holed as an ingenious example of that British speciality "High-Tech".

In part this was fair: details of aircraft and ships rub shoulders with architecture and landscape in Avery's sketchbooks, and from his student days he had been fascinated by the industrialisation of building and the potential of new materials.

But there was far more to MOMI than constructional ingenuity; not least an almost uncanny ability to cope with difficult sites. Amidst the cramped, unprepossessing location under Waterloo Bridge Avery sought to regulate the construction with 'ideal' geometric proportions and, simultaneously, to forge an architectural language that echoed both the image-conscious glamour of film and the serial repetition of the still frames from which moving images are conjured.

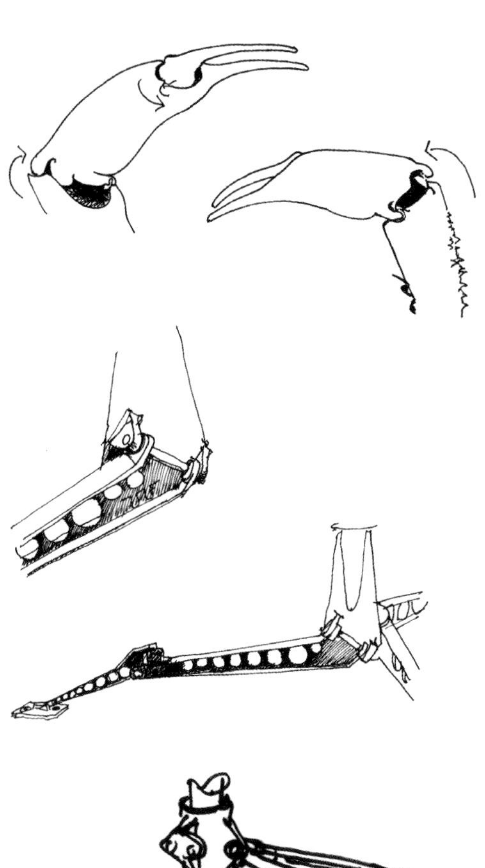

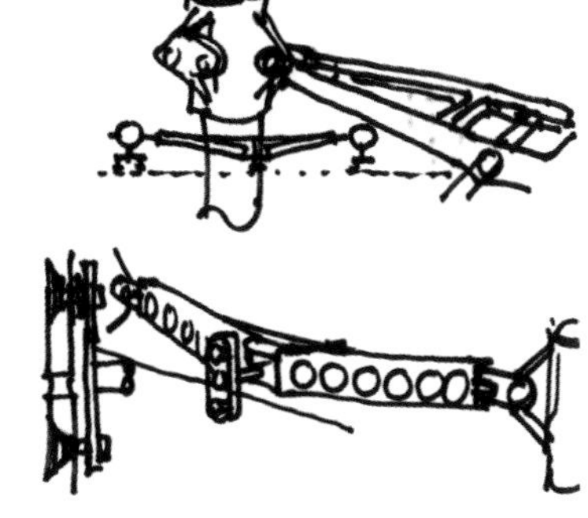

This Page
Clockwise from top left:
Sketches; Schinkel's Altes Museum; Berlin:
Aircraft undercarriage:
Crab's claws:
Lightweight military tripod:
MOMI structural sketch details 1984–1988:
MOMI photos; gallery and eye/lens roof lights 1988.
Opposite Page
MOMI facade photo

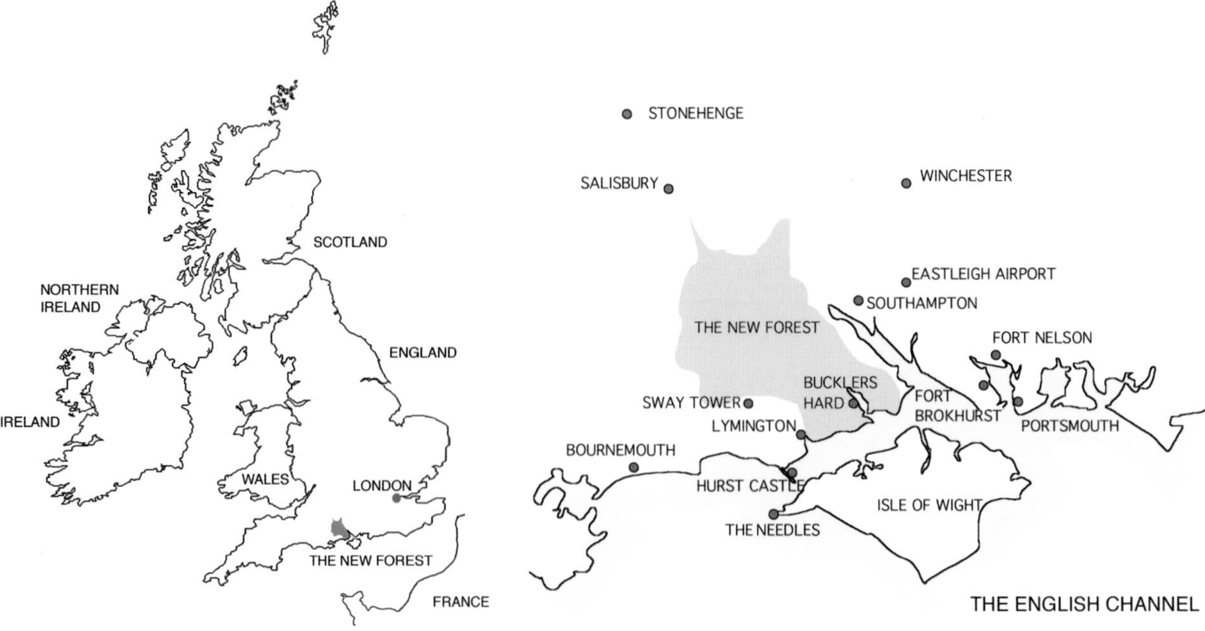

What is most revealing is not so much that this improbable synthesis was achieved, but that it was attempted at all—and it is in such conjunctions of apparent opposites that clues to understanding Avery's at times bewilderingly various output are to be found. Exploring 'the Englishness of English art' Nikolaus Pevsner suggested that the uniqueness of the national sensibility lay in the ability to fuse a pragmatic approach with the contradictory delight of fantasy and the irrational. One thinks immediately of the crowded intricacies of Sir John Soane's house that were matched, at the Bank of England, by some of the most eloquently blank walls in the history of architecture. Or of Lord Burlington, whose Chiswick House and grounds married Palladian clarity to the dawning of the Picturesque style of gardening—whose relaxed, rambling manner would in turn influence Soane and, later, yield the rigorous functional planning, responsive to nuances of use and orientation, of the English Free Style.

That Avery delights in similar, seemingly contradictory impulses will become apparent throughout this book. Equally clear is his refusal to accept the widespread narrowing of the architect's role as innovator across every scale, from chairs to city planning, that is typical of our times. The Victorians, by contrast, saw nothing odd in a "gardener" designing what subsequently became the world's most compelling example of industrialised building. Paxton's Crystal Palace may have been exceptional in scale, but it was typical in conception, in its delight in new technologies and in its designer's determination to break new ground.

A similar spirit of adventure informed a less well known Victorian folly, completed in 1886, that lives large in Avery's memory. Known today as Sway Tower, it rises to more than 60 metres above the New Forest where Avery was brought up, and was the work of the wealthy spiritualist lawyer, Andrew Peterson. The alliance of square shaft and hexagonal stair turret offered Avery an early lesson in the elemental power of geometrically controlled form, and both were capped with domed 'hats' that seem to anticipate Lutyens' work in India—not altogether coincidentally, perhaps, because Peterson had served in the Raj and discovered there concrete, practically unknown in England at the time, with which his tower was built. Doubling as mausoleum and launch-pad to the next world, Peterson's tower soared high above the New Forest, home to pagan worship long after England had been Christianised, a place, as Philip Hoare has written, "of sanctuary, mystery and magical transformation... our lost and ancient Eden".

If Jay Appleton's contention that designed landscapes around the world are unconscious recreations of the qualities of "prospect and refuge" to which the earliest humans were adapted on the plains of Africa, then the New Forest, with its striking contrast between open heathland and tight thickets of trees, offers England's closest analogue of that natural Eden. It is not quite so surprising, therefore, that the primal contrast between architecture and nature encountered at Peterson's tower would eventually serve as an inspiration for Avery's ongoing project for a Wilderness City (Chapter 2), that envisages a wholesale restructuring of our sprawling, increasingly formless occupation of the land into a sharp contrast between compacted settlements and restored wilds.

This Page
Above left: Map of the United Kingdom.
Above right: Map of the New Forest.

Opposite Page
Top: Sketch of the savannah, Kenya.
Middle left: Watercolour of Lymington 1962.
Bottom left: The New Forest.
Far right (top): Watercolour of forest hamlet (Pilley) 1961.
Far right (smaller images)
Clockwise from top left:
Oil painting; Hurst Castle and Fort Albert, Isle of Wight 1961;
Sway Tower;
Hurst Castle;
The Needles;
Forest stream;
Fort Brockhurst.

Such formative experiences are often, in the long run, more decisive in the development of a genuinely original talent than a formal education.

Avery's schooling followed, initially at least, a conventional path, courtesy of the Leicester College of Art—which, when he enrolled in 1962—was amongst the country's most highly regarded. The course combined a traditional, almost Beaux Arts approach to composition with a Bauhaus-inspired attention to learning to work in the 'nature' of materials.

While at Leicester Avery became keenly interested in the aesthetic ideas of Wilhelm Worringer, which centred on the idea of 'empathy', and his tutors included David Greene, already famed as a member of the Archigram group, and the celebrated historian of theatres, Richard Leacroft, whose use of cut-away axonometric drawings to explain the workings of complex buildings left an indelible mark. This was doubtless helped by the fact that architecture's most celebrated 'built axonometric', Stirling and Gowan's Engineering Building, was just a mile up the road at Leicester University—and may well also have been a stimulus to Avery's lifelong fascination with crystalline glass.

It can be dangerous to read too much into student work, but in Avery's case some of his earliest projects do seem like pointers to the future. There was an adventurous essay in concrete shell construction that could almost pass muster as an example of today's 'blobitecture', while a third year design for a boat club contains hints of much that was to come.

Formed with a triangulated prefabricated structure, it featured—like many of the projects documented here—faceted glazing, geometrically controlled proportions and picturesque siting, artfully rendered in a watercolour style Avery had mastered, and publicly exhibited, as a schoolboy.

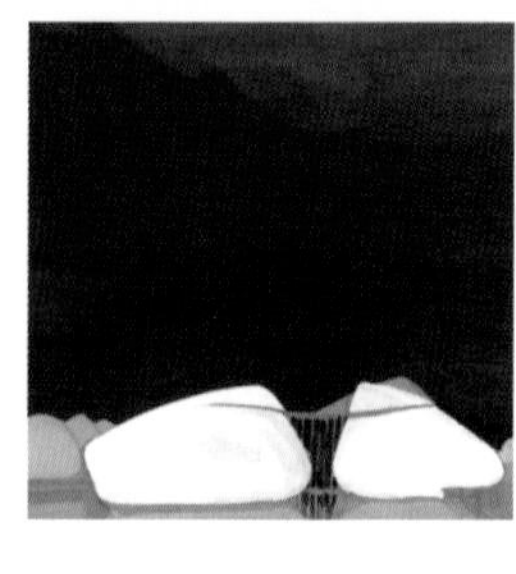

Equally, given his holistic concerns, it seems entirely appropriate that Avery should use a Travel Award from the local branch of the RIBA not to study the compositional or technical aspects of architecture that preoccupied him in the studio, but to head off in search of alpine villages to explore "The Relationship of Architecture to the Environment": a determination to address what are now commonly termed "environmental issues" informed his work well before these imperatives became inescapable.

During his time at Leicester Avery also developed what has proved to be a lifelong admiration for the buildings of Frank Lloyd Wright. But although his library now boasts some 30 books on the American master, the lessons

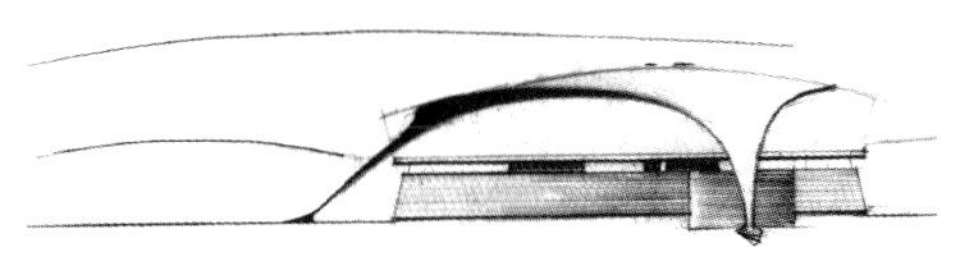

This Page
Third Year Project: Sailing Club: Swithland Reservoir; Leicester 1964. *Above:* The first contiguity study referencing the soft rounded hills and bridge arches. *Left:* The second contiguity study referencing the trees and reflections on the lake, 1964 (p. 138).
Middle: diagrammatic perspective showing the diagrid, faceted glazing and the golden rectangle proportion.
Bottom: Watercolour of Zernez, Switzerland in the Worringer manner 1964.

Opposite Page
Top: Falling Water; Frank Lloyd Wright.
Upper middle: The Engineering Building, Leicester by Stirling and Gowan.
Lower middle: Second year project Holiday Centre 1963.
Bottom: Sketch of house at Scuol, Switzerland, with Piz Lischana behind.

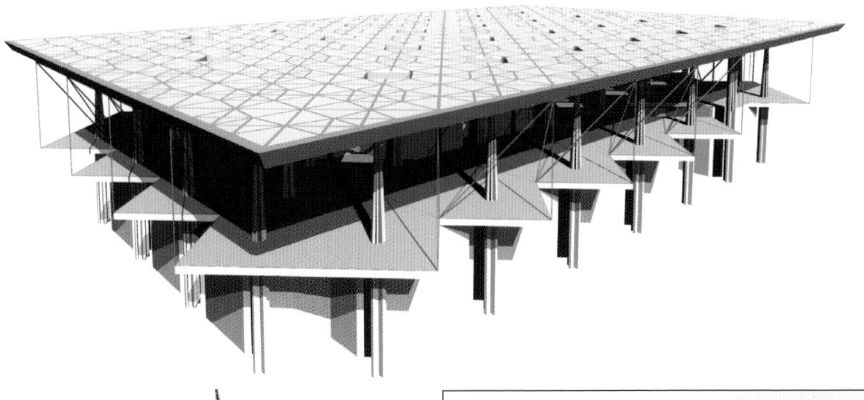

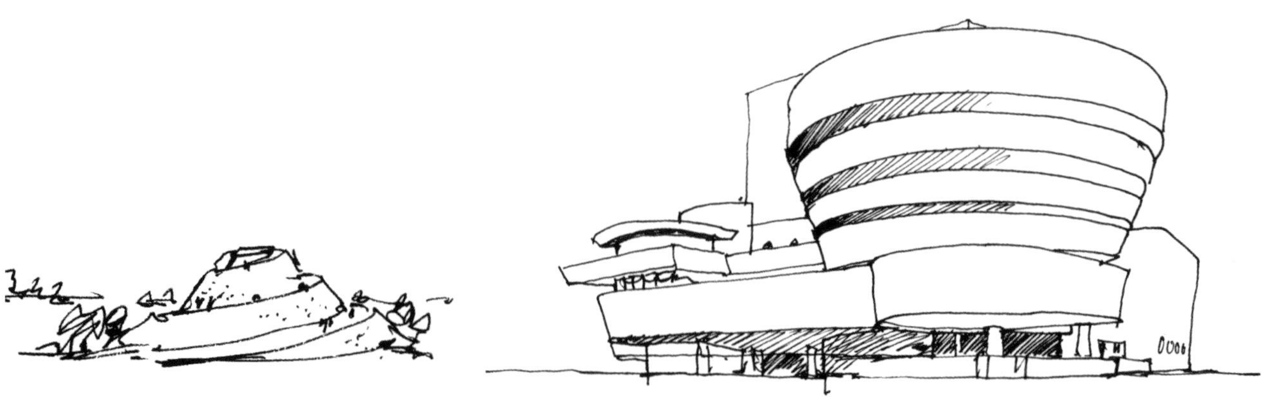

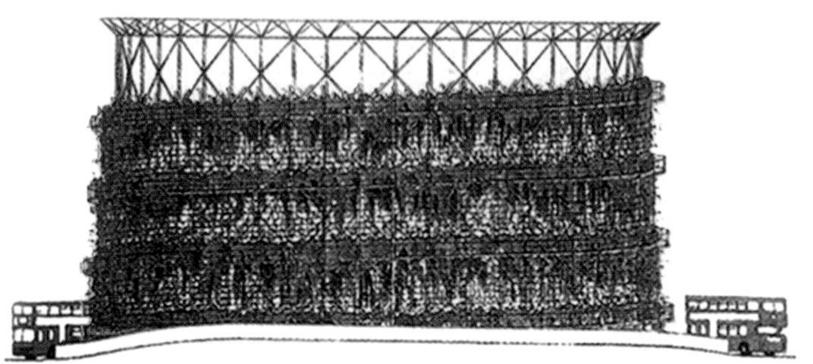

drawn from his work have now been so completely absorbed as to escape easy recognition. He shares with Wright an occasional fascination with unorthodox triangular geometries, and a debt to the Prairie Houses can, perhaps, be discerned in the stratified composition of an early project for an office building at Heathrow. Beyond this, the connections seem remote, unless the obvious Neolithic precedents for the spiralling mounds proposed for the Millennium site at Greenwich (p. 151) and in Green Park left) find, like the great drum of London's IMAX cinema (left), an echo in the 'automobile objective' that Wright designed for Gordon Strong—which, of course, proved to be the unwitting primer for the Guggenheim Museum.

After Leicester, Avery decided to pursue a unique, then newly established Masters course in architectural history and theory at Essex University. It was dominated by three academics who would subsequently become major figures in architectural education: Joseph Rykwert (Chapter 3), Dalibor Vesely and George Baird. Grounded in French and German theory, in particular the ideas of Roland Barthes and the phenomenology of Merleau-Ponty and Martin Heidegger (later to prove so widely influential), the course emphasised the 'relatedness' of architecture to the human subject, to programmatic content, and to

physical and social contexts.

In addition to a heavy dose of theory, uncommon in mainstream education at the time, Essex also deepened Avery's love of history by introducing him to works that would resonate through his career. It was there that he fell in love with circular buildings such as San Stefano Rotundo, Santa Constanza and Bramante's Tempietto in Rome, not to mention the more exotic delights of the Teatro Maritimo at Hadrian's Villa, which later served as primers for projects as various as the Dubai IMAX cinema (p. 168) and the small but powerful arts building at Oakham School (p. 160). In a similar way, an unbuilt theatre by Inigo Jones eventually provided the springboard for the Vanburgh Theatre at RADA, (p. 108) and the space-expanding mirrors of the Salle des Glaces at Versailles came to mind when renewing the performance space in the Royal Overseas League. (pp. 170–171)

This Page
Top left: Baptistery Duomo and Campanile, Pisa;
Middle left: Santa Constanza, Rome;
Top right: The Tempietto; Bramante; Rome;
Middle right: San Stefano Rotundo; Rome.
Right: Island Pavilion, Hadrian's Villa, Rome.

Opposite Page
Top left and upper middle: The Spiral Mound, Green Park 1996.
Top right: The Guggenheim museum; New York; Frank Lloyd Wright.
Lower middle: The IMAX Cinema; early design 1991–1992.
Bottom: Model; office building; Heathrow 1972–1974.

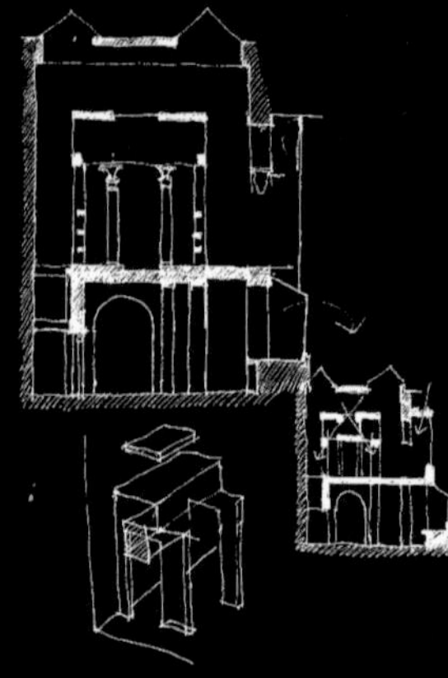

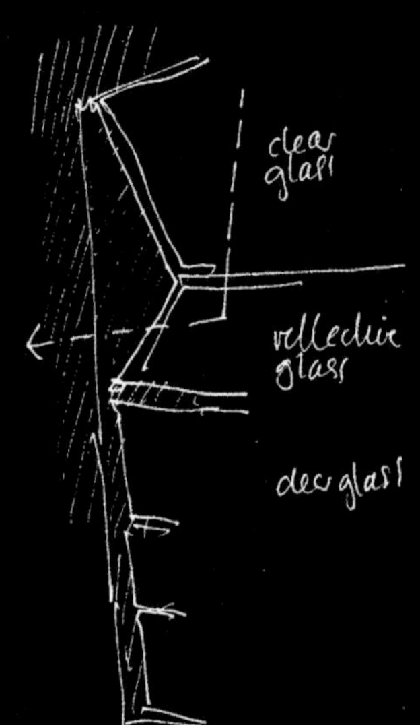

It was at Essex, also, that Avery developed his fascination with the work of Soane, which epitomises the contention of that influential theorist of the English landscape garden, the poet Alexander Pope, that "He gains all points who pleasingly confounds, / surprises, varies, and conceals the bounds". By hiding structure, slashing unexpected vistas through his sections, concealing sources of natural light and multiplying the resulting effects with mirrors,

Soane brought to architecture the confounding variety of the Picturesque landscape—and bequeathed to Avery a repertoire of ideas that have informed many of his most successful built projects.

From the mirror-enhanced interiors of Plantation House (pp. 68–69, 140) and Charterhouse Mews (pp. 66–67, 144) where, in the latter, reflections transform a space with 2:1 proportions into a calm 'virtual' cube—to the drama of the taut cleft between the swelling auditoria at RADA that is animated, on mid-summer's day, by a raking shaft of sun that slices through the space to touch the bust of George Bernard Shaw, Soane's influence is pervasive.

The often bewildering variety of Avery's work is not, however, attributable solely to his wide-ranging love of architectural history.

Far from indulging in some form of gratuitous postmodern eclecticism, he has always sought to address problems on their own terms, not his—or at least 'not his' in the way that is now almost ubiquitously understood: by passing them through the filter of a personal style.

Avery's 'style' is not a predetermined formal language, but a way of working that begins with a close interrogation of brief and site, seeking to find there the stimulus for something new and particular. In this he can also be seen to be following Alexander Pope's most celebrated advice: "consult the genius of the place in all".

This Page
Top: Three sketches from John Soane's House, London.
Right, above: RADA 1994–2000: The Cleft; view from an oriel window.
Right: RADA: The Cleft approaching the summer solstice.
Above left: RADA: The sun touching the base of the statue of George Bernard Shaw at the summer solstice.
Opposite Page
The Cleft.

For Avery, the 'in all' implications of programme and site are notably far-reaching, embracing not only the physical character of the locale, but also its 'spirit', mediated by imagination and memory—an approach exemplified in the later writings of Christian Norberg-Schulz. Avery is always alert to inflections that tie project to place.

The formal repertoire ranges from abstractions derived from the immediate landscape—as, for example, in the cliff-like forms proposed for the Turner Museum at Margate (p. 157) and as a line of exploration for a theatre in nearby Folkestone (p. 168) to a rich range of responses to complex urban sites.

In the competition design for the Channel 4 TV Headquarters, for example, (p. 144) the principal facade was conceived as an almost independent screen of Avery's familiar angled glazing (of which more later); the secondary side elevations were to be 'greened' with foliage; and to the rear an arc of stone addressed a civilised crescent of cafes and shops in an elegant 1:1 proportion of width to height.

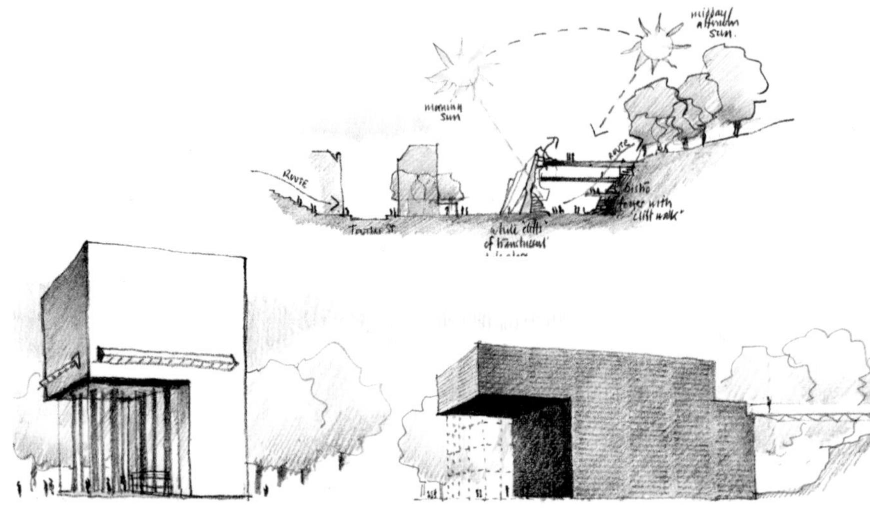

This Page
Top left: Conceptual sketch of the cliff forms, Margate 2001.
Top right: Diagram of the gallery as 'cave'; Margate.
Middle: Concept model, Margate.
Bottom (top): Section of the cliff-form at the Folkstone Theatre 2005.
Bottom (right): Scheme referencing the local black tar-painted fisherman's houses.
Bottom (left): Scheme referencing the re-planted public park behind the site.

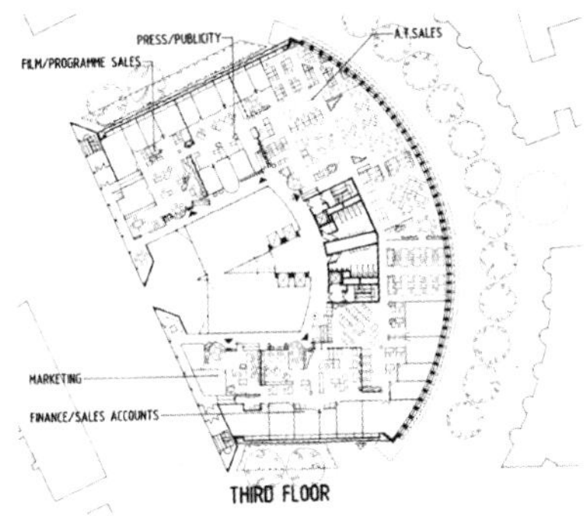

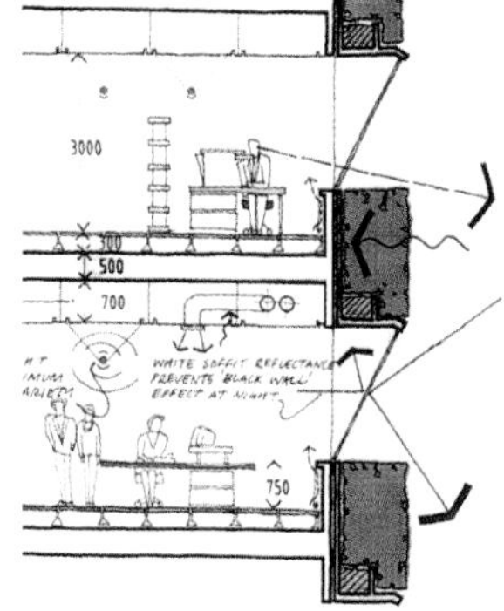

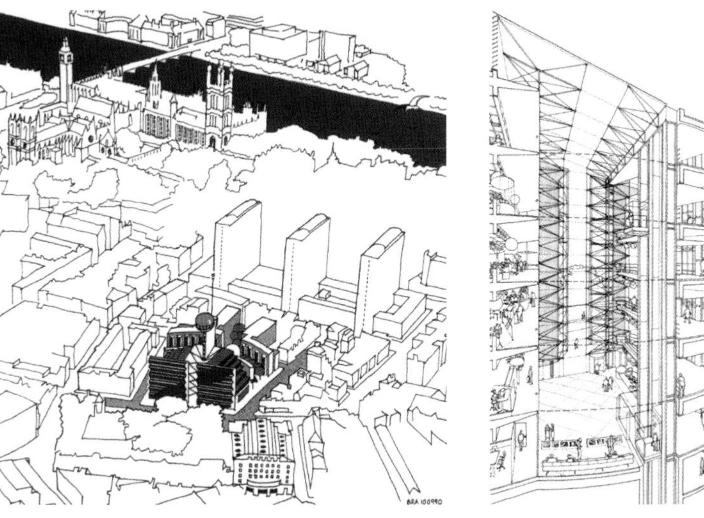

This Page
Clockwise from top left:
Sketch; Marine Patrol Craft.
Channel 4 Headquarters; 1990:
The rear quadrant;
Typical floor plan;
Developed section through planter facade;
Section through atrium;
Aerial concept drawing;
Perspective from Horseferry Road.

A recent project for offices adjacent to the Old Bailey (p. 172) is similarly inflected to mediate the contrasting scales of the adjacent courts and a surviving fragment of the City's Roman wall to the rear, generating in the process an intriguingly bent atrium. The principal elevation is furnished with groups of balcony-like projecting windows, while to the rear deeply recessed openings maintain vision through a plant-covered wall courtesy of a boldly projecting stainless steel 'ruff'.

Finally, at Neathouse Place, (pp. 70–77, 89–92, 147) where most architects, like its original designers, would see the need only for a 'universal' shaft articulated, if at all, by considerations of solar control, Avery again deployed two contrasting window forms. Addressing Victoria Station is the angled glazing explored in several earlier projects, while to the other side you discover a procession of faceted oriels. In both, unusually for an office building, technical issues—daylight penetration and solar control—and experiential opportunities, are combined: the oriels draw the eye towards a glimpse of nearby Westminster Cathedral, while the unequal planes of the angled glazing are calculated to frame the sky and direct the gaze down to the public space of the street below.

Avery's love of angled glazing as a counterpoint to an opaque building

This Page
Main picture: the continguity—the new/old dialalogue
Top left: 7–10 Old Bailey 2006–2009; First design study with raked solar control glazing.
Above top: Detail of the window oriels.
Above: View of the oriels juxtaposed to the Court entrance.

Opposite Page
Top: Cross-section, 7–10 Old Bailey.
Far right, top: Raked glazing at No. 1 Neathouse Place (1994–1996).
Far right, middle: Eastern elevation, zig-zag glazing, No. 1 Neathouse Place.
Far right, bottom: Inside view of zig-zag glazing.

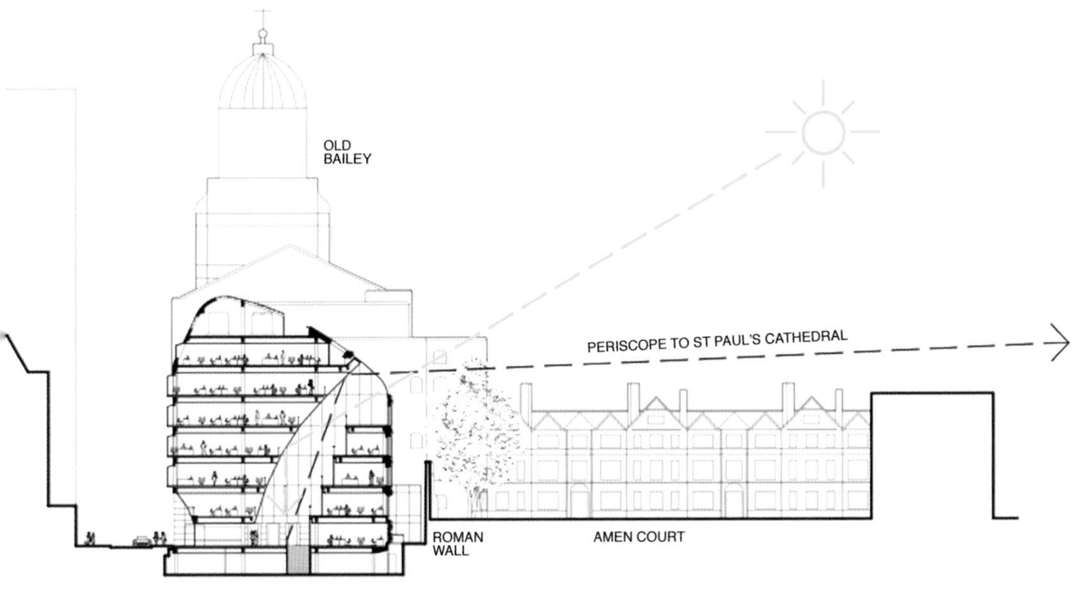
OLD
BAILEY
PERISCOPE TO ST PAUL'S CATHEDRAL
ROMAN
WALL
AMEN COURT

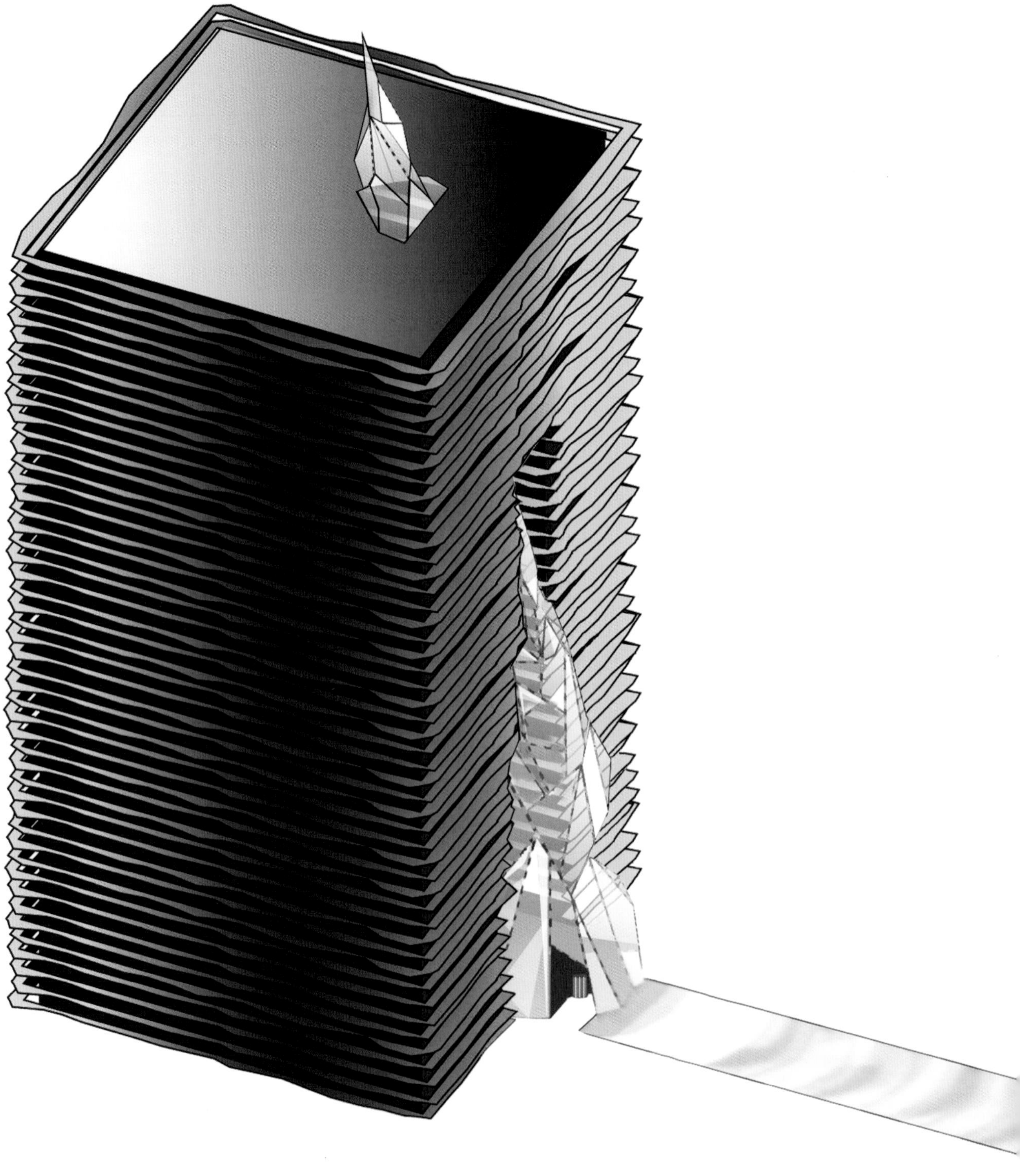

mass may, ultimately, derive from Stirling and Gowan's Leicester Engineering Building (p. 6 and 134), but it has developed far beyond these formal origins into one of the many ways in which he seeks to interrelate buildings and users. Not least amongst these is an almost atavistic desire to engage our bodies and cultural memories in the shaping and experience of architecture: hence the continual renewing of his vision of Wilderness City and love of large-scale earthworks. And hence, also, his fascination with buildings conceived as surrogates for, or abstractions of, land forms.

Several urban projects—one thinks immediately of the competition designs for the Cardiff Opera House (p. 147 and right) and Museum of Scotland (p. 145)—appear as constructed landscapes reminiscent of both Jørn Utzon's platforms and James Stirling's German museum designs of the 1970s, while Avery's abstractions of land forms range from the almost minimalist expression of a new office building near Euston Station (Regents Place: See left and right and p. 164), rendered as a sedimentary block of stone riven by a quartz vein, to the place-specific narrative developed for a Central Area Development in Kolkata in India (pp. 166–167 and right). There, the complex was cast as an abstract representation of the floodplains, tea-growing terraces and snow-capped Himalayas of West Bengal. What is implicit, ultimately, in all these projects is an invitation, in the heart of the city, to renew our relationship with Nature, a relationship at once physical and cerebral whose importance and scope Avery came to understand in the New Forest and which is central to his most potent theoretical projects, from Wilderness City to the vision of a network of Ecological Beacons (pp. 86–87, 148) to stand watch, like ancient megaliths, over our global environmental impacts.

Opposite Page
Isometric view of Regents Place office tower, 2003.

This Page
Top: The Cardiff Opera House sketch 1994.
Middle: Sketch, Regents Place office tower, 2003.
Bottom: Sketch, Kolkata New Town, India

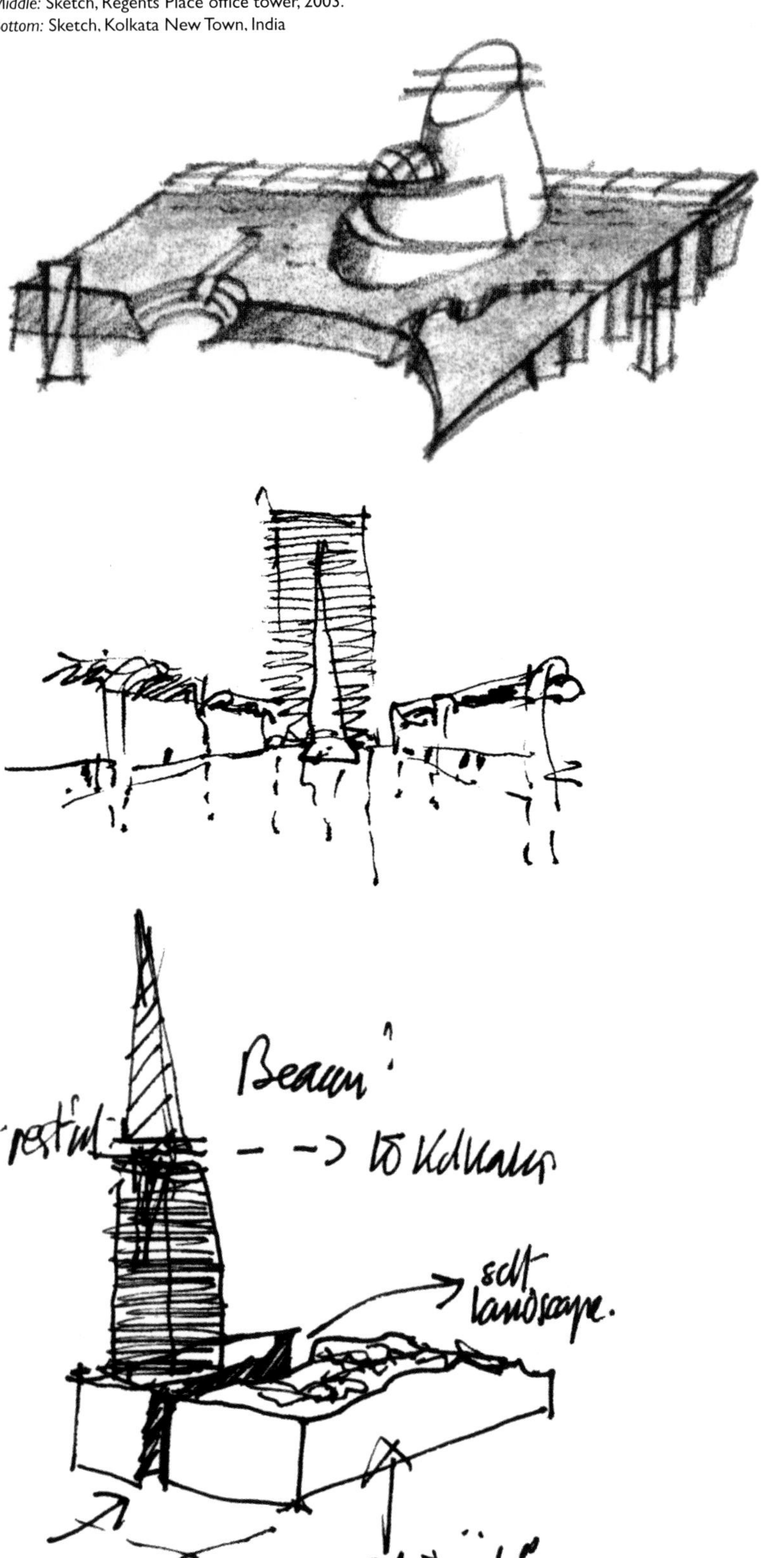

Avery's Romantic love of landscape is matched by a Classical concern with systems of proportion—rare amongst contemporary architects but evident, as we have already noted, since his student work. He breathed surprising life into this perennially vexed issue with an original and provocative speculation—first published in the Architectural Review and reprinted here (Chapter 6 p. 95)—about the possibility that the seemingly universal appeal of the Golden Rectangle may lie in the physical economy of human vision.

The exigencies of actual building have, throughout history, impeded the construction of 'ideally' proportioned buildings and Avery's work, so frequently involved with existing structures and complex urban sites, is no exception.

His first built project, the British Carpet Trade Centre 1976–1978, used 1:1 and 2:1 proportions throughout (opposite and p. 136) but the unrealised Rank Xerox Headquarters (right and pp. 64–65, 145) of 1991 promised his most thoroughgoing exercise in geometric control, with such rhythms ordering everything from the intervals between buildings to the proportions of spaces and details. And Pantheon-like, the volume of the Jerwood Theatre at RADA (pp. 104–111, 148) is described by a double sphere, while the new elevation forms a Golden Rectangle. For the most part, however, it is only in small interiors—such as those in Plantation House (pp. 68–69, 140) and Charterhouse Mews (pp. 66–67, 144) and in the detailing of elements such as windows that he has been able to achieve his ideal.

Most architects today eschew such systems, and yet we seem to sense in spaces conceived in this way, from the grandeur of the Pantheon to Sigurd Lewerentz's diminutive Resurrection Chapel at Stockholm's Woodland Crematorium, a life-enhancing calm and composure. We may no longer believe that our bodies are shadows of some ideal geometric figure—as famously depicted by Leonardo da Vinci—but the feeling of gentle control and inter-relatedness that carefully studied proportions can bring has been a recurring objective for those in search of beauty and that attendant reciprocity between subject and object that lies at the heart of aesthetic experience.

For the Neo-Platonists of the Renaissance, 'ideal' geometries were means to deeply human ends, and similar concerns inform Bryan Avery's work across the entire scale of architectural endeavour. His range is almost unique in recent British, if not world architecture, and he has won acclaim for graphic and product design as well as buildings and planning.

Inventions such as the now ubiquitous external up-downlighter were quickly exploited by manufacturers in contravention of his patent—confirming the impossibility, without vast financial resources, of protecting something so self-evidently useful.

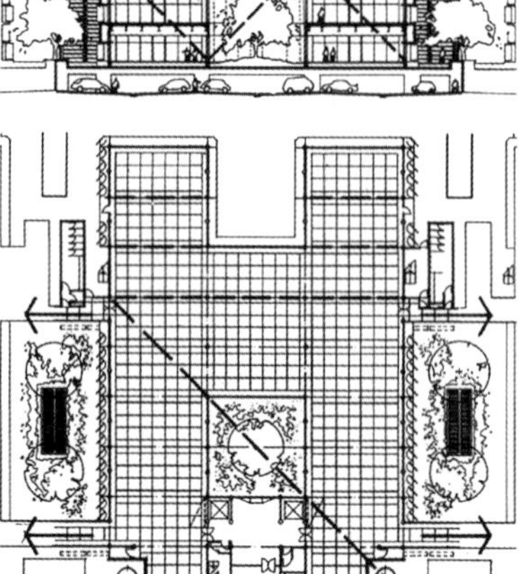

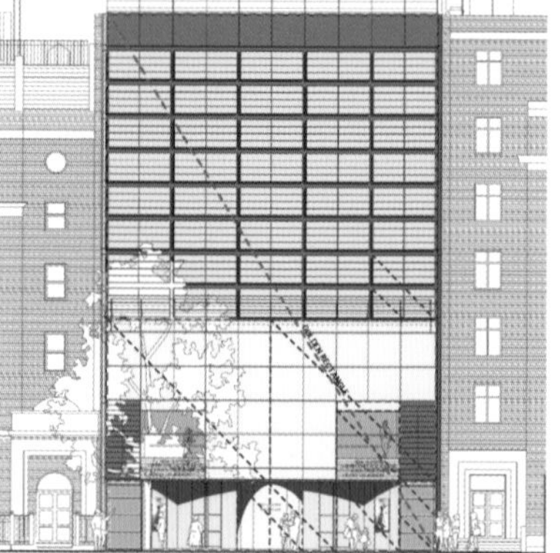

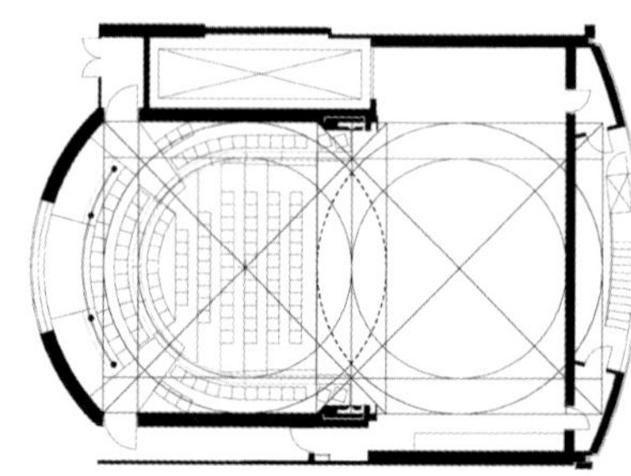

This Page
Right; from top down:
Rank Xerox UK headquarters1991, typical facade;
Rank Xerox, plan and cross-section;
RADA, the Malet Street elevation and proportional diagram 1994–2000;
RADA, the Jerwood Vanbrugh auditorium plan.

Opposite Page
Upper half: Interior photographs of the British Carpet Trade Centre.
Lower half: Internal elevations and proportional diagrams.

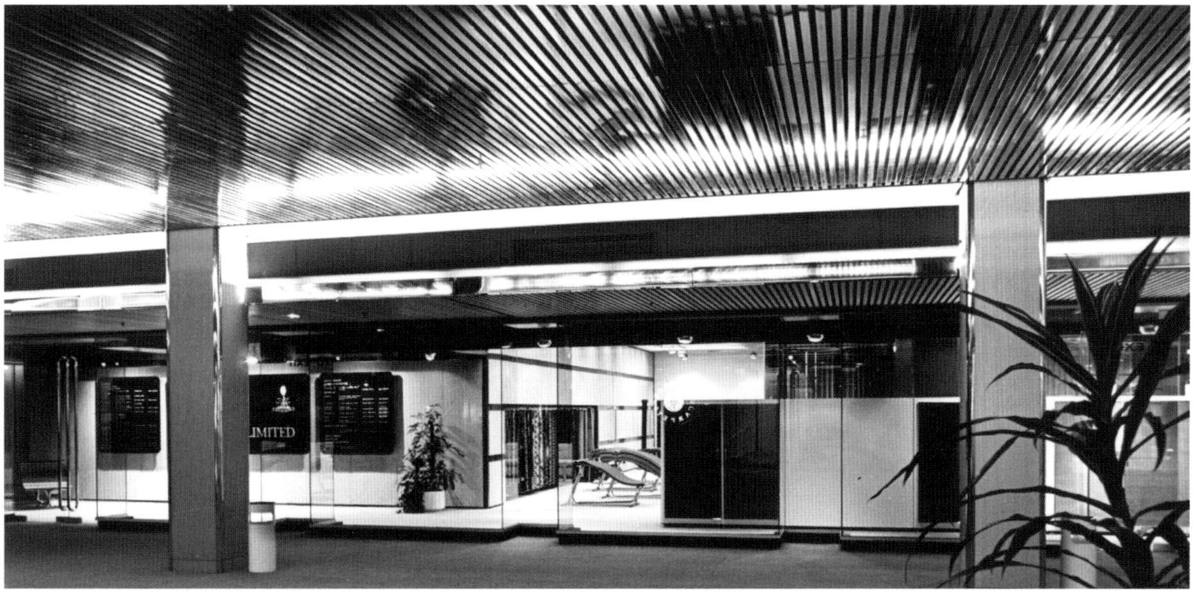
LIMITED

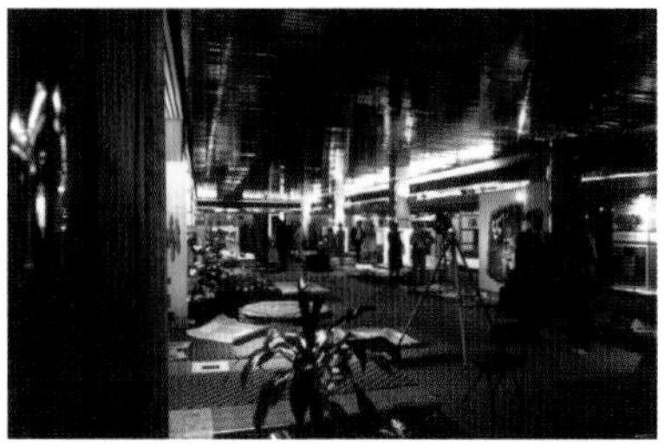

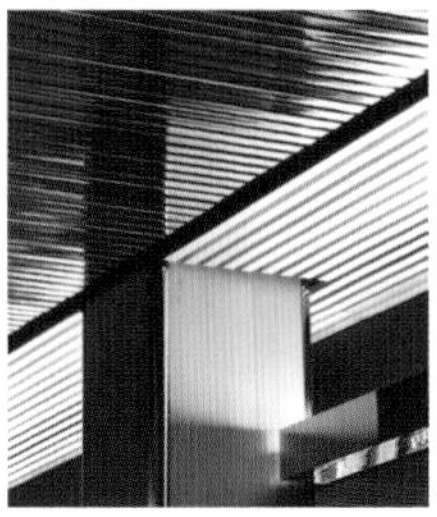

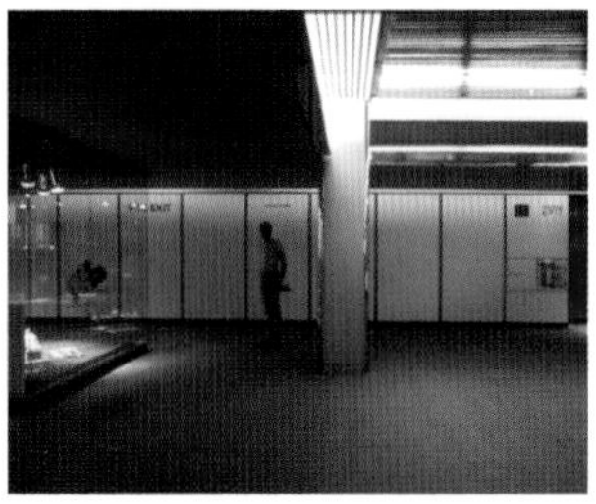

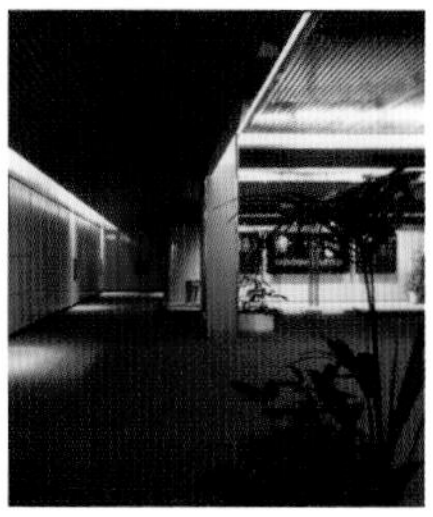

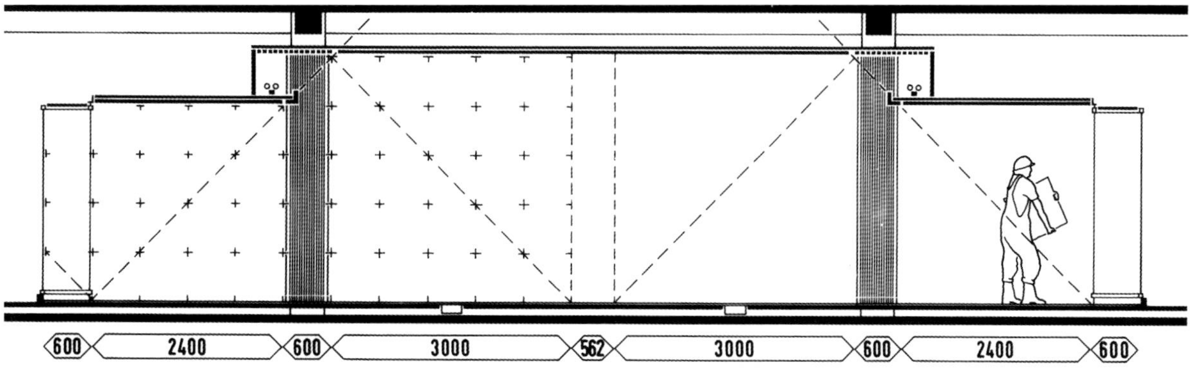
600
2400
600
3000
562
3000
600
2400
600

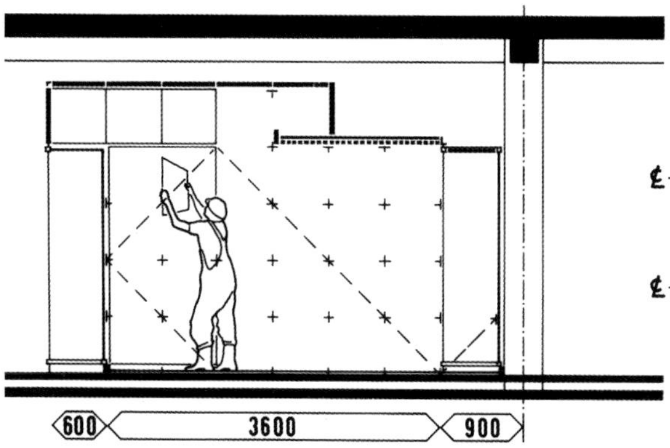
600
3600
900

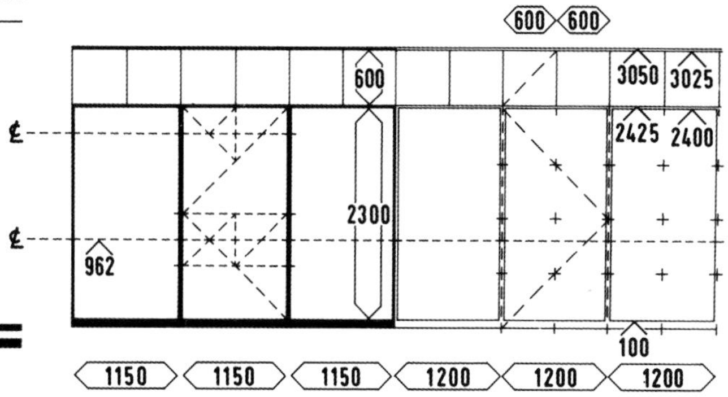
600
600
600
3050
3025
2425
2400
2300
962
100
1150
1150
1150
1200
1200
1200

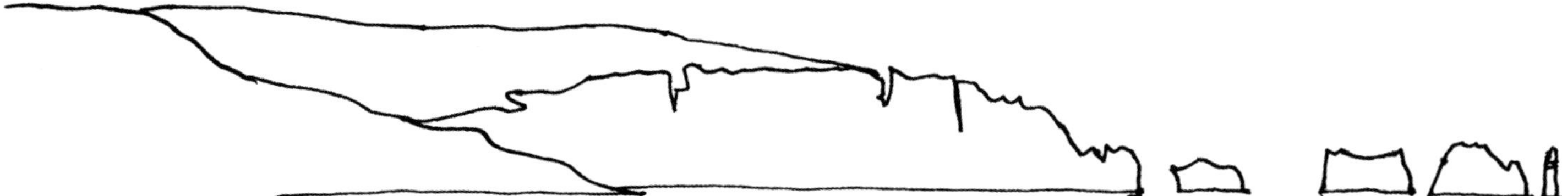

Other ideas, like Wilderness City, probably struck many as hopelessly ambitious when first proposed, and attracted interest from geographers before architects. 20 years on, with the industrialisation of the Far East already underway and the global environmental crisis looming large in the collective consciousness, his ideas on urban intensification and rural de-settlement now seem universally and urgently relevant.

In an era of specialisation, when architects increasingly devote themselves to a particular sector of work such as housing, health or education, Avery's eagerness to range freely within and beyond the supposed limits of the discipline is both refreshing and, one suspects, as professionally precarious as his refusal to promote a 'signature' style.

But such, surely, was always the way of the twentieth century's major architects: what they envisaged was a new world, not merely new buildings, a "total architecture"—to borrow a phrase from Walter Gropius—whose scope embraced every aspect of how we construct a shared world. Ironically, in countries dominated by ephemeral media and the machinations of global capital, the scope of architecture seems to be diminishing just as rapidly as the societal and environmental challenges are expanding.

Against this background, Avery's work remains a beacon of hope, inviting us to reject the foreclosing of the discipline around questions of style, and to marshal our technical and aesthetic resources to address the major issues of our time.

No single project, arguably, better sums up Avery's lifelong concerns than his design for the British Pavilion at the Shanghai Expo 2010 (for Avery's description of this see the footnote on p. 26).

Responding to the Expo's theme of "better city, better life", Avery proposed a poetic distillation of Britain's most influential contribution to urbanism and landscape—the Garden City and Landscape Garden. The support spaces were to be housed in an ivy-covered base that filled the available site and supported various archetypal gardens—rose, cottage, herb, etc.—through which ran a picturesquely meandering path.

At the centre of the roof-top 'park' was to be a lake, and in the lake a mysterious glass island, housing the main exhibition and shaped like a dream-distorted memory of the British coastline. As visitors approached, the island was to be shrouded in mist and protected by choppy water, but after a period of disorientation, they would be admitted across a metal grid rising up from under the water as a bridge into the pavilion.

Had it been realised, Avery's richly-evocative structure might well have proved to be Britain's most significant contribution to the architecture of such events since Joseph Paxton's Crystal Palace sheltered the Great Exhibition of 1851. The contrast between the two is telling: whereas Paxton gave dazzling expression to the global aspirations of the world's dominant power and, more broadly, of an emerging technological civilisation, Avery proposed to harness advanced technology in the service of a vision of our re-engagement with Nature. Rooted in the perennial British concern with the particular and the local, this fusion of the ecological and the technological, the pragmatic and the poetic, epitomises Avery's growing body of work and offers a compelling architectural vision for the twenty-first century.

See Nikolaus Pevsner, *The Englishness of English Art*, London: The Architectural Press, 1956, esp. pp. 163–192.
See Philip Hoare, *England's Lost Eden Adventures in a Victorian Utopia*, London: Harper Perennial, 2005, p. 7.
See Jay Appleton, *The Experience of Landscape*, London: Wiley, rev. ed., 1993.

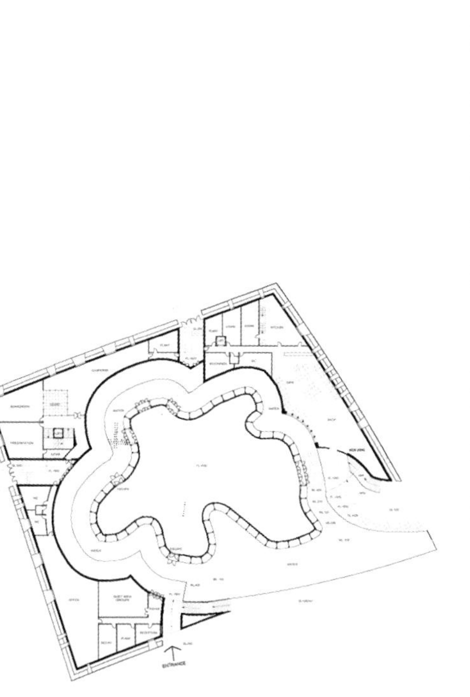

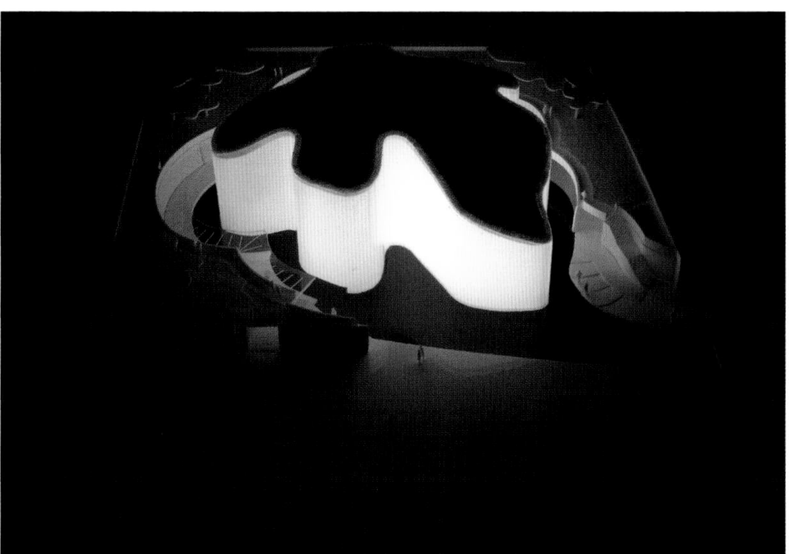

This Page
Above left: British Pavillion: Expo 2010, Shanghai 2007–2008; Ground floor plan.
Above right: View of the pavilion across the water.
Left: Model.
Below: Vegetation wall at the Citadel; Horseguards Parade; London.
Bottom (left): Elevation with vegetation wall.
Bottom (right): Section.

Opposite Page
Sketch of the chalk cliffs and Needles; Isle of Wight.

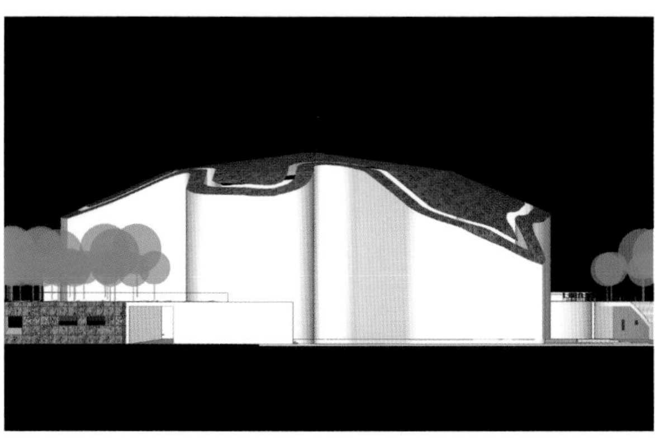

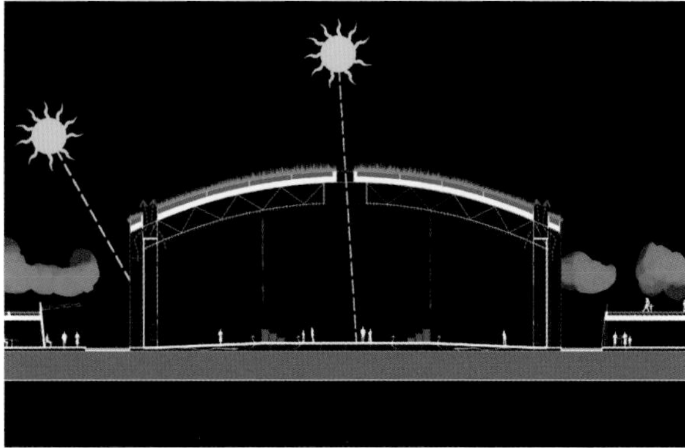

Footnotes to Chapter 1
The British Pavilion at Expo 2010

Britain was the world's first country to industrialise so it was also the first to confront the issues of urban alienation. In so doing, it pioneered what is arguably the most successful, and most emulated new model for modern urban development—that cities work best when they address the human need for a small scale local identity and a rapprochement with the natural world.

The British Pavilion is thus to be seen as a metaphoric public park within the urban context of the Expo site. Its base is covered entirely with planting like the ivy covered walls to the secret garden of Frances Hodgson Burnett. Its roof is landscaped with a variety of British garden types, a rose garden; cottage garden; herb garden and an allotment perhaps. Through them a route meanders in the manner of a London park and at its centre, there is a lake… and in the lake… an island.

The Island is the allegorical heart of the project. It refers to the 'island nation' and the extraordinary impact that the island has had on world affairs, and to the 'island pavilion', that seminal space inside Hadrian's Villa, wherein the emperor would seek creative distance from the world outside.

The approach to the Island thus suggests both a journey and a crossing.

As the pathway winds out of view, a cooling mist comes up from the water and down from a canopy to create a fog, and the disorientation that this generates causes the homogeneity of the crowd to be broken up and individuals to be isolated.

When those leading the queue reach the end and can go no further, the water, previously placid, now bubbles like a choppy sea and up through it comes a metal grid to offer a crossing like stepping stones to the other side. As this happens, the glass walls to the Island open up and the queue crosses into the Pavilion. The grid then lowers back down into the water and disappears.This is the entry to the citadel, like Xanadu, a fabulous island city.

A favourite fable of Taosm, the traditional Chinese philosophical system founded by Laozi in the sixth century BC, speaks of the 'Immortals'—"perfect beings who dwell in a far away place"—celebrated in poetics and painting as the "Isles of the Immortals". These fabled Isles had high mountains, lush vegetation, misty valleys, blue rivers and the most desirable flora and fauna imaginable. (pp. 20–21, 177)

Chapter 2

Fragments of Wilderness City
by Bryan Avery

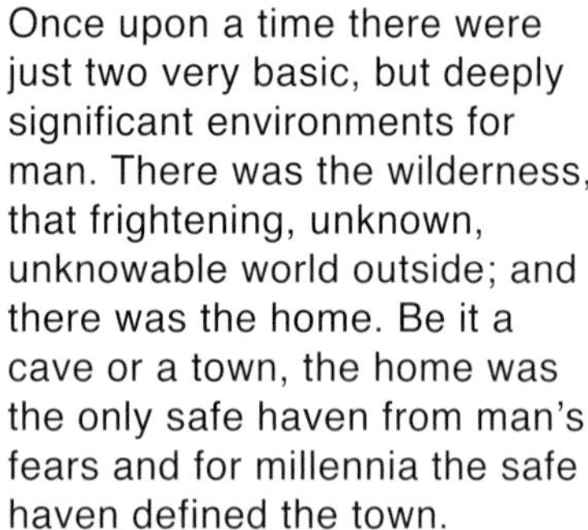

Once upon a time there were just two very basic, but deeply significant environments for man. There was the wilderness, that frightening, unknown, unknowable world outside; and there was the home. Be it a cave or a town, the home was the only safe haven from man's fears and for millennia the safe haven defined the town.

The security of the home-town freed its people to nurture the intellectual talents that had hitherto been a liability and thus began the long process towards a cohesive and mutually beneficial social structure which would eventually allow a level of prosperity to develop in the towns impossible to imagine in the wilderness.

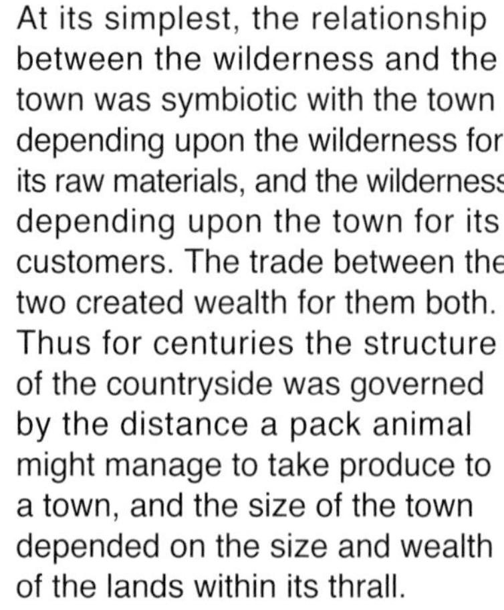

At its simplest, the relationship between the wilderness and the town was symbiotic with the town depending upon the wilderness for its raw materials, and the wilderness depending upon the town for its customers. The trade between the two created wealth for them both. Thus for centuries the structure of the countryside was governed by the distance a pack animal might manage to take produce to a town, and the size of the town depended on the size and wealth of the lands within its thrall.

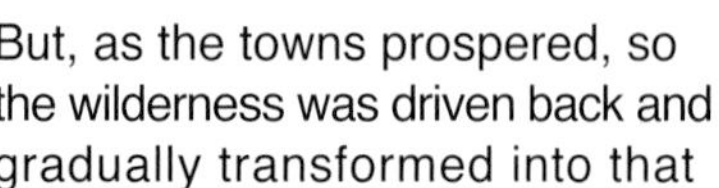

But, as the towns prospered, so the wilderness was driven back and gradually transformed into that

quasi-natural world of field and farm that we now call countryside.

This was the stasis reached in England by the eighteenth century. It was an extraordinarily subtle and complex structure of ownerships and mutually beneficial sound husbandry and as the population expanded and new techniques permitted the cultivation of hitherto unprofitable land, it transformed the entire topography of the United Kingdom into a managed landscape. This was the 'old England' of the poets, the 'garden England' that we so much revere to this day. It is still embodied within us as the ideal pastoral landscape of our national imagination.

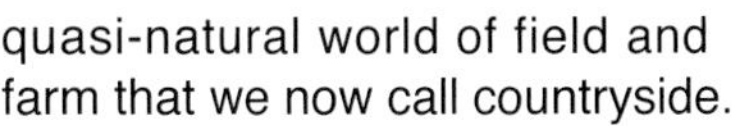

This Page
Right: Selbourne, Hampshire.
Above left: A tree lined lane, Surrey.
Above middle: South Downs; Sussex.
Above right: South Downs; Sussex.
Top centre: Sketch; Bucklers Hard, New Forest.
Top right: Sketch; Lachendorf, Austria.

Opposite Page
Top: Sketch; Penne, France.
Middle: Village, near Dijon, France.
Bottom: Gold Hill; Shaftesbury; Dorset.

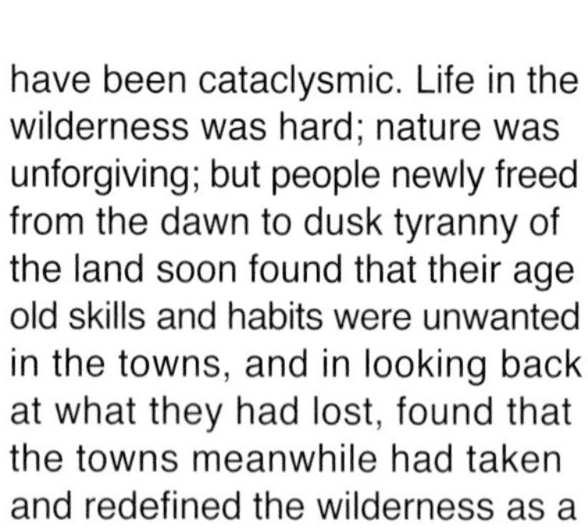

Its death knell was the Industrial Revolution. Pastoral wealth was suddenly eclipsed by industrial wealth. The countryside was denuded of labour, mechanisation took command, and new towns sprang up for industrial purposes almost entirely unconnected with the rural economy. The local interdependencies upon which so much of the landscape of the past had depended were broken. Mechanised transportation and communication systems at first linked towns locally, then nationally, and then within a century, the economies even of the villages were linked globally. The result was not so much a cerebral 'global village' or even a small-scale software driven utopian vision of a decentralised and pastoral cottage industry—but a 'global metropolis'.

93 per cent of the UK's population now already live officially in towns and when the farmers depart and the townsfolk move in, the countryside quickly becomes only another name for a town. And the farmers have been departing. Forced out by competitive world markets, it is said that the net worth of farming in the UK has sunk to a little more than half that of the ready-made sandwich industry.

However, whilst the UK has had almost 200 years to adjust to this process; in the countries of the developing world the changes have been cataclysmic. Life in the wilderness was hard; nature was unforgiving; but people newly freed from the dawn to dusk tyranny of the land soon found that their age old skills and habits were unwanted in the towns, and in looking back at what they had lost, found that the towns meanwhile had taken and redefined the wilderness as a countryside in its own image.

There was now no safe haven. That deep bond between the wild places where man is not the master and the safe havens of our towns had been broken.

Moreover, that exhausting but satisfying physicality of the natural world of which, until a minute or two ago in geological time, man was so much a part—that world of myth and legend, of heroic feats, dark forests and fearsome encounters that still resides in the dark recesses of our minds is such a stubborn part of our culture that it cannot be ignored.

We have no adequate words to describe this. The terms "Environmental" and "Ecological" suggest little of the real torment that afflicts us, for there are deep structures to man's existence which bind him to the natural world and, for all our delight in the cerebral aspects of our art, until we can also forge some rapprochements with these, our lives will forever be in tension.

The trouble is, the towns are pitiless and voracious competitors with the natural world and forever getting bigger. London, one of the first to industrialise, now has over seven million people and is some 40 miles across. It already holds economic sway over the entire country—and is still growing. But London is made small by comparison with some others. Around the world there are already several towns of 20 million—and some are forecast to grow to 50 million or more.

How are we to define such structures? Simply calling them cities, conurbations or metropolitan regions isn't helpful because at root such structures can no longer be considered safe havens—the people within them do not feel attached to a singular and familiar place nor do they feel secure.

Where then did it all go wrong? The foot-trodden wilderness paths that lead through the defensive gates into the social spaces at the town's heart provided an admirable model but only for as long as it was constrained in size by its walls. As soon as the walls had been breached and development had accreted beyond them, it generated a density of traffic between

This Page
Flyover; Cairo, Egypt.

Opposite Page
Clockwise from top left:
Sketch of Hong Kong; Elderly Moroccan: Rus in Urbe; Cairo and Hong Kong; Residential district Hong Kong.

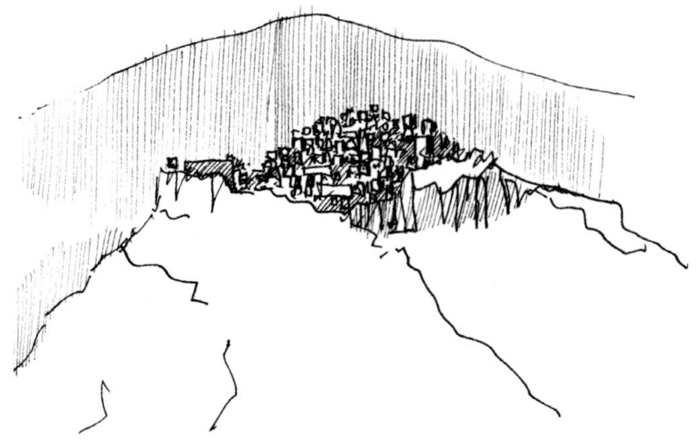

the perimeter and the centre which couldn't be accommodated by the old pathway structures. Nor could the increased size and density of uses in the centre be accommodated in the older buildings already built there. They had all to be modified or rebuilt.

Thus the pressure for change began and the whole structure of the modern town has evolved as a dynamic, never-ending system of infrastructural redevelopment. With this comes upheaval, danger and the dependency upon systems we cannot comprehend and which are as uncertain as the vagaries of nature we had left the wilderness to escape.

It is no surprise therefore that, if we can afford it, our 'escape' now is to the suburbs and beyond, to the countryside—or better, to a continental countryside where the pressure from the towns may not yet have been so keenly felt.

We are still looking, of course, for our own individual safe havens and no matter how futile it may appear, the need to do so is very strong within us.

This Page
Top left: Sketch, Comares, Andalusia. Spain.
Top right: Sketch, High density town house-walling; Yemen:
Middle left: Cairo, Egypt.
Middle right: Udaipur, India.
Bottom: Athens, Greece.

Consider, even within the towns themselves we prefer to identify the places where we live as small, semi-autonomous units, not as the constituent parts of a greater urban whole. We give such units names and a defining character and we fiercely defend it. Moreover, the more detached the unit, and the more independently cellular it can become, the higher its perceived value. In this we are re-tracing the patterns of habitation of the wilderness. We frequently refer to the urban cells as villages. We still hold annual country fairs with sheep-shearing and hay making in that most urbanised of London boroughs, Lambeth; and 200 years after their foundation, we still hold village fetes in the great London squares.

This Page
Top: Sketch, Cordes-en-Ciel, France.
Middle left: Ennismore Gardens, London.
Middle centre: Pimlico Road farmers market.
Middle right: Annual summer parade. Pimlico, London.
Bottom: Annual 'village' fete, St George's Square, Pimlico, London.

It has often been concluded from this that we in England have never been very good at creating truly urban environments, at least not in the continental hard paved social city sense, but our contribution has been arguably the more significant —the creation of the suburban garden, public parks and garden cities, all attempts, like our famous fondness for pets, at keeping man in touch with nature. As urban aesthetes we may not value this but we have nonetheless created here in the UK, a paradigm for urban living which accords with deep instincts.

This Page
Left: St James's Park, London.
Below: St James's Park, London.
Bottom: Royal Crescent, Bath.

This Page
Top: Petworth Park, Sussex.
Below right: Stourhead, Wiltshire.
Below left: Sherbourne Castle, Dorset.

But what then of the wilderness—that necessary natural counterpoint to the town?

Once, not so long ago, within living memory, when cars were not so readily available, it was not uncommon for the average person's experience of the world to be limited to perhaps a few square miles. The train and coach might connect to the town, but the hinterland, the wilderness itself, was impenetrable except on horseback or on foot. Beyond five or ten miles, knowledge was confined to rumour, not experience, and for as long as such places existed only in the imagination they remained objects of mystery and wonder. The wilderness was still the great frontier in microcosm, between what was known and what remained uncertain and for as long as this existed the landscape had an epic scale quite unrelated to its size and our delight in it could never be exhausted.

But, easy access has now brought a density of use to the wilderness with which it cannot cope, supplanting remoteness and tranquillity with congestion and bustle, bringing danger and destruction and beauty spots worn thin by over use. City dwellers come for recreation. They bring to the wild places their microlights, hang gliders and Pitts specials; they take to the paths with mountain bikes and motorbikes and quads; they fill the forests with the sounds of picnics and paintball parties.

Is it any wonder then that the perception of the wilderness has changed and that people still questing their right to fulfilment from the proximity of nature must travel ever further afield, destroying in their frustration the very thing they seek? Transmuted into 'countryside' the wilderness is already an endangered experience.

This Page
Top left: Pylons powering the rural idyll in the Appalachians, USA.
Middle: Quad-bikes at an off-road rally in the Appalachians, USA.
Bottom: City cyclists passing through Chipstead, Surrey.

Opposite Page
Top left: Eagle Owl;
Top right and bottom: Pine Forests, New Forest;

So, preserve and conserve the wilderness and countryside? yes of course, but question first the value of a husk of a hamlet used only by wearied weekenders. Ask what the countryside is, what it means to us and what we would like it to be. We could conclude that we have it all wrong. We could find that, with the break-up of the historic estates, the land husbandry ways of the past are over and, with the advent of the agri-business tenant manager, the countryside can no longer be entrusted to country folk. Certainly the countryside and all in it are now in service to the towns and the towns' values are prevailing.

Consider, roads trod out in Medieval times now widened, straightened and levelled; distinctive features, blind bends, narrow bridges and tunnelled hedgerows all now subsumed within a common standard set by the townsfolk's engineers for suburban safe passage. The villages have been held to ransom by the highways men. Little hope here for the rural idyll.

We should be resisting, be saying "hold on, this isn't the countryside we came for"; this is not the connection we seek with the slow changing natural rhythms of the seasonal order of things; This is not the "long green delirium like a vision of paradise" that Nan Fairbrother, author of *New Lives New Landscapes* told us of in her childhood expeditions from the post-war Coventry slums.

We should insist that the countryside should be, must be, beautiful, but also a little bit dangerous; that its by-ways should quagmire, have sheep barring passage and be ever so slightly smelly. Our bicycles, motorcycles and cars can cope and curiously are designed to cope, to judge from the advertisements, but even if we were to go one step further and to insist upon a return to the full and unexpurgated rural idyll of our dreams (and we could easily do so if we so wished), we could ask for peace and tranquillity again in our countryside, and then declassify the lanes, dig them up and pot-hole them. That would slow things down a little and we could dispense then with the speed humps, white lines, signposts and lights.

Not that we need be inconvenienced, for we could then demand drive-by-wire suspensions, satellite navigators and four-wheel drives for all our cars. We could ask for non-rusting bodies and easy-clean wheels too. We should not be intimidated by the technical or financial difficulties. After all, if one automotive nation (Germany) can manufacture cars which require the rest of the world to provide millimetre-precise cambering on all its roads for them to perform to specification and if another automotive nation (the United States) could insist that as its cars need catalytic converters because of an environmental problem in Los Angeles we must pay hugely for one too—why then cannot we ask for such a car here? We (almost) already have it. It sits, docile and unextended, in the supermarket car park.

This Page
From the top down:
An unaltered bend and bridge at Boldre; New Forest.
Village street rent apart by a through-route; Dorset.
Weekender's cottage near Winchester; Hampshire.
The 'high' street at Buckler's Hard; New Forest:
Sheep barring passage; New Forest.

Opposite Page
Top: Sketch. Ancient South Downs 'High' way.
Upper middle: Limited access motorway conserving the countryside in southern Germany.
Middle left: An engineering solution for speed control, Dorset.
Middle right: A psychological solution for speed control; New Forest
Bottom: A country highway of the future; New Forest.

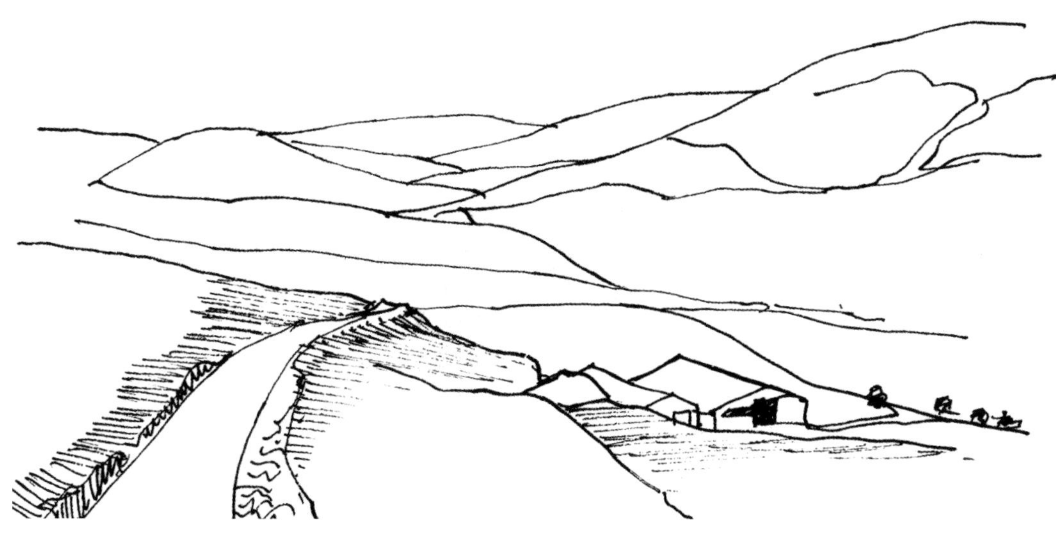

Consider too, that of 345,000 km of roads in Britain, nearly 300,000 km are minor roads, and uniquely in the world, the vast majority of these are tarmacadammed to a high surface standard permitting universally high average speeds. Why?

Imagine then a countryside in which the high speed roads do still exist but only as limited access de-restricted expressways between the major towns and most of the rest of the highway system is left to regress to the condition it was in before the Model T Ford, the original boneshaker, required something a little smoother to run on. Something like the New Forest perhaps, where two-way roads have been pot-holed on both sides such that on-coming cars are forced to a centre-of-the-road confrontation or go off-road to pass. It has slowed speeds dramatically. It also brings back something of the original skill and delight of motoring —as an experience in itself and not as a means to an end. We could, with such an approach, begin to restore the natural rhythms of the countryside so that we may again experience its pleasurable essence and stop just cutting through it in our cars in a vain search for ever more distant distractions.

We might also demand that our villages be made into autonomous economic units using fresh local produce, not refrigerated deliveries from town. Our homes could also be provided with walk-in cold stores

and, with teleshopping for staples delivered weekly by van, the local market could again become the social focus of a region.

This countryside of ours is too small to be opened up to full gaze from car windows at 60 miles per hour. With the hedgerows gone, its intimacy and privacy has been violated. Its character exists solely in its tiny scale and its labyrinthine mystery is proportional only to its inaccessibility. A wilderness which is inhabited becomes countryside and inhabited countryside soon becomes only another name for a town.

We have an opportunity now: under the twin pressures of the changing global economy, and the move towards more sustainable organic farming methods, highly intensive farmland is coming out of production and we should grasp the opportunity, mechanise more inventively, decentralise, and use 'just in time' seasonal production methods to make efficient the small fields and meadows of a new garden England —and return the rest to nature.

The structure of the landscape with its 'figure and ground' pattern of fields and meadows defined by hedgerows and coppices, provides in effect a township-like structure of walls and rooms—a green labyrinth, within which a multitude of the township's recreational functions could be concentrated. This might

leave the rest of the countryside to be re-forested and returned as a truly wild wilderness from which we need never again feel the need to escape. We might even imagine a return of the wolf and bear to lowland England. That would spice things up a little. We could then re-shape the landscape to our dreams. All we need to do is say how poetically we wish to live.

However we are, in a sense, still only toying with this issue. The towns remain the problem. For as long as we fail to structure their growth the countryside will always be under threat, and ultimately the wilderness too.

This Page
Top: Sketch, South Downs way near Chichester, Sussex.
Middle: The downland labyrinthine landscape as it was pre-war.
Bottom: The landscape created by agri-business with the hedgerows and coppices removed.

Opposite Page
Top: Sketch of 'Wolves' a sculpture by Sally Matthews at the Goodwood Sculpture Park: Sussex: 2003:
Middle: Advanced technology (ATH) Village proposal of 1984–1985 (pp. 4–5, 56–57, 80, 140).
Bottom: The ill-fated Africar designed by Tony Howarth in the 1980s was before its time, made of wood and designed to operate off-road using a lorry-wide high clearance wheelbase and a 2CV suspension; with a different power plant it would be ideal for the new countryside.

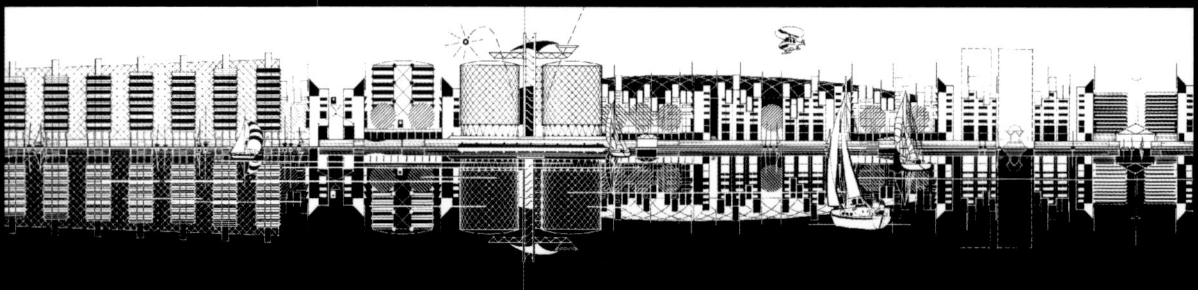

We need therefore to make our towns very much denser than they are today. There is no escaping the fact that land is a finite commodity and we must use it sparingly. We should at least double the present densities. We need to develope lift-access medium rise back-to-back mixed-use developments of combined workspace and residential units. (ATH housing studies (p. 46, 54–55,140). These would cut commuting, create huge energy savings and be especially attractive to the new generation of singletons and retirees. For the latter a private lift access direct to each flat, once considered an unaffordable luxury as electric windows in cars once were too, will become a necessity. (Kolkata project p. 173)

The towns must be kind to families too. It is the high cost/ low space standard equation, together with the noise, lack of privacy and the unreliability and fearfulness of the transport systems that is driving families out. We need to design our town houses and flats more generously; with good acoustics, play spaces and privacy which in effect, means that we need to break the land cost spiral caused by the economic attraction of the town centre and break therefore with the centripetal plan.

This Page
Above top: Long elevation; Silvertown masterplan 1990–1992.
Above right: Typical ATH waterside elevation.

Opposite Page
Top: Axonometric of the Silvertown masterplan. Middle and bottom: Millennium Exposition structure, section and elevation.

Footnote:

An invitation to prepare a new master plan for Silvertown in London's Dockland, (1990–1992: see p.145) provided an opportunity to apply the lessons learnt from the previous ATH (Advanced Technology Houses) research projects to an existing urban problem.

The site was divided in two by an east-west dual carriageway, so this was raised up as a viaduct to allow people to pass under it and integrated with a rapid-transit tramway shielded from the rest of the site by a protective wall of multi-use buildings. Passing quietly and now all but invisibly through the development, this new viaduct was then provided with six ramped access 'gateways' which connected in turn with the principal north-south avenues and east-west local roads in a descending order of traffic densities and speed.

A total of 1540 ATH were proposed, of several types, with and without gardens, some back-to-back, but most fully integrated into other structures, including car parking, industrial and commercial buildings - and an 80,000-seat sports stadium. Unlike contemporary stadia with their remote location and acres of wasteful car parking, this stadium (at right in aerial view opposite), is carved out from within the city block. Its main approaches are from the two civic ends - the riverside walk and the square, whilst on the two other flanks the stadium is wrapped in noise sheltering multi-story carparking hidden behind a residential facade.

This ability to juxtapose what hitherto had been considered entirely incompatible uses is a key factor in the plan. As such, it was the first demonstration of how cities of the future might be condensed and revitalised; ideas that were to reappear in the later Wilderness City projects.

At the heart of the scheme was a building of more than local significance. Intended as the location for an 'end-of-millennium exposition' that would inaugurate the development (later to become the brief for the Millennium Dome). This huge structure had an air-supported, cable-stayed fabric roof that covered 5.9 hectares. With a maximum span of 310 meters, it would have been by far the largest such structure in the world.

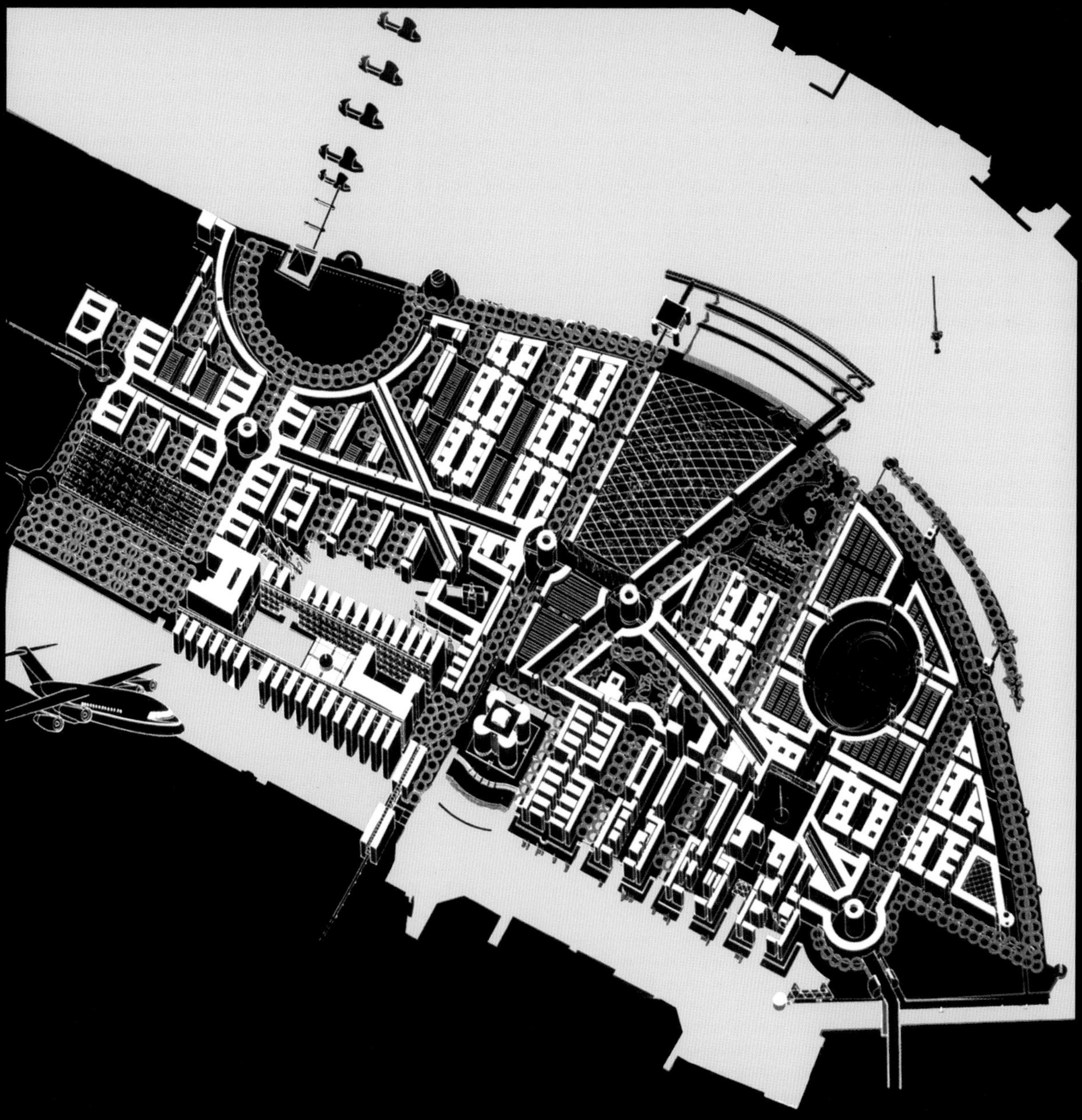

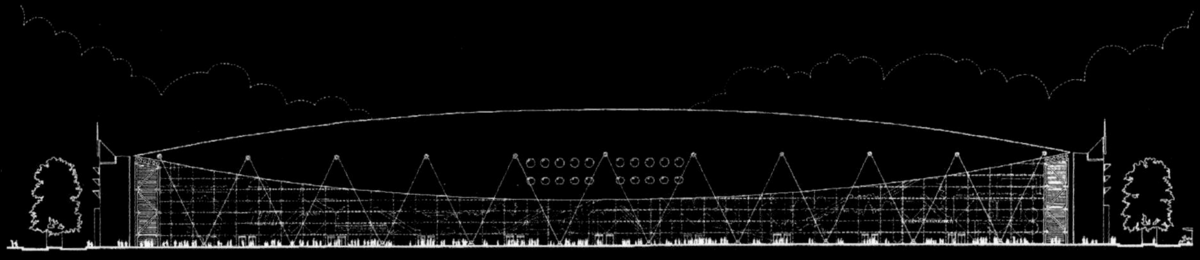

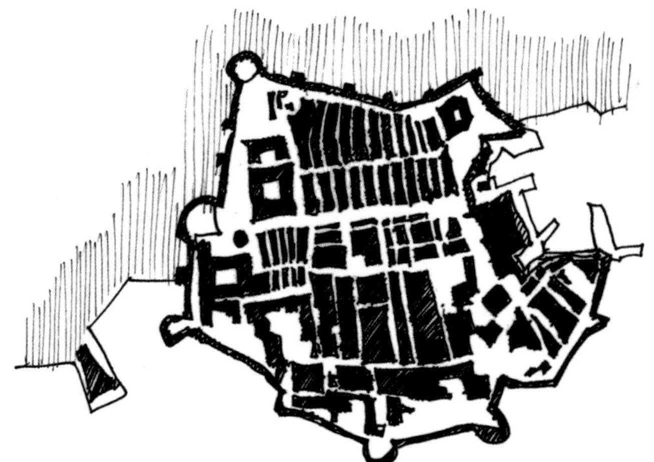

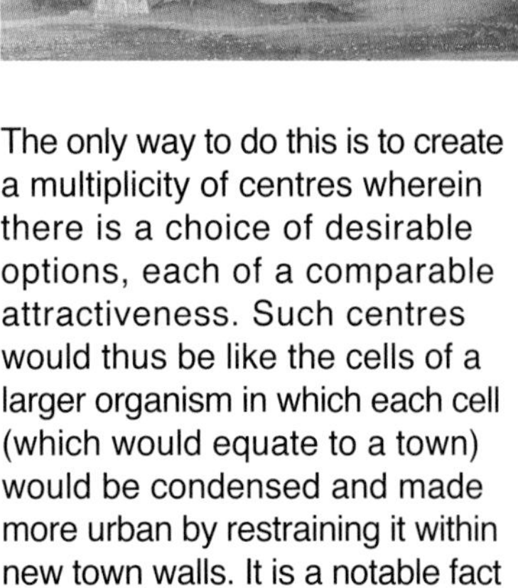

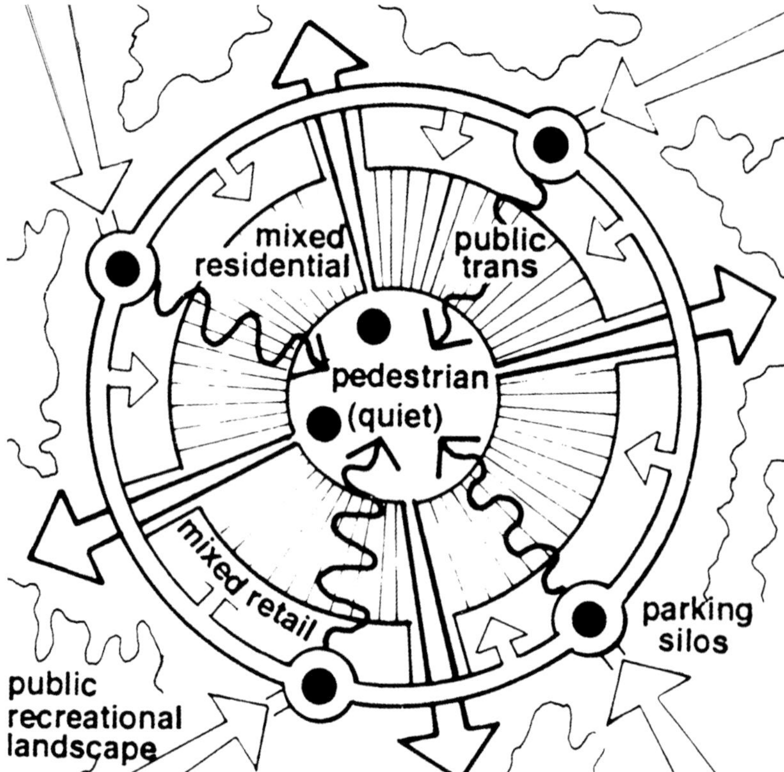

The only way to do this is to create a multiplicity of centres wherein there is a choice of desirable options, each of a comparable attractiveness. Such centres would thus be like the cells of a larger organism in which each cell (which would equate to a town) would be condensed and made more urban by restraining it within new town walls. It is a notable fact that almost all of the world's most cherished urban environments have been constrained in some way, usually by a natural circumstance of geography or by a man-made defensive wall.

The 'walls' in this case would in fact be raised roads, viaducts which would contain below them the main shopping and commercial districts and made back-to-back perhaps with housing too. The walls are thus permeable to pedestrians at ground level and, to maximise the development potential, the perimeter of each cell would be built to the highest densities. This would free the centre to become the cultural and socio-political heart of the community. The spaces there would be tranquil and of public scale.

The entire town could then be pedestrianised except for emergency services and at each gateway there might be an expandable

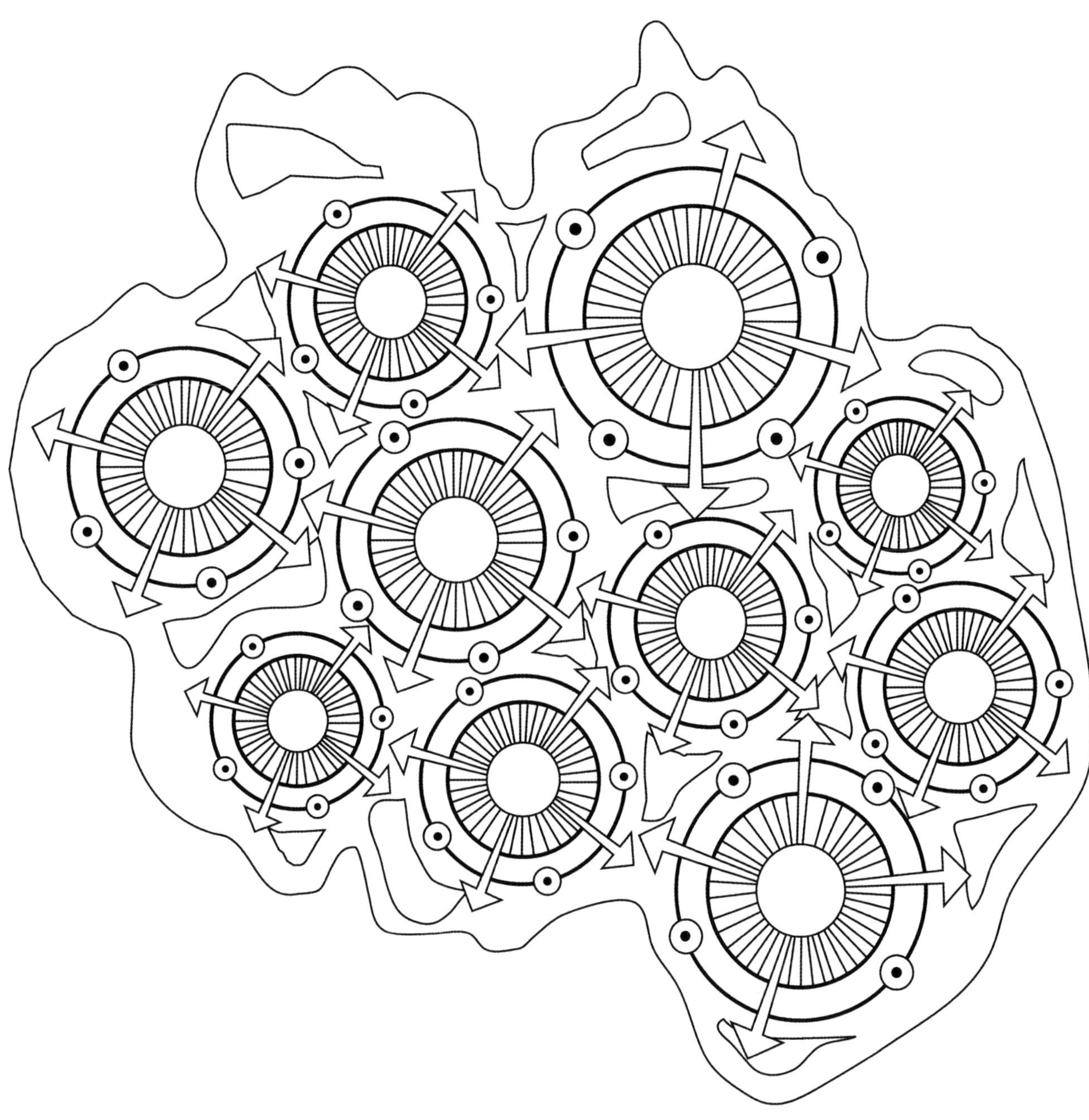

parking 'silo' beyond which private cars would not normally go. The town is thus made small, to a scale that suits the pedestrian—a half hour walk across—in a complete inversion of the Garden City plan.

Within such a proposal, urban growth would occur not by adding land-hungry, low-density developments to the edges of existing centres, but by constraining these to their existing size such that the residents would be obliged to be inventive in order to increase the density and when this has been exhausted then new autonomous townships would be founded, each kept separate from its neighbour by landscaped public parkland open to all. Such townships could have their own political and economic structures and would thus have their own identity and character. However, interlinked one with

This Page
Above: Diagram to illustrate city cells coalescing into a cellular city.

Opposite Page
Top left: Plan of Dubrovnik; Croatia.
Middle left: Cordes-en-Ciel; France.
Bottom left: Early map of Florence (Vatican Collection).
Bottom right: Diagram of a typical city-cell.

Overleaf
Main image: Eagle's eye view of the Helsinki-Tampere Wilderness city plan 1993.
Bottom: Sketch of perimeter viaduct and parking silo.

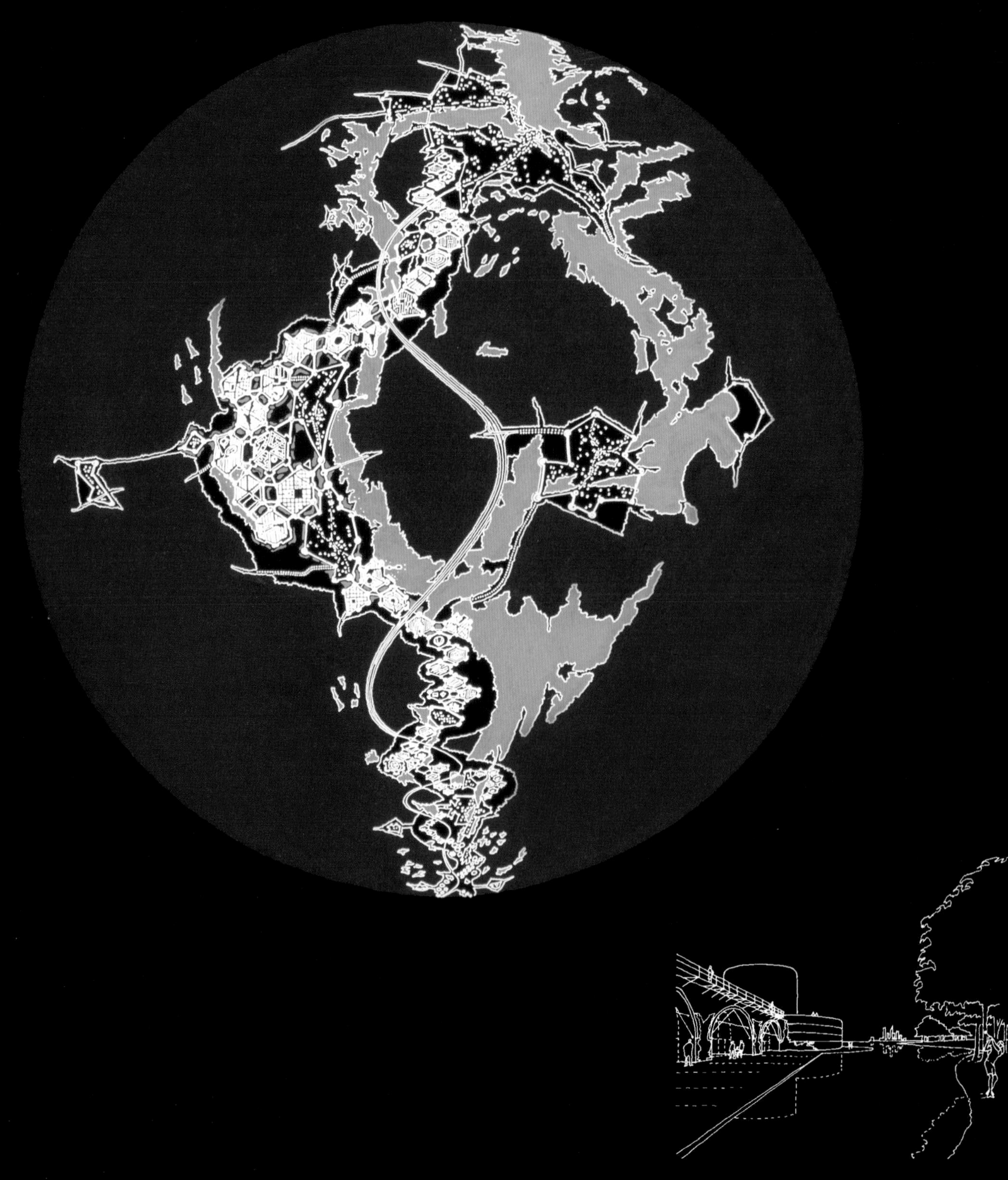

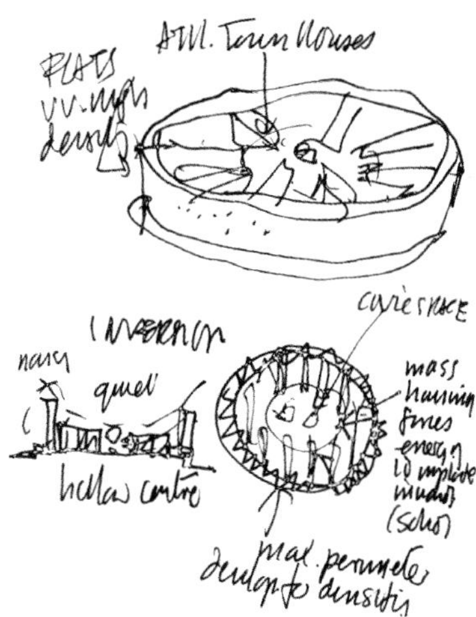

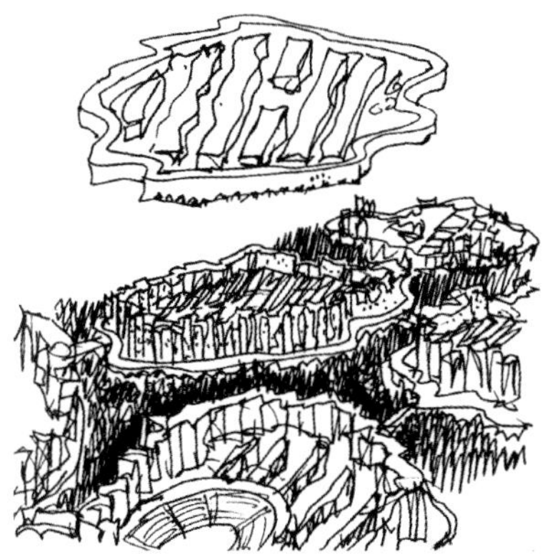

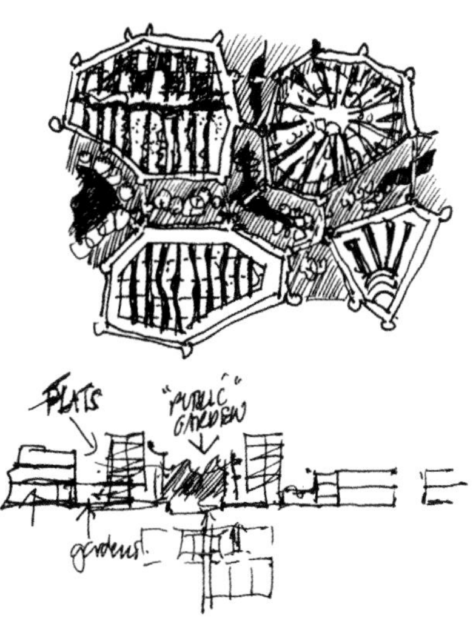

another by rapid expressways and public transit systems, they would together constitute a major metropolitan region in which each township could support specialised city-scale facilities.

This cell-like network would be more responsive to growth and change, and would be less disruptive to the whole when the economy of one cell burgeoned or foundered. It creates, too, a real sense of place, an urbane urban environment in close contact with the natural world; a place small enough to relate to, yet with all the facilities that a modern metropolis can offer.

Such a city would have cells of different characters much as Soho, Covent Garden, the City of London, Belgravia, and so on, comprise London itself, except that each cell would be separated by a mildly tamed wilderness, a public parkland, a cordon sanitaire, to protect its individuality. The cells, being autonomous can even die without the need to cauterise the city.

If the cells of such a city could be made desirable in the way that say small market towns are desirable, it might thereby release pressure upon the countryside and the countryside can then revert to its original status, as the necessary wilderness in counterpoint to the town.

This may seem utopian, but it could well become a necessity. We are already finding it difficult to support a growing social infrastructure from a declining tax base. We have a progressively ageing population yet we seem curiously unwilling to extrapolate from the demographic changes taking place and to re-configure our environment accordingly. And yet if we are to believe the statistics, there are now some 2.4 metres less young adults in the population and 1.2 million more in their early 60s and 80s than in the 1980s. We have seen how the young adults and their purchasing powers helped shape the physical environment of our cities in the 1980s and we should expect no less a change as the elderly take over.

But make no mistake. The elderly are not what they used to be. With a life expectancy in good health to the age of 75 or 80, they are not the helpless souls we imagined in our youth: they are still at the peak of their powers, and with a choice of how and where to live. They are not even constrained to these shores.

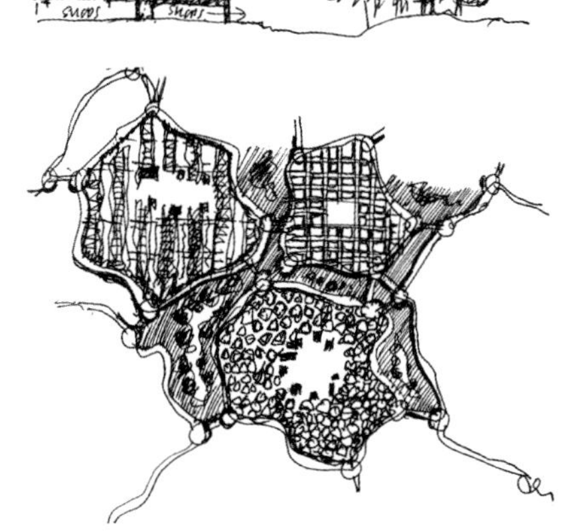

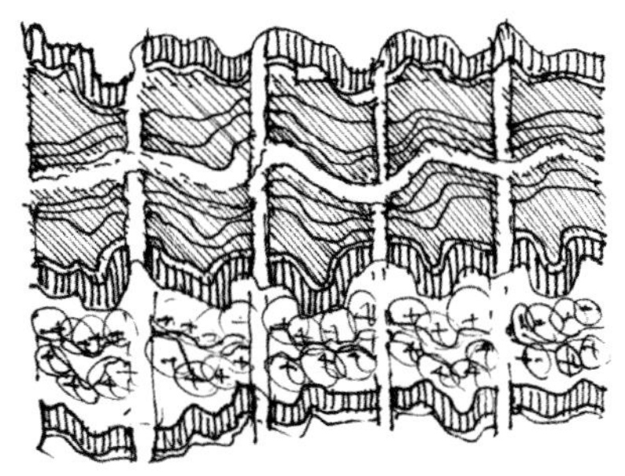

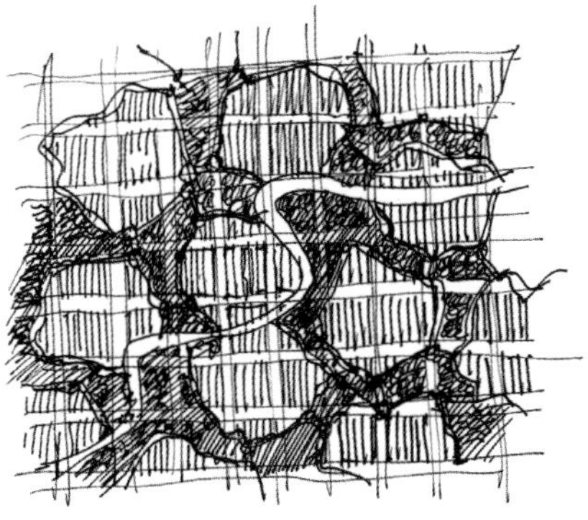

This Page
Development Sketches:
Top left: The doughnut plan.
Top middle and top right: High density perimeter blocks
Right top: Paradigm plans.
Right middle: Back-to-back residential/ commercial structures.
Right bottom: Grid-cells.

Maybe therefore we should forget for a moment our urban design conventions, and look instead at ourselves, our origins, and the economic and demographic changes taking place and let these be our inspiration.

Illustrated opposite is a miniaturised Wilderness City on a plot destined otherwise for the conventional suburban solution—individual villas on half an acre of land. Instead we have the plot as hamlet, a community set in its own small wilderness with quiet, traffic free, internal public spaces for social encounters, and dwellings with spacious ground floor family rooms and roof top gardens. Each plot has a lift-accessed tower for the more private areas—the bedrooms, studies and viewing loggias—and thus the elderly or infirm will have no steps to climb and can seek help next door when needed. The house is a safe haven, a place for poetic isolation or for social exchange and the towers are both refuges and watch-towers.

The 'wilderness' here is as wild as we can make it—a managed coppice which could be harvested for materials and fuel and would provide protected habitats for wild flora and fauna. It would be big enough for fox and badger perhaps, and small deer too, but the wolves would have to wait until a few more such settlements could be built. The lake between the two 'hamlets' is intended as a vestigial 'sea' or 'moat' whereby to set up an oppositional tension between the two communities and thus to create, over time, a strong sense of identity and character for each. One can imagine the children of these communities coming together here for ice-skating in the winter and for picnics and boating in the summer. More prosaically the lake would collect the run-off rainwater from the two settlements and thus provide a fresh water reservoir and a source of fresh fish.

Our forebears would have understood this. It connects directly to the deeper underlying rhythms of life on this planet.

"Once upon a time there were just very basic, but deeply significant environments for man. There was the wilderness, that frightening, unknown, unknowable world outside, and there was the home. Be it a cave or a town, the home was the only safe haven from man's fears and for millennia the safe haven has defined the town."

The Wilderness City Project developed out of the earlier ATH projects of 1984–1985 and was published in Housing and Planning Review *Vol 40, Nos 3, 4 & 5, 1985. This text is based on lectures given during that period and subsequently updated for* 'Made' Magazine, *Issue No. 1: 2004.*

This Page
From top left: Two sketches of San Gimignano, Italy; two sketches of Cordes-en-Ciel, France; Sketch of Fources, France.

Opposite Page
Top: Wilderness Hamlet plan 2000;
Below: Wilderness Hamlet aerial view.

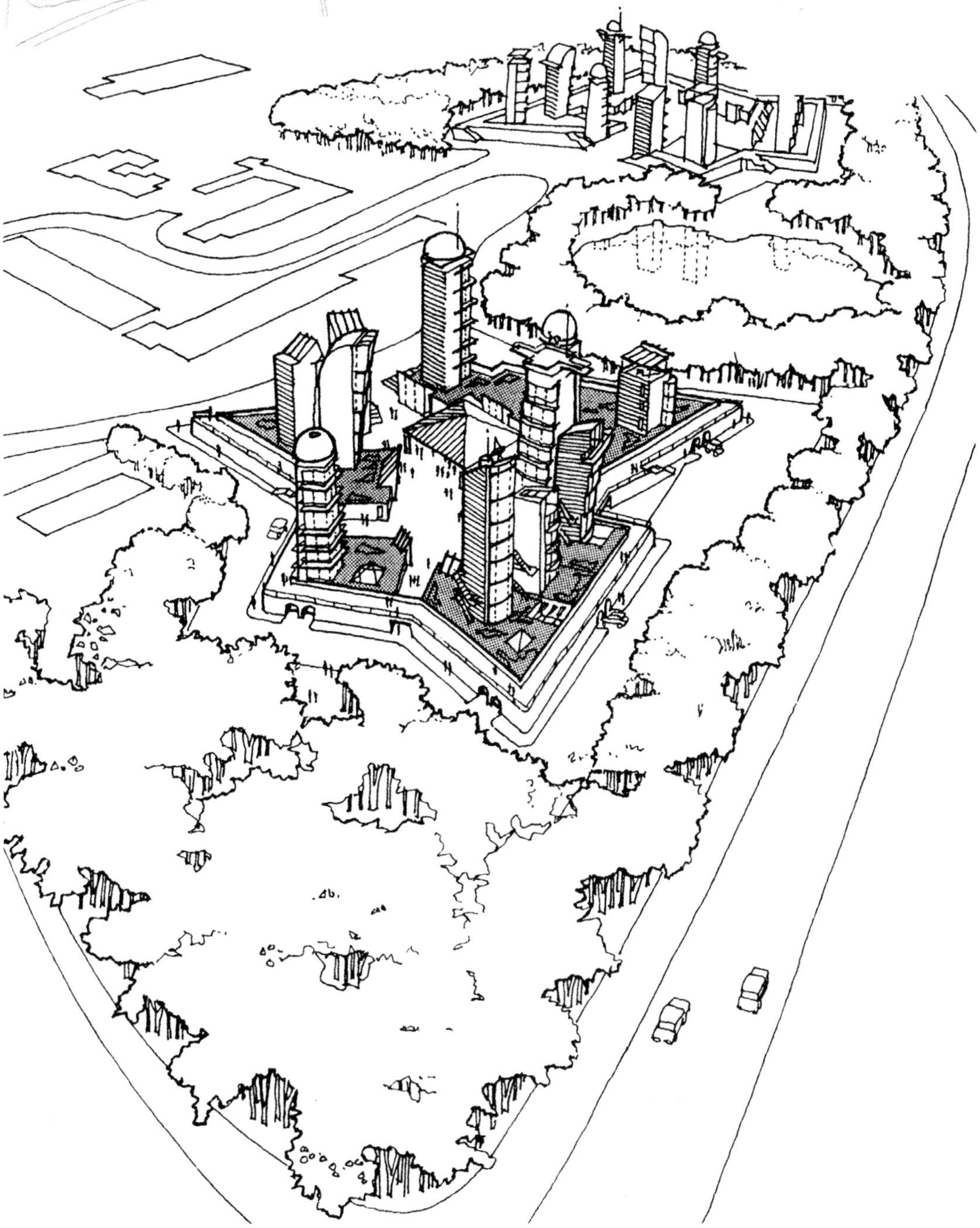

45

Footnotes to Chapter 2
Advanced Technology Housing: The Future of the Suburbs: A proposition: 1984–1985

The proposition was that as family sizes decreased and both parents could be freed sooner to seek income and fulfilment through work, the home would quickly burgeon, first with labour-saving devices and then with leisure and pleasure goods—all of which would demand space. Furthermore, as more people take up the opportunity to work from home, the house would cease to be merely a dormitory and could become instead the permanent setting for a total working-family life.

Consider, in this context, the 'new-old' terrace. Its plot measures six metres wide and 36 metres deep. The frontage is a quiet, traffic-restricted avenue onto which the solar-shaded and soundproofed windows of the bedrooms face. All the houses are raised to overlook off-road parking places and to provide ready access to the under-floor services. The parking places are sloped up to distance the living accommodation from the pavement and have troughs for the front wheels to lock into and be electronically monitored.

At the rear, to allow for growth, the garden walls are designed to support a future roof. The houses can now be expanded at any time with ease, to provide accommodation for any amount of domestic equipment or for embryonic business and manufacturing ventures.

In an inversion of the traditional suburban pattern, these activities now open onto a comfortably wide and partially covered alley at the back. This will encourage social and trading encounters within the community and thereby help establish an electronics-age equivalent of the medieval market street.
(pp. 144)

Advanced Technology Housing: The Future of the City: A proposition 1984–1985

In the next century (2000), when with technology's help many of mankind's most pressing economic concerns may at last have been resolved, these will be seen increasingly as mere frameworks within which life takes place. Perhaps then we will come to listen more to our environment and, in trying to understand its genius, we will be forced to turn towards a more poetic use of technology in search of meaning in our lives.

In 1984 it was thought that as the electronics revolution took effect, industrial production facilities would become ever smaller and more environmentally benign. Linked by global communications and rendered autonomous by cheap business machines, industries would become more and more decentralised and decreasingly dependent on historical and geographical factors. Consequently, they would become less constrained to the town.

If the town was therefore no longer the centre of production sustained by a daily repopulation from the suburbs, it would be freed to become again what it once was: a stable community of town-liking people, a stage-set for social encounters and a forum for exchanges in commerce, culture and politics.

Such a town would require a new form of housing, a 'new-old' design for very small plots, to realise a new urbanity—a rich multi-role environment wherein families could once more live in privacy and tranquillity.

The advanced technology town house is thus a single aspect, narrow fronted unit between four and four and a half metres wide—the width of one room—and up to eight metres deep. It is exceptionally energy efficient, sharing walls and recycling heat to a thermal store. It sits on its own freehold plot, with or without a garden or garage, and the units can be set side-by-side or back-to-back (back to back-to-back) or backed on to other urban structures to suit any urban form.

The house would be prefabricated in room cell sizes, such that a young couple starting with a one-room unit could eventually expand their home to multiple levels to accommodate a family, an office, a work-room, or any number of ancillary facilities. Within such a structure it would thus be possible for families to remain rooted in their neighbourhood, if they choose, for the rest of their lives.

The maximum number of stackable rooms has been limited to nine including the roof-top utility room or terrace so that facades are restricted to no more than 24 metres in height, the historic limit for cities such as London or Paris.

To reach the upper floor, the houses are fitted with integral stairs, furniture hoists and interactive, 'intelligent' lifts. The lifts are driven by linear motors activated by voice command and controlled by household management microprocessors that track the occupants and respond instantly on call. The room-to-room travel times are less than with a flight of stairs and, with no motor rooms, cables or counterweights, the lift-shafts take up little space. The lift-cars are lightweight and inherently safe, relying on inductive effect to descend in an emergency.

For a sophisticated, demanding but demographically ageing population where proximity to the town's facilities will become increasingly essential and inter-dependencies within flats increasingly intolerable, such high-density autonomous dwellings with lift access may ultimately be considered a necessity.
(pp. 38–39, 54–55, 140)

Chapter 3

The Civic Dimension

by Joseph Rykwert

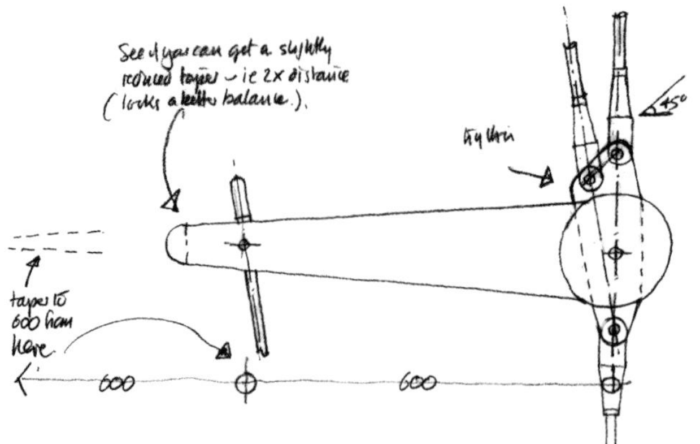

To encompass the whole range of design—from industrial production to the city—has been many an architect's ambition: Bryan Avery seems to have achieved it without really trying. Product design seems like second nature to him, and he has applied himself to it as problems have come to mind, while the urban dimension has always been integral to his thinking, even when he works at a domestic scale. How conscious he is of it can be seen in his early and unrealised design for the Repertory Theatre at Keswick, 1980 (opposite and p. 136) where the link to the town, and the 'walk-through' patterns of movement are essential to the project. He has even been guided by urban considerations when reworking existing buildings, so that the knottiest problem in the conversion of the feature—and comfort-less slab office block at No. 1 Neathouse Place (pp. 14–15, 70–77, 89–92, 147) was its adaptation to current demands of climatic comfort and energy saving—which also, incidentally, allowed an enlargement of the original floor area. The way in which this was achieved also involved re-organising the two long sides of the office space in relation to the surrounding urban landscape, and this was achieved by re-organising the framing of the view, as well as distinguishing the north-east face sharply from the southwest one, although both sides had been treated in the same way in the original building. The wide roadway over which the office block formed a bridge would fill with a forbidding whirlwind at the slightest air-movement, so a canopy was inserted beneath the soffit of the motorised passage and it now makes the space easily accessible to pedestrians.

Avery is very clear about the difference between the two spheres of the designer's activity. This is not a common virtue—and I certainly count it as one—at a time when too much designing is done as if a building is much like any industrial product, an isolated object such as might fit into any context. This makes Avery's deliberate involvement with, but also conscious distinction between, the different aspects of the design process admirable, and gives weight to his thinking about the nature of urban living.

It is generally recognised, even if many developers and politicians have not got round to the idea, that the way in which we occupy urban space is being dramatically transformed, and that for a number of reasons. Some approaches are due to climate change, and others to the shift of demography towards an older population in the Western world, but above all it is the lasting and radical impact of electronic media which has already altered work patterns

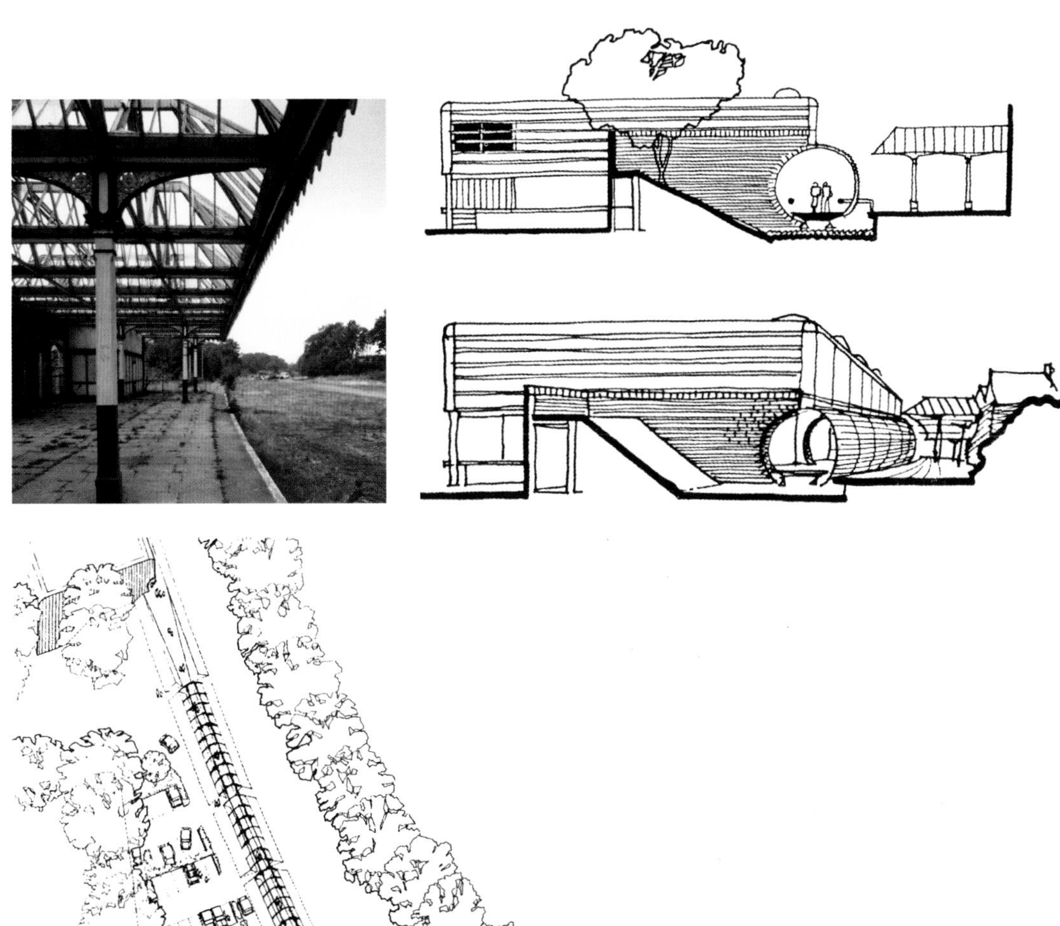

This Page
Top left: The disused Keswick railway station.
Top right: Keswick Repertory Theatre 1980; section and perspective.
Left: Axonometric.

Opposite Page
Top left: Sketch of Rotunda structure: No. 1 Neathouse Place 1994–1996.
Top right and bottom left: Photos No. 1 Neathouse Place, London.

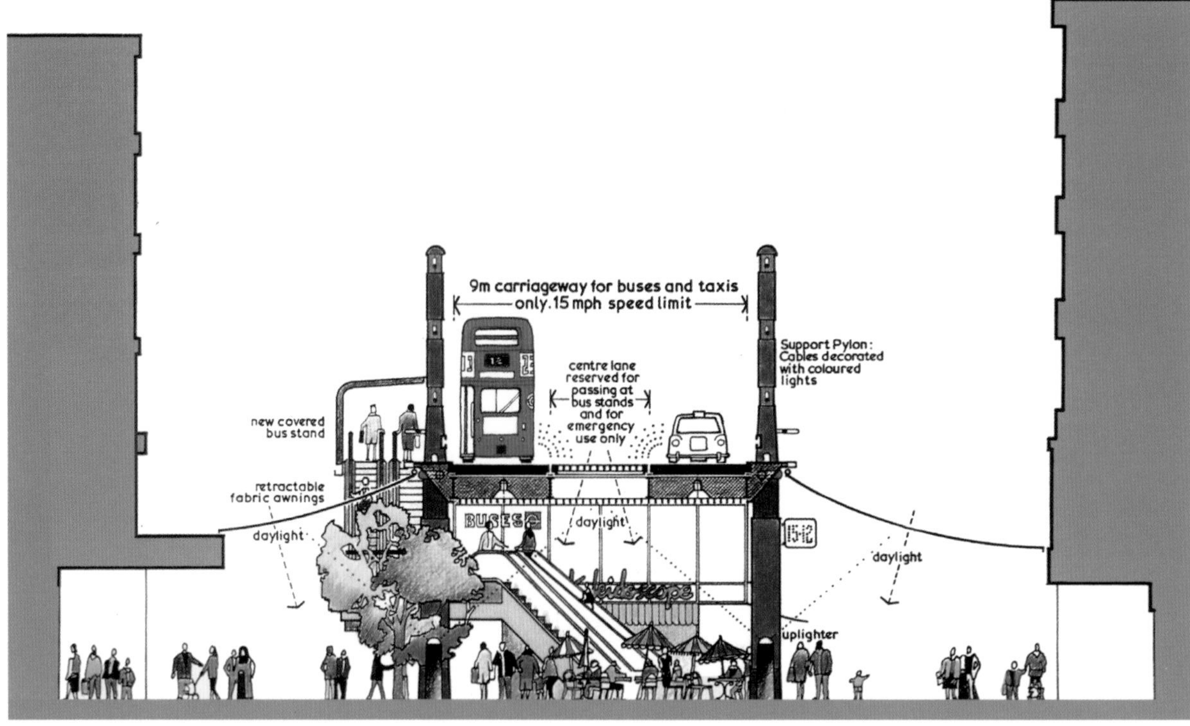

irrevocably—and will continue to do so increasingly in the future. The 'Global Village' which Marshall McLuhan imagined as his own living reality 40 or 50 years ago may not quite have worked through our social fabric, but the polarity between office, workshop and home has already been eroded. Which, strangely enough—and Avery is to be credited with having realised it early—gives some century-old ideas unexpected relevance. Their sometimes quite dramatic re-interpretation, stimulated by social and technological change, is very much part of what he calls his new-old approach. So the two-level traffic streets Eugene Hénard proposed for Paris about 1900 are ambitiously adapted in Avery's project for a light-metal raised traffic highway to take public (and semi-public, such as taxis) transport along Oxford Street; the technology is much more feasible than that which was available to Hénard and it would allow the present street level to become pedestrianised—in part at least—so as to give new life to the venerable London artery with its well-established emporia. Avery adapted this project later to the conditions of the Avenue of the Emirates in Abu-Dhabi. Such a scheme, light in structure, permeable to light, and relatively quiet would have all the advantages of the old American elevated railway without its many disadvantages.

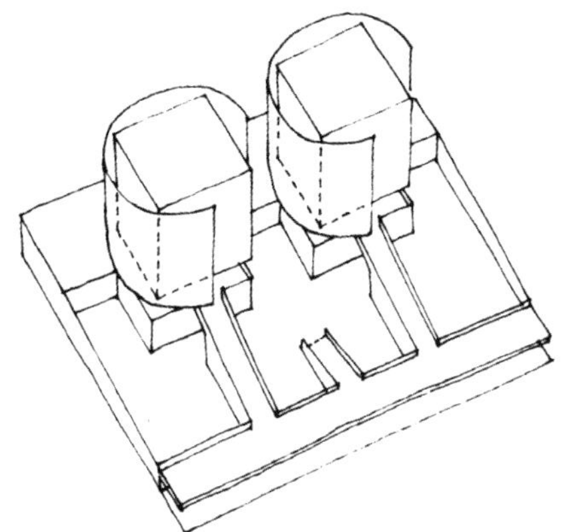

This Page
Above: Abu Dhabi, the Avenue of the Emirates 1982; model of proposals;
Above right: 120m square city block.
Right: Civic building elevation and plan.
Below: Master plan.
Bottom: The Oxford Street Mall project 1981–1983; typical elevation.

Opposite Page
The Oxford Street Mall project; cross-section.

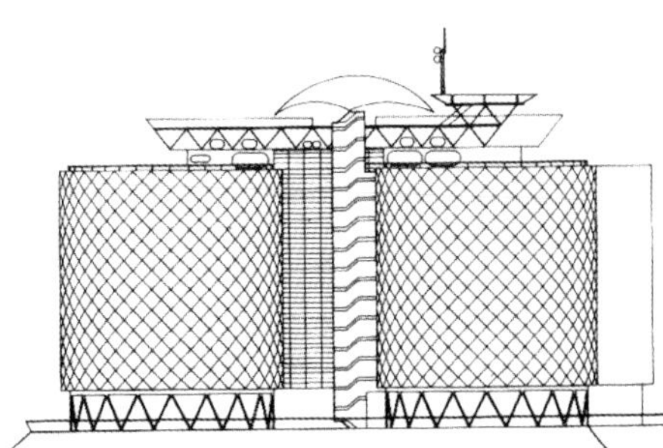

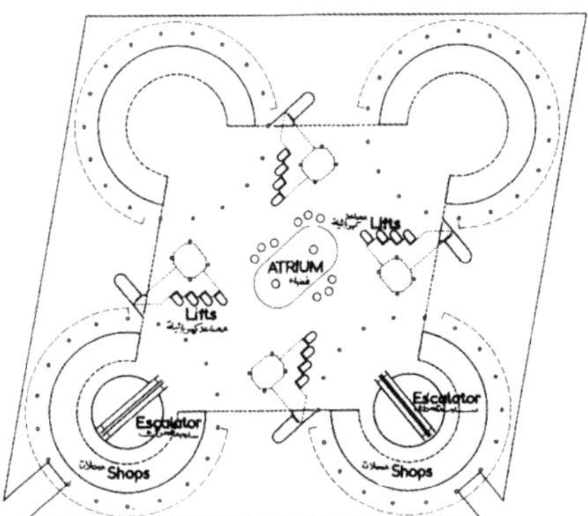

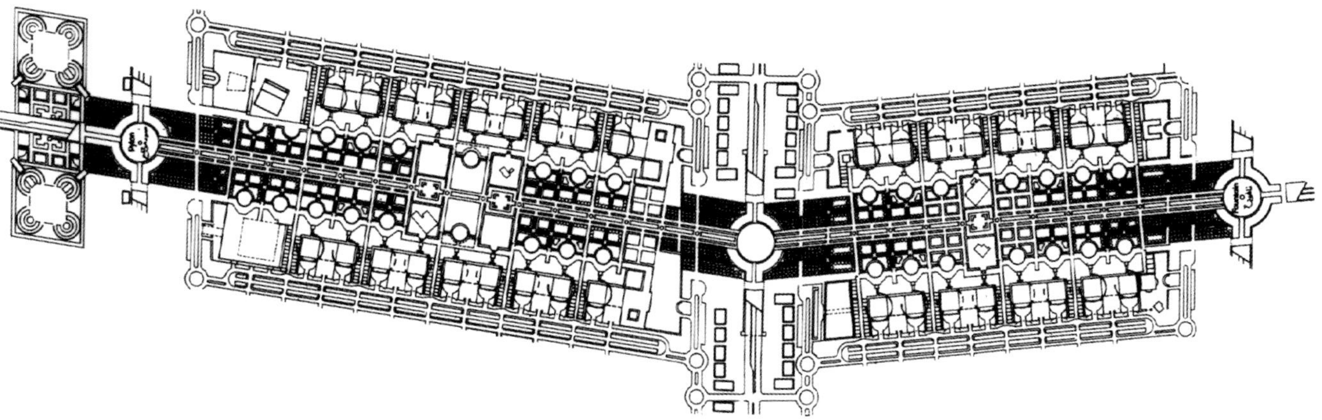

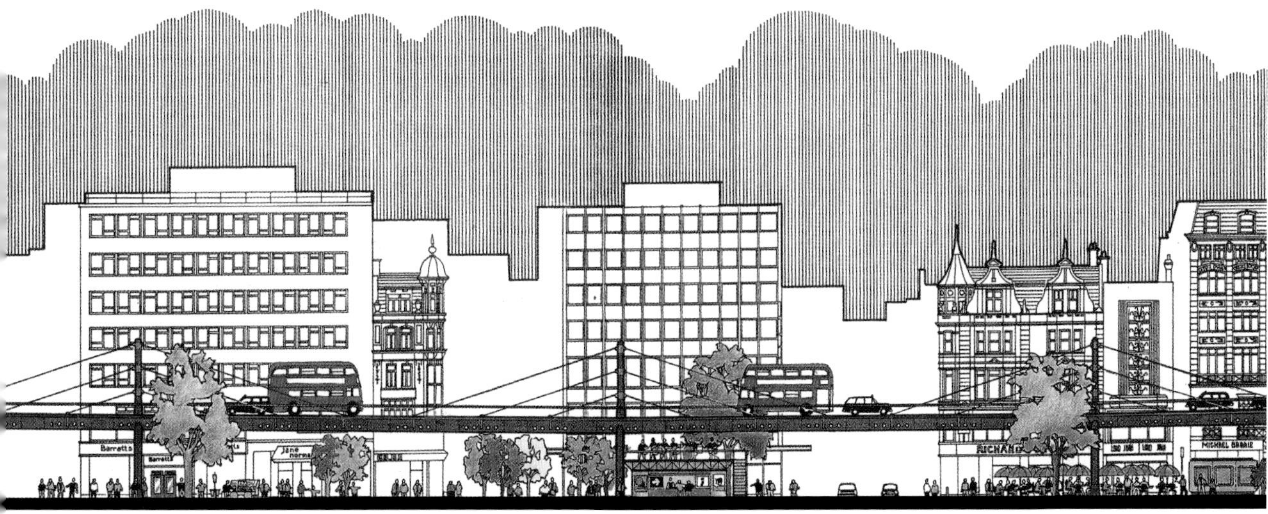

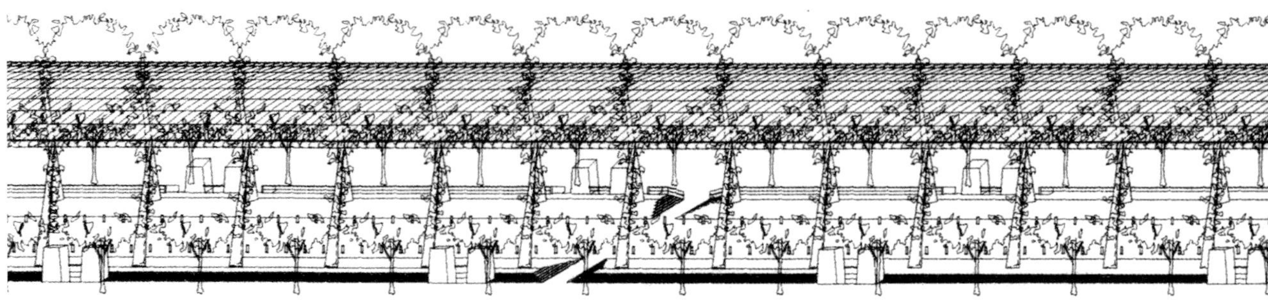

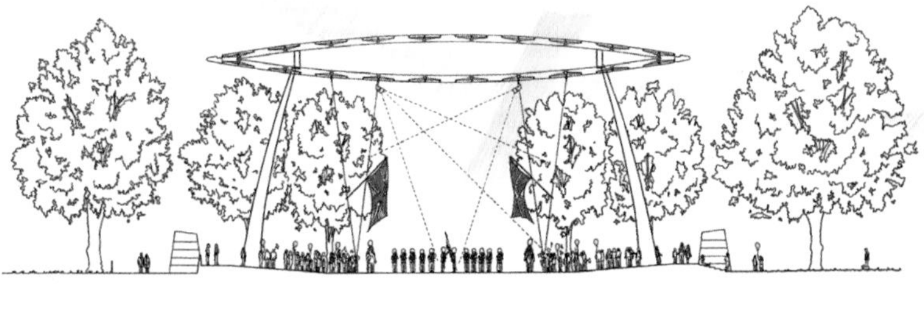

A few years later, Avery floated a project to roof the Mall between Admiralty Arch and Buckingham Palace. Had he been allowed to carry this out, London would have acquired the largest covered pedestrian space in the country—perhaps in the world. It would have united Green and St James' Parks; at the same time he also suggested closing Constitution Hill to traffic so as to turn it into a long parking area for buses; it would be served by a mini-tram, while the north edge of Green Park, bordering on Piccadilly, was to be given a new treatment and both parks re-landscaped. The main feature of the project was of course the light metal structure to carry the roof over the Mall, which was to be partly transparent, partly translucent, its soffit 18 metres above the pavement. It was to rise over the trees that line the Mall now, though additional,higher planting was also suggested. When the weather required it, the sides of the structure were to be screened by rolled blinds in inclement weather. Together the Oxford Street and the Mall projects would—at a relatively low cost—have provided London with sheltered, public and pedestrian space such as no other world city could offer (for Avery's notes on this see p. 58).

This Page
Top: Part-axonometric of the Mall roof 1992.
Middle top two: Sections with canopy open and closed.
Middle: Perspective down the Mall.
Bottom, left and right: The pageantry for which the Mall is famous.

Opposite Page
Aerial view of the Mall looking towards Buckingham Palace.

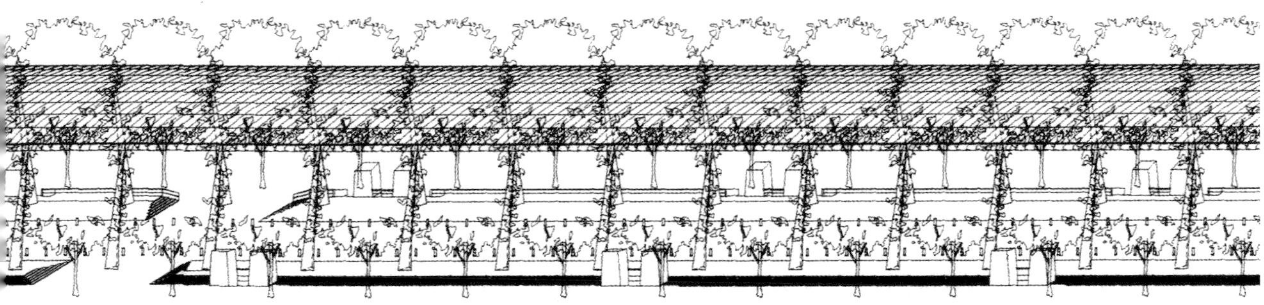

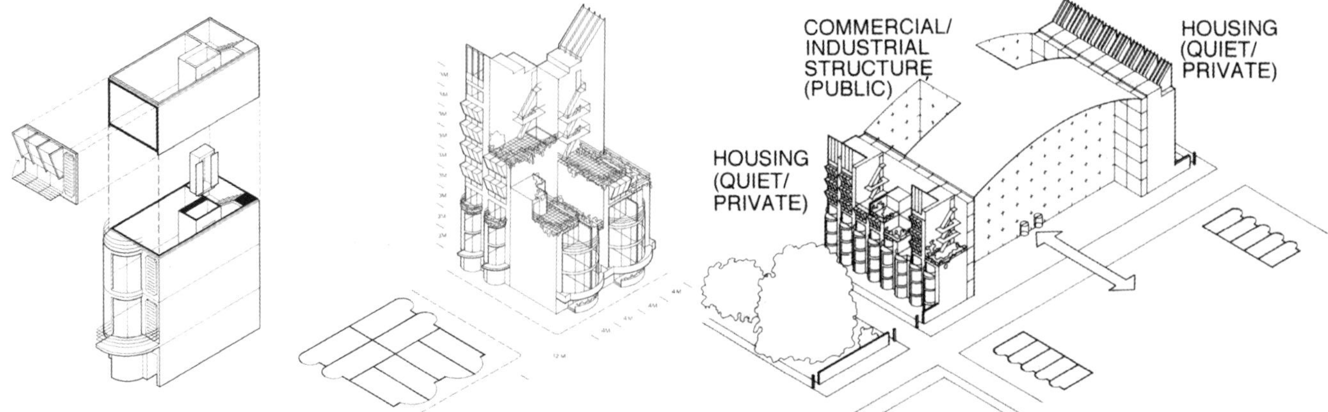

These were highly ambitious, long-range schemes requiring public, or even government support. But at the same time Avery was rethinking the problem of urban accommodation. He considered that the individual —or the semi-detached—house could not fulfil the requirements we place on our environment. Higher densities, even in low-rise building, would be the order of the day; he therefore concentrated attention on the unrecognised potentiality of terrace houses, which were to be made up of industrially prefabricated units which could be combined, stacked and unstacked as families grew and later contracted. And of course they were so designed that the street facade could be varied according to height, orientation and the inhabitants' circumstance. Several of such apartments could be arranged round an internal communication and service core provided with linear-motorised lifts as well as stairs and hoists. This allowed both for a richly varied exterior and also for plans in which work-spaces could be integrated with housing.

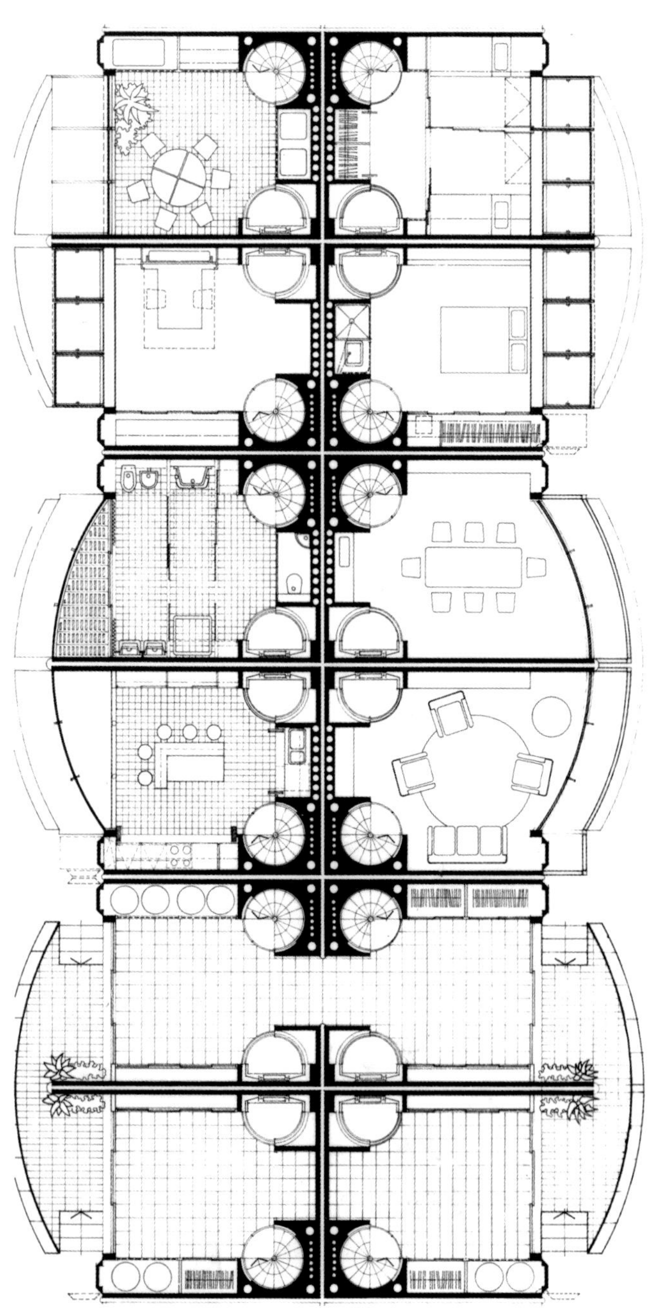

This Page
Top left: The prefabricated, double cube ATH unit construction.
Top middle: The units stacked back-to-back and of varying heights.
Top right: The residential units stacked back-to-back with commercial structures.
Right: Plan of the original 1984 high density back-to-back residential units.

Opposite Page
Isometric of a 'mature' back-to-back Advanced Technology Housing (ATH) terrace 1984.

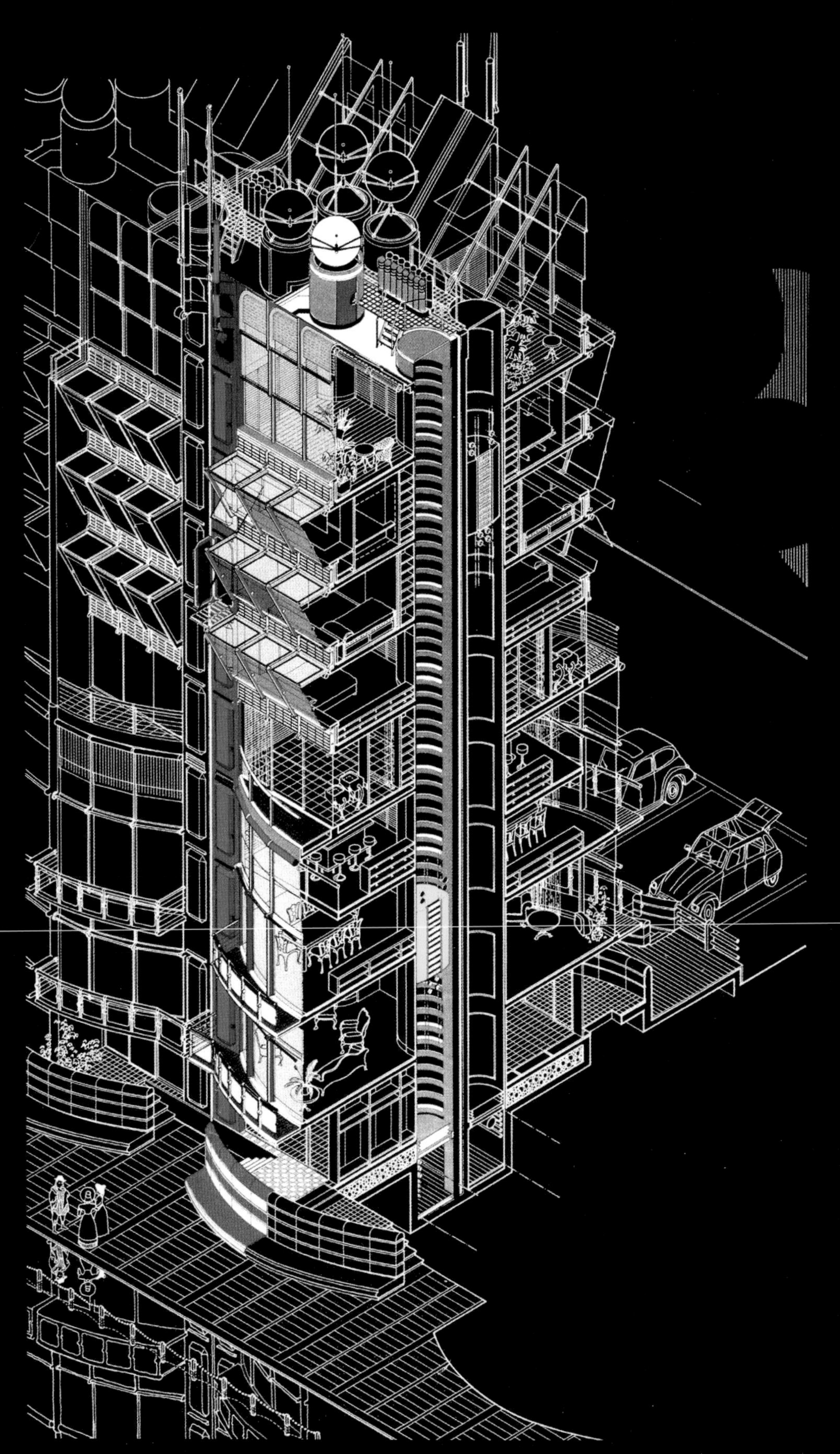

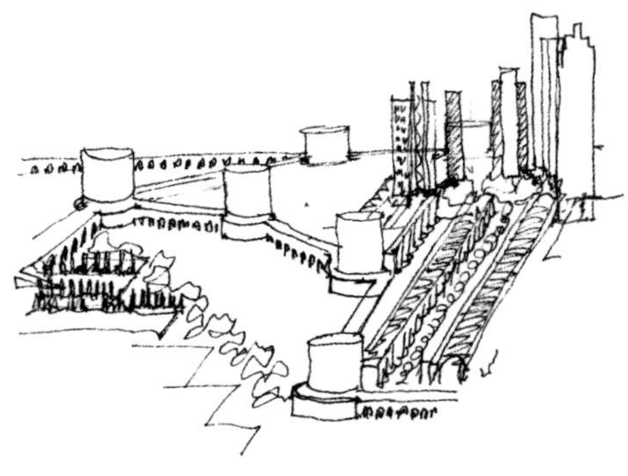

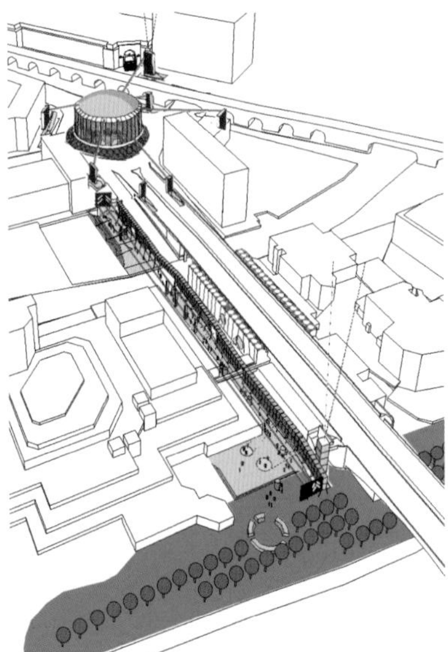

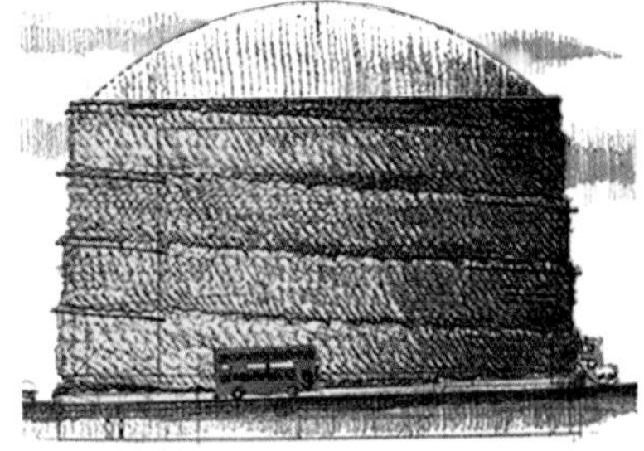

This Page
Above from top down: Wilderness city sketch;
Sketch of the final form of the IMAX;
The IMAX and MOMI masterplan linkage (Electric Avenue);
The original IMAX concept sketch (1991)—a spiral hydroponically watered vegetation covered drum.

Opposite Page
Original (1984) sketch of a Wilderness Hamlet.

From these projects, Avery moved on to a more ambitious re-interpretation of Ebenezer Howard's garden city ideal, whose proposals have often been wilfully misunderstood.

Howard's town plans, which he drew as circular diagrams, have been lampooned, though he himself was quite explicit that they were never to be read as such. Avery, well aware of Howard's essential message, adopts an analogous diagrammatic approach in his development scheme for the Helsinki-Tampere region (pp. 40–42).

The hilly Southern Finnish landscape is broken by a network of picturesque lakes and Avery proposed to link them to a number of separate, interconnected townships, each one outlined and encircled by a by-pass road; unlike the English ones, these do not ramble through the countryside, but form a sharp, if pervious, high-level edge to the township, sheltering workshops, industrial and commercial enterprises.

Within this outline, each town can develop its own civic and spatial organisation. At the junction of the high-speed road and the by-pass, as well as at certain nodes, Avery placed cylindrical parking silos—and so provided yet another re-interpretation of the round-about type. The vehicular traffic within the Finnish townships was to be limited to supplies and emergency services; normal internal circulation would be pedestrian. Though each of them could have a different plan, the model projected views of the towns do look surprisingly like those of some sixteenth and seventeenth century fortified cities, the ring-roads like bulwarks, while the traffic silos occupy the place of bastions.

His traffic silos and junctions are therefore a re-examination of another Hénard urban device, the traffic roundabout, which Avery stands on its head in one of his best-known schemes, the IMAX Cinema, whose projection system offers a complex filmic experience on a very wide screen.

The cylindrical building is sited on the existing 'bull-ring' roundabout at Waterloo, and its shallow dome roof suggests the unified space within. The structure had to offer sonic isolation from the complex of railway tunnels and other city services that run under the site, as well as from the heavy traffic that moved round it. The auditorium was therefore raised clear of the ground, and this created a large, low-level foyer linked by underground passages to the surrounding institutions: the National Theatre precinct, the National Film Theatre (Avery's earliest major London project—tucked under the southern end of Waterloo Bridge) and the Underground and railway stations.

The main—formal and urban—problem was the proper figuration to give this very prominent but eccentrically sited building. Avery had originally proposed a spiral ramp climbing up to the dome, with continuous planting as a green skin (p. 118). But his final project has a complex glass outer skin suspended on brackets beyond the blank inner walls that were wrapped originally in a vast, dramatic painting by Sir Howard Hodgkin—an under-appreciated landmark of South London.

The scale of the image allows passing motorists a clear view of it, while the space between the roadway and the edge of the building is a public area into which the underground access passages feed. It is sheltered by creepers which turn it into a pergola, and also provides the passer-by, as well as the motorist, with a view of the cylindrical structure rising from its green base. (pp. 8, 118–125, 146, Footnote p. 186)

While working on such realisations, Avery continued to speculate on urbanistic problems. He was well aware that Ebenezer Howard's notion was that the garden city should be productive and should never act as a dormitory whose occupiers would need to travel to the nearest city to earn their living.

Hampstead Garden Suburb, a conspicuous piece of planning and building that claimed to apply Howard's principles, therefore perpetuated a misconception. Howard had insisted on the urbanity of his satellites as he did on the rurality of the green spaces that separated them (though he did not quite use those terms, which—before the advent of industrial farming—may not have been needed, in any case). Rurality, however, is very much part of Avery's programme, which he has called "Wilderness City" and I (for one) find his vision of a countryside criss-crossed by unpaved, potholed and un-signposted roads very appealing—an emphatic extension and intensification of the green belt.

He is also concerned to emphasise the contrary and very urban character of his proposed satellites, which he wants considerably denser than Howard ever did. The clusters of relatively low (under ten-storey) towers, like a San Gimignano transferred to the much more lush, gentler English countryside, would be surrounded by further clusters of low-rise terraces.

The occupation of the towers would be dependent on a rapid link to ground level through small and low-energy lifts. The buildings would also be interconnected—rather than separated—by paved pedestrian areas, shopping, public spaces—to provide the essential urban buzz.

Such concentration would allow much of the countryside to return to a wild, or at least a semi-wild state, the wilderness about which Avery writes so lyrically. It would also encourage food-production in allotments and orchards, forms of localised husbandry related to adjoining markets (some of which could, of course be sheltered under the bypass-'wall', to which he attaches great importance, realising as he does that retail trade is the urban lifeblood).

The autonomy of such enclaves seems to me an essential virtue of the whole project—and the condition under which the green spaces in between can really return to their primal wilderness condition has an immediate, powerful appeal. The hierarchy of towers will therefore have to be a feature of any detailed design of the 'town', and will be developed when the specific design of each particular site is detailed and refined. I look forward eagerly to Avery being allowed to apply such ideas in his practice, though his projects require a political will and involvement which seems absent in our world. Nor do I think changes of government in this or any other country can bring them about. The political will of which I speak has little to do with party-politics, but is much more concerned with the relation between development finance and local authority. In this climate, the work of Avery's office, which offers a mix of hard-headed—even if rather dramatic—realisations such as the Neathouse Place office building and the IMAX Cinema, as well as highly worked-out, and very ambitious, visionary urban proposals, and even more speculative texts (his remarkably original essay on the physiology of proportional perception is an instance) is of outstanding importance, offering, as it does, an example both his more pedestrian and his more 'theoretical' colleagues might follow. Such a fruitful combination of themes and approaches can make a definite contribution to a change in the climate of patronage—especially official patronage—in this country and perhaps also elsewhere.

Footnote to Chapter 3
The Mall Project 1996

The project proposed closing the Mall to traffic and covering it with a half-mile long glass canopy. This would be a gift to the nation, creating a special place unlike any other in the world, wherein people could congregate in safety all year round—to promenade, to celebrate, and to enjoy a spectacular new setting for the ceremonies and pageants for which London is famous. The plan required removal of all through traffic from the Mall and Horseguards Road. Of all London's roads, these are arguably the easiest to pedestrianise as they are already restricted to light vehicles and are periodically closed to all traffic for special occasions. To improve access, Constitution Hill would be restructured for coach parking, and linked to Trafalgar Square and Westminster by an electric shuttle service.

With the Mall pedestrianised, there would no longer be a barrier between St James' Park and Green Park, and the latter could be re-planned to form a new social environment—one-mile long, quiet and traffic-free—stretching all the way from Hyde Park to Trafalgar Square.

The Mall would be resurfaced for pedestrian use and on each side, the ground would slope up gently to afford visitors better views of ceremonial events. Small kiosks, public lavatories and facilities for the disabled would be provided at regular intervals. A generous stepped terrace would be created on the St James' Park side, running the full length of the Mall and this would become a venue for promenading or for simply sitting and enjoying the views of this, the most beautiful and romantic of all London's parks.

The canopy is 46 metres wide and approximately 825 metres long. It was designed as a prefabricated, double-skin planar-glazed structure, suitable for rapid assembly and providing maximum lightness with minimum maintenance. Rising some 18 metres to its underside, the canopy would sit above the inner (lower) row of tress and be fitted with integral spot-lights, sound systems and supports for flags and banners.

While the canopy was primarily a roof, open along both sides, it also included tracks into which removable synthetic membranes—clear or translucent—could be fitted, thus creating an enclosed space of 39,600 square metres, or nearly ten acres. Such a space could transform the civic life of London and provide a new social focus for the nation.
(pp. 52–53, 61, 149)

Chapter 4

The Workplace
by John Worthington

Digital communications have had a profound effect on how we define work and the way it is organised. Over the last 25 years how we work has changed dramatically, but over the same period of time office buildings and the way they are planned have changed little. Frank Lloyd Wright's Johnson Wax Building (1936–1939) (left, top), Foster's Hong Kong and Shanghai Bank (1985) (left below), and the more recent offices in the City of London all follow a similar paradigm, of large open-plan floor areas, serried ranks of desks and centralised control.

Bryan Avery's work, disappointingly much of it never built, has nonetheless been a beacon of innovative thinking over the last thirty years. The work has explored the impact of new technologies and has been prepared to speculate on the impact that the blurring of functions will have on buildings, their construction and their wider urban context.

In the last 50 years we have shifted from manufacturing, through service to a knowledge-based economy. Today many of the clerical functions of the office are computerised and value is added through know-how, creativity and innovation.
The new office paradigm is one of decentralised power, flexible working and a diversity of settings for collaborative working. Work is now structured as a pleasure, in a playful environment, and leisure looks more like hard work. The new communications technologies have allowed us to work where, when and how we like. The increased freedom of communication has allowed for 'distributed working' and the choice of the most appropriate locations across a networked conurbation. Some would claim that we are in danger of creating a semi-urbanised, placeless sprawl. Or it could be argued that the challenge is to create new types of places in a new type of urban structure. The new paradigm, as reflected in Holland's Randstad, is a low density city in a high density landscape with distinctive high intensity urban nodes. In his essay "Fragments of a Wilderness City" 1984-2004, (Chapter 2), Avery prophetically visualises a post-industrial urban landscape of 'distributed' living and working in a 'rural' bliss connected by a network of de-surfaced country lanes.

His work has, since the practice began in the early 1970s, been intuitively grappling with four major themes that face urbanists and architects in the twenty-first century. First, a world of paradox where the resolution of problems is not seen to be a 'binary' choice between either this or that, but a balance which allows for both this and that.

This Page
Top: High density mixed use walled city; Essaouira; Morocco.
Middle: Frank Lloyd Wright, Johnson Wax Building; Racine, Wisconsin, USA.
Bottom: Norman Foster; Hong Kong and Shanghai Bank HQ; Hong Kong.

The work of the practice does not reflect a neat classification into building types. It is interested in both the detail and the big idea. It is both ‘high tech’ and ‘high feel’.

Secondly, we live today in a world that is both real and virtual. Instant cheap communication has allowed us in real time to be part of an event at the far side of the globe. Football fans don their tribal paint to join a virtual global crowd, whilst sitting in their very real English village pub.

Avery, in his proposals for communities in an age of advanced technology, 1984–1985, and his later 1993 versions of Wilderness City, is at the heart of this, explaining real and the virtual in these plans for the cities of the future.

Thirdly, we are faced with the paradox of valuing distinctive permanent places which can respond to continuous change. This is a recurring theme in the workplace projects of the office, from the Spiral mixed use office building proposal of 1973 (pp. 63, 135), to the later competition entries for the European Patent Office, 1988 (pp. 64, 141) and Rank Xerox European Systems HQ, Welwyn Garden City 1991 (pp. 64–65, 145).

Lastly, Avery’s work has addressed the challenge of making places that are both enhanced by, and enhance, technology. Proposals for the Avenue of the Emirates 1982 (pp. 51, 138); the adaptations underneath Waterloo Bridge for the Museum of the Moving Image 1984–1988 (pp. 2–3, 84–85, 112–117,186), the European Teleport project 1994 (p. 148); Ecological Beacons, 1994–1996 (pp. 17, 86–87) and the Mall, 1996 (pp. 52–53 and Footnote p. 58),are all fascinated with an understanding of emerging technologies and expressed meanings.

The portfolio of work reflects an enquiring mind and facility of expression that is equally at ease with concepts as with detail. What were the foundations for this breadth of awareness? After studying at Leicester College of Art, then one of the foremost art schools in this country, Avery worked with Anthony Williams Burles, a practice specialising in component design, where he was immediately introduced to the pragmatic world of the manufacturer and the detailing required for the reality of production. However, after a year of being immersed in such detail, he joined the recently established masters course in Architectural Theory and Criticism at the University of Essex. Here he studied under Professors Joseph Rykwert and Dalibor Vesely, whose phenomenological approach brought new perspectives and depth to his thinking.

I first met Bryan Avery when Frank Duffy, Colin Cave and I were preparing a series of technical articles for *The Architects’ Journal* on office design.

In the late 1960s, office design was seen by the majority of the profession as uninteresting and commercial. It was a delightful surprise, as I scoured practices for interesting examples of innovative office design thinking, to meet Bryan, who at that time was working for Raymond Cecil on a proposal on the Bath Road adjacent to Heathrow airport (pp. 8, 62, 135). The proposed office building, located 350 metres from the end of Runway One and directly under the flight path of Runway Two, was heavily constrained by public safety regulations and flight safety contours. In this hostile, noisy and polluted environment, Bryan showed his innovative ability to find opportunities in the most unlikely circumstances.

To control the high-frequency airborne noise, the roofs of the building were designed to be double skinned and cantilevered out and down at the edges like aerofoil flaps to protect the walls. The walls were inclined inwards at an angle of 16 degrees to further reduce exposure to noise and sun.

This Page
Top: One of several civic spaces within the commercial matrix of Essaouira, Morocco.

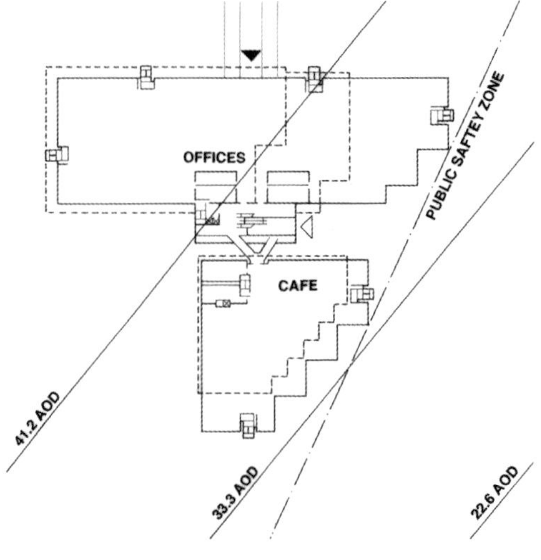

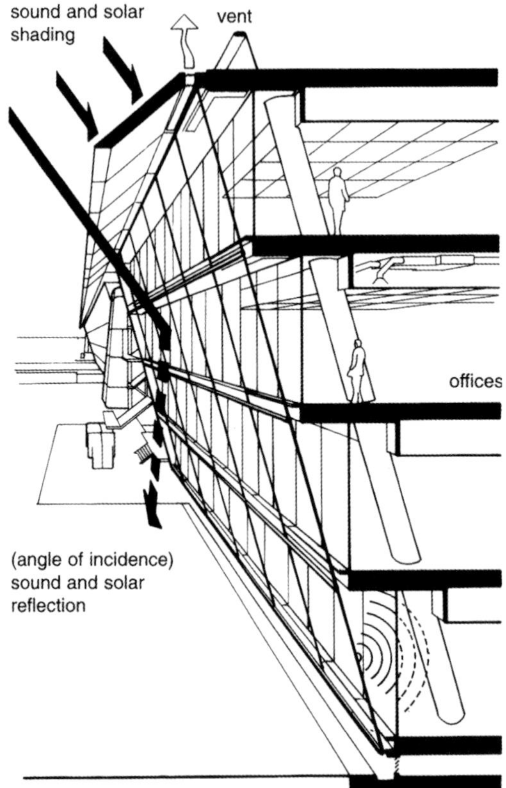

Such angling, combined with a double glazed profiled cavity, provided the acoustic performance equivalent to a 600 mm thick solid masonry wall. The project, although never constructed, showed Avery's grasp of technical detail whilst never losing a concern to create meaningful, elegant and enjoyable places. Moreover, the lessons learnt here about solar and acoustic attenuation have continued to inform subsequent projects, and the characteristic angled glass profile has recurred in many of the practice's best-known buildings.

In the same period, Avery's involvement with the world of commercial, speculative office design raised his awareness of the need for flexibility and adaptability in use. The 'Spiral' multi tenanted project, 1973, was an exploration into how companies could expand, shrink and reconfigure within the same block. The requirement was to allow tenants to have direct public access to their own reception area whilst at the same time allowing for private and secure access to all parts of their domain without entering the public area. The solution was to arrange the offices as three autonomous blocks, each reducing in area towards the top to create ten different sized floor plates, spiralling down at one-third storey heights around a central point. The blocks themselves are separated one from another by a narrow atrium, open to the street and accommodating the main vertical circulation.

The "Spiral" was an intelligently intuitive architectural response to what, 30 years later, was to be recognised as the emerging office typology. Today, the property industry is recognising the value of separate but interconnected floor plates, to allow for independent small lets or security between departments within the same organisation. Circulation space linking between floors is slowly being perceived as an asset to foster informal communication and collaboration, rather than a loss of prime lettable space, and the standard repetitive floor height is being questioned, to be replaced by more dynamic sectional forms which allow for a wider range of settings and connections within.

Footnote:

Comprising 14,771m² of commercial space, of which some 8,500m² was to be dedicated to offices, the 'Spiral' project was an exploration into the nature of speculative office design.

Research indicated that offices are nearly always in a state of flux: expanding, shrinking or just being reconfigured. At the same time, companies rarely have the same space requirements. However, they all prefer direct public access to their own reception area, whereafter they ask that there be private and secure access to all parts of their domain without recourse again to the public areas.

In the Spiral project, the offices were arranged as three autonomous blocks, each three or four storeys in height and each reducing in area towards the top to create 10 different sized floor-plates. The floor-plates were then 'spiralled' at one-third storey heights around a central point, the blocks themselves being separated one from another by a narrow atrium, open to the street.

This simple planning device allowed individual floor-plates within each block to be linked across the atrium, either up or down the spiral, making it possible to provide private and secure links between adjacent floors throughout the building.

Such was the flexibility of the design, that within a three-to-four storey building, 55 different permutations of space could be provided within one change of level. Allowing a two-thirds or full-height storey change, the permutations increased exponentially.

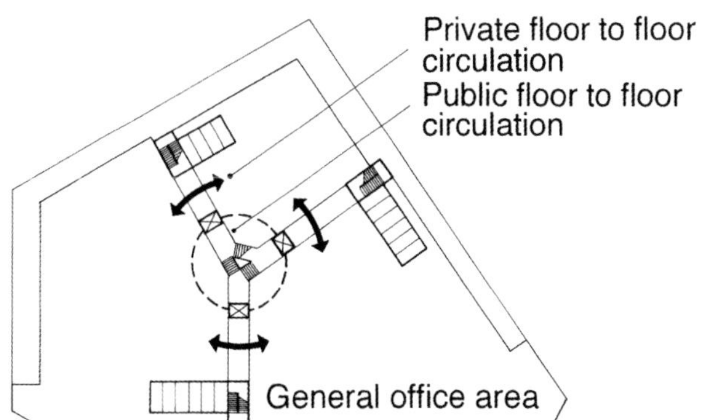

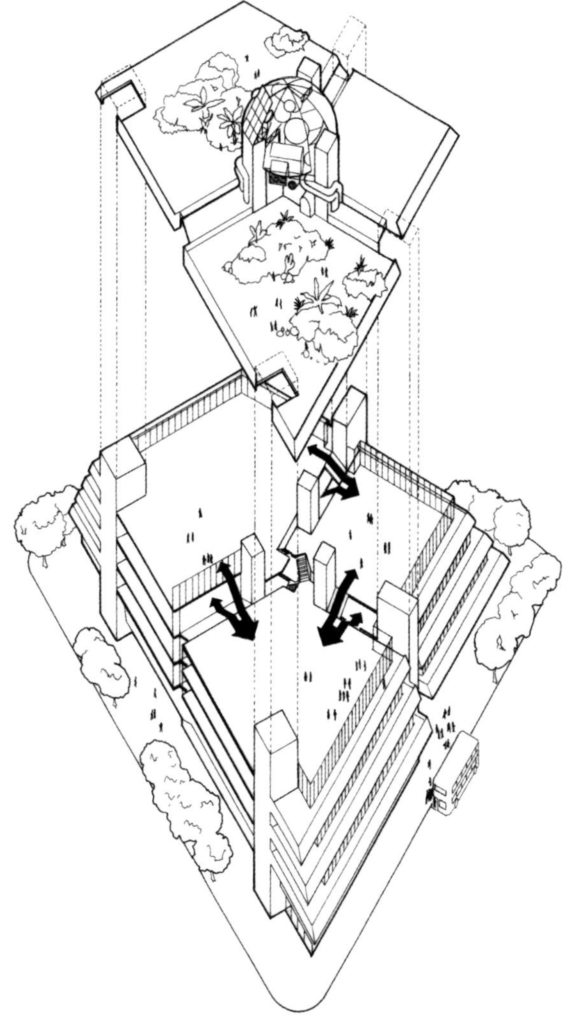

This Page
Top: The Spiral office project 1974–1975. Office floor plan;
Middle: Axonometric;
Bottom: Model.

Opposite Page
Top: Offices at Heathrow Airport; London 1972–1974; plan.
Middle: Cross-section.
Bottom: Model.

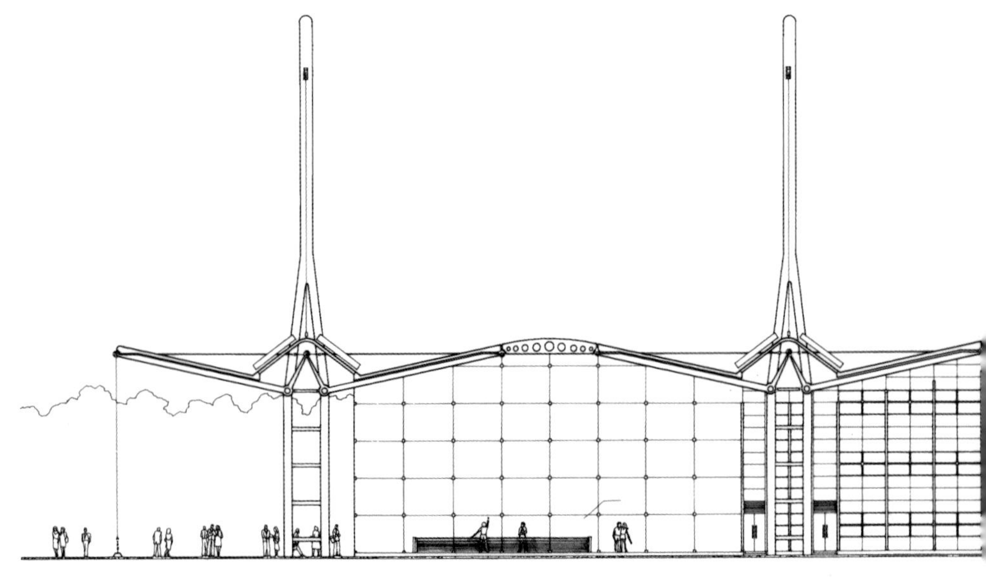

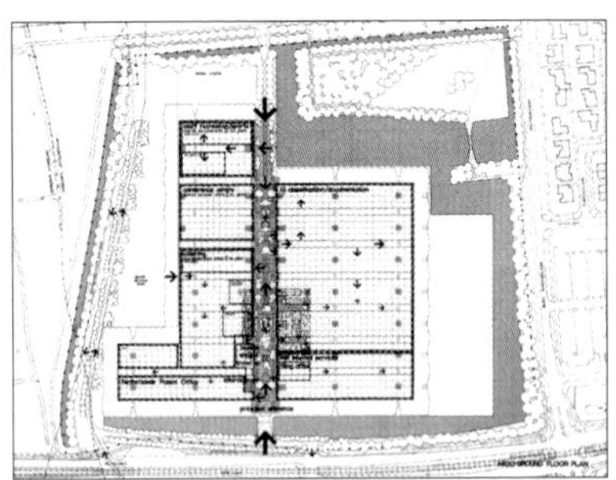

The European Patent Office Competition, 1988, explored the theme of growth and change from another perspective. Stimulated by the agro industrial glasshouse landscape of central Holland, the competition entry proposed a vast 116,000 square metre covered space within which an independent community of streets, squares and blocks could be formed. The proposition was a "self-contained environment of lightweight two and three storey structures... sheltered by a single all-encompassing roof, supported independently from cable-stayed masts set at 30 metre intervals... the separation of the two structures allowing greater flexibility, in both plan and section, such that the building could be expanded over time with minimal inconvenience".

Rank Xerox's invitation to undertake a feasibility study to restructure their existing manufacturing site at Welwyn Garden City for the relocation of its European Systems headquarters, 1991, was an opportunity to explore further the expression of growth and change in site planning and building form (p. 145). "The challenge was to give expression to Rank Xerox's corporate character, while allowing for probable expansion or contraction and, in extremis, for possible separate lettings or even freehold sales".

The site was organised with a strong corporate façade and a clear public area to the front, comprising a landscaped berm with a pergola topping to contain the carparking. The rear provides

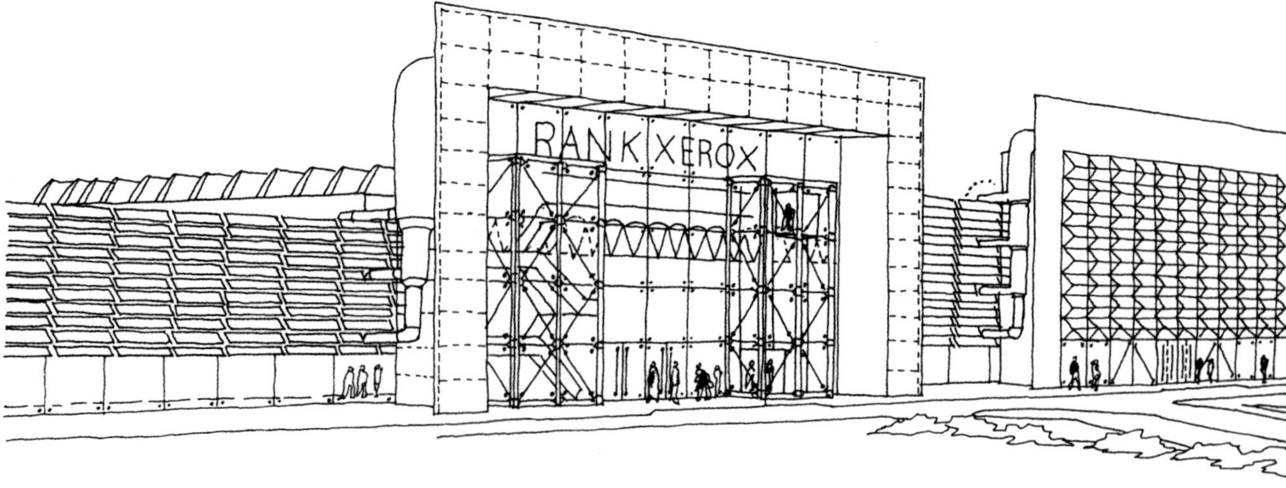

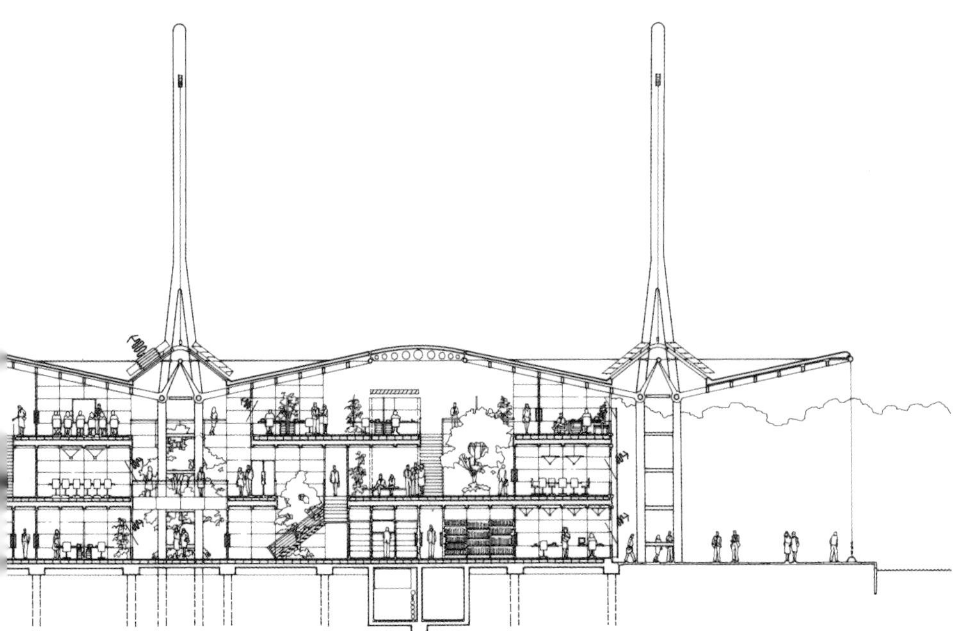

private, more intimate, spaces for staff relaxation. The scale is reduced by the rear blocks terracing down to the sheltered gardens behind.

The building complex is a set of four H-shaped, three-storied blocks, each with their own dedicated site, complete with car parking, access and services. The separate building blocks are interlinked front and rear, the front providing continuous semi-public access between all five blocks, and the rear providing a secure link for staff inter-departmental circulation.

The building complex provides for over 18,000 square metres of flexible floor space in an articulated collection of interconnected spaces that can be separated or combined to form larger or smaller units, each with their own distinctive identity as required. The proposals are a logical development from the earlier propositions of the 'Spiral', combining the flexibility of contiguous, undifferentiated space with the need for character and identity. The proposals provide a clear conceptual framework, with a legible articulation of the real estate agenda for flexibility of tenancies and fit out.

This Page
Rank Xerox HQ, 1991, right (masterplan), below and opposite (perspective).

Opposite Page
European Patent Office, 1988; Above (section), left top (plans) and bottom (model).

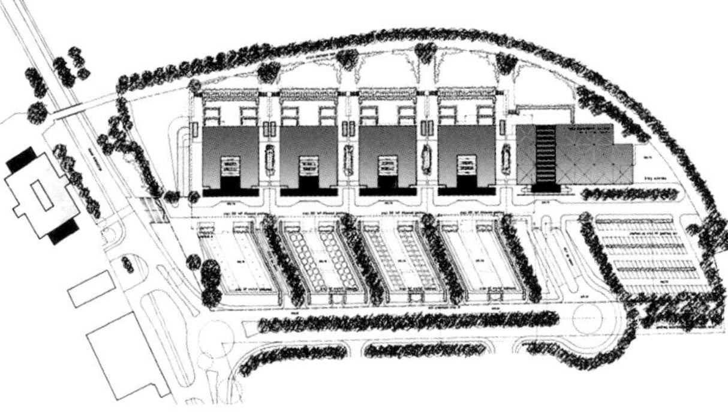

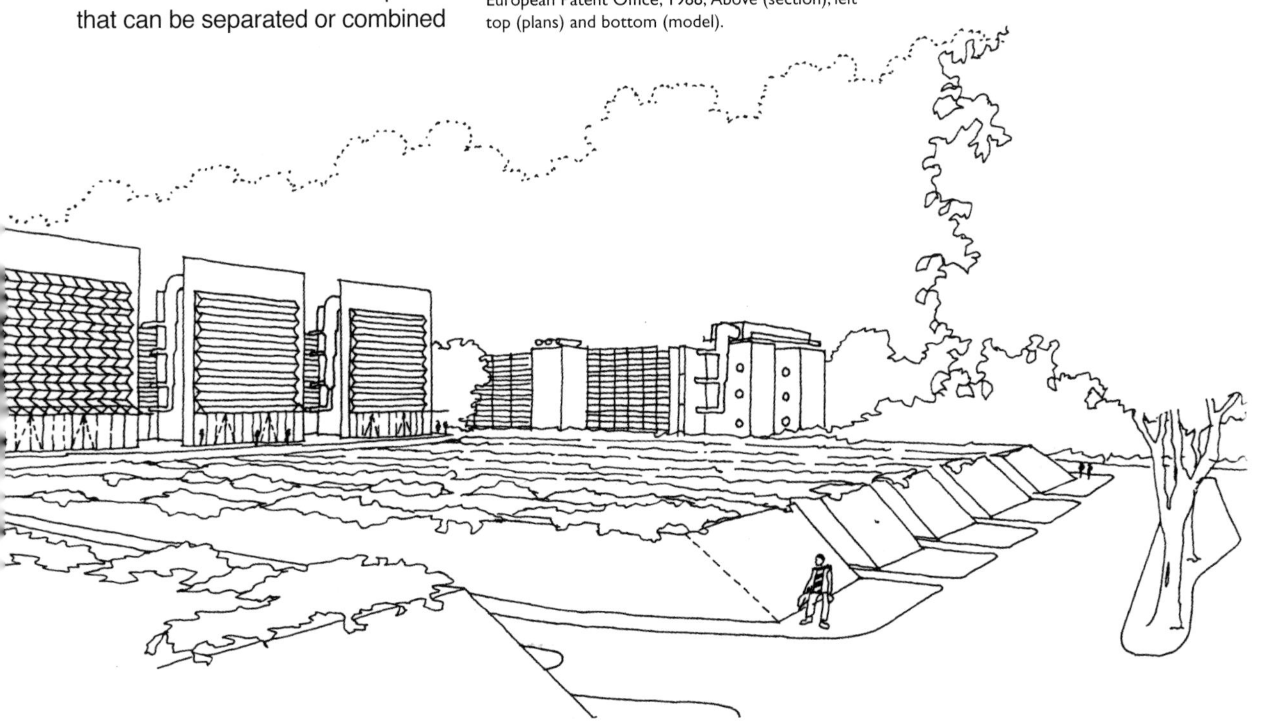

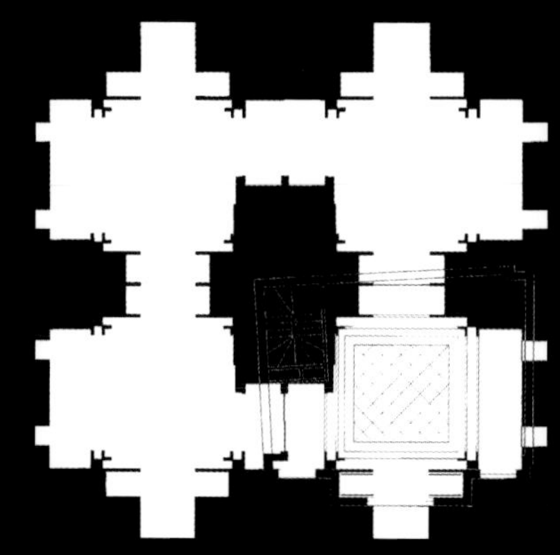

In parallel with a continuous flow of innovative feasibility studies and competition entries, the practice was also involved with several high quality commercial interiors.

Charterhouse Mews for Hewitt Associates, a leading American management consultancy, involved the conversion of a three-storied mews house into a 'pied-a-terre' base for their London operations. Two of the floors were reorganised to provide a combination of workstations and enclosed offices and the third floor was re-planned to provide a confidential meeting room. Although a small project in a domestic building, Avery approached it as an architectural challenge. He was concerned to give the room presence and dignity despite the low height, awkwardly shaped space. A recurring theme of Avery's work and writing, is the use of a 1:1 and 2:1 proportional system developed here to great effect, with the central space being transformed through the use of mirrors from a square plan with low ceiling into a 'virtual' 4.7 metre cube. The design owes much to Soane and his early studies at Essex and "the resultant space has an intimacy, and a grandeur, that belies its size, while at the table there is a palpable calm".

This Page
Top: Charterhouse Mews, 1989. Floor plan depicting the mirrored pochés.

Opposite Page
The poché and mirrored ceiling.

Plantation House in Fenchurch Street, subsequently redeveloped, was a six-year programme of upgrading the office tenancies to a modern commercial specification and revitalising the internal public environment. The complex, with 32,500m2 of multi tenanted space and a public thoroughfare through the building at ground level, was a dynamic business community.

With five separate entrances and the same number of independent lift cores, of which only three were associated with specific entrances, the challenge for the architect was to create 'one place' legibility and orientation.

To resolve this, emphasis was placed on the five vertical lift cores, using colour, texture and lighting to identify the different localities. A separate project was to design an internal signage system "to create a comprehensive method of orientation which, eschewing convention, relies on a series of line-of-sight wall signs and purpose made company logos over each door. Colour-coded directories at every entrance allow each office to be located quickly and with minimum inconvenience." The results showed the value of a good designer who brought order, meaning, discipline

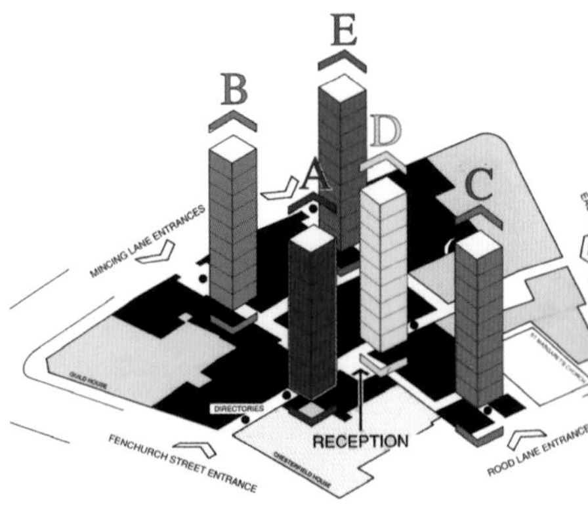

and elegance to what many other professionals might have seen to be just another job.

This Page
Clockwise from top left:
The signage system, Plantation House 1985–1991 (p. 85); The colour-coded lifts, pink, yellow, green and red; Handrail detail; Typical ground floor corridor; The conference room.

Opposite Page
Top left: The facade; Plantation House;
Top middle: The colour-coded locator board at each entrance;
Top right: The colour coding principle for the lift cores.
Bottom: The new 'gentleman's club' reception area.

Avery's interest in the office as a building type finally found physical expression at No. 1 Neathouse Place, Victoria, 1994–1996. The building, a typical 1960s speculative office block with a narrow depth and low floor to floor heights, had been lying vacant for several years as recurring feasibility studies proved the building to be too expensive to demolish and too low in floor height to be converted to meet modern office specification. The problem was seen to be compounded by the building spanning one of the busiest traffic routes into central London.

In the end, the developer, who had been involved with Avery's RADA (the Royal Academy of Dramatic Art) project, asked him for suggestions. What others, through conventional wisdom, had seen as insurmountable problems, he saw as opportunities. The gateway effect of the road underneath was seen as an opportunity to create a landmark and celebrate the entry to the Victoria station precinct. By moving the entrance to the south of the building and creating a separate entrance pavilion, he has articulated a meeting point of routes and a change point from the transience of the station precinct to the neighbourhood scale of Pimlico and Wilton Road.

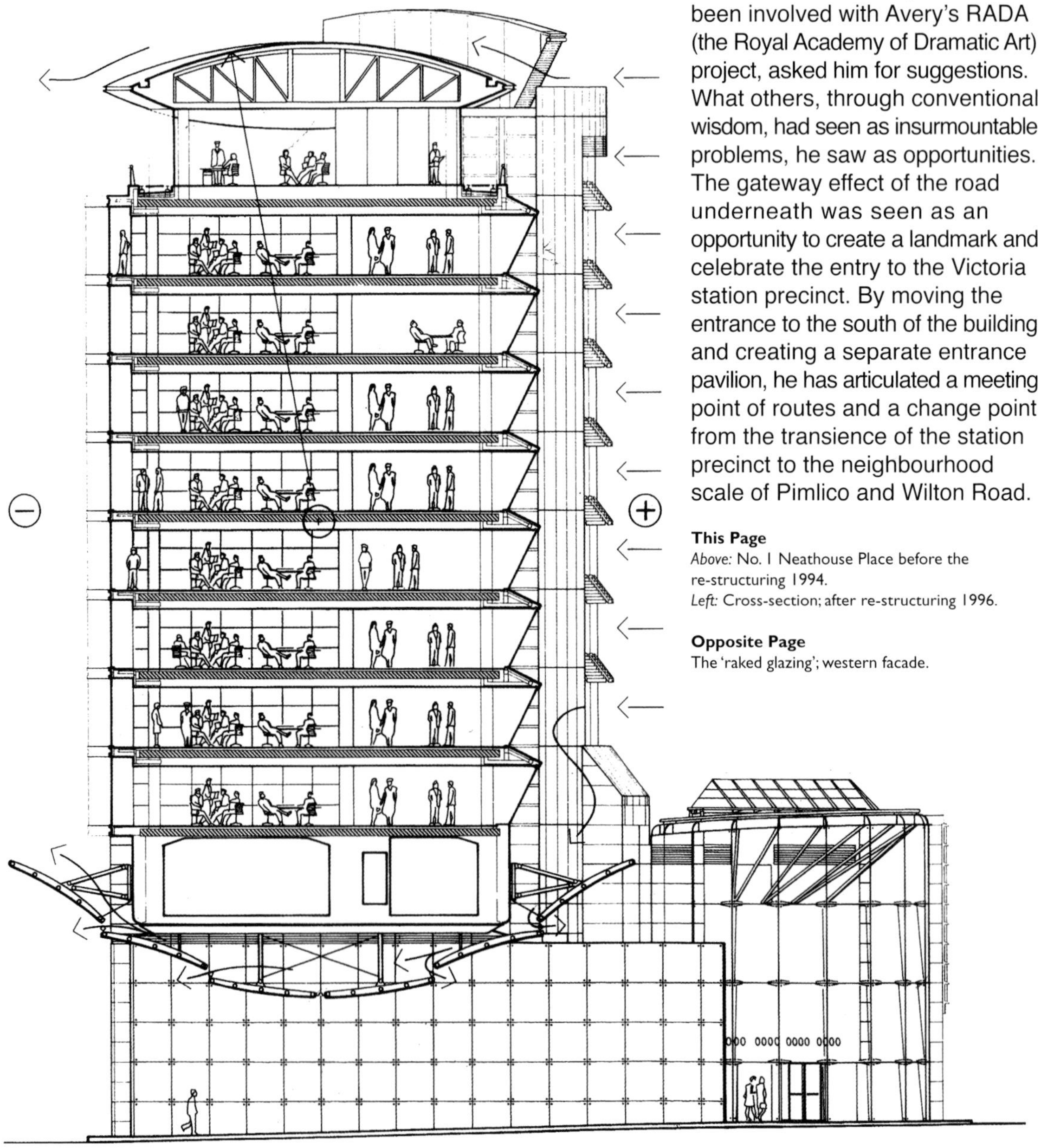

This Page
Above: No. 1 Neathouse Place before the re-structuring 1994.
Left: Cross-section; after re-structuring 1996.

Opposite Page
The 'raked glazing'; western facade.

The drab sixties slab block was given a new character and a distinctive identity by the well judged addition of four key architectural elements; a dramatic entrance rotunda connected to a new lift core and external stair tower; an independent floating roof structure over valuable new "penthouse" offices; two vertical services towers placed externally at either end of the block to provide localised air handling plant and thereby overcome the need for deep ceiling voids; and two new but completely different facades. Internally, undaunted by the low floor to floor heights, Avery recognised the opportunity to add floorspace to the perimeter and articulate the facades to reflect local conditions.

On the south elevation, the solutions reflect lessons learnt from his earlier Heathrow office project. Raked glazing controls solar gain and glare, provides a visual focus internally to counteract the low floor to ceiling height (2.45 metres) and creates a striking external facade which is seen in glimpses by those hurrying to and from the station.

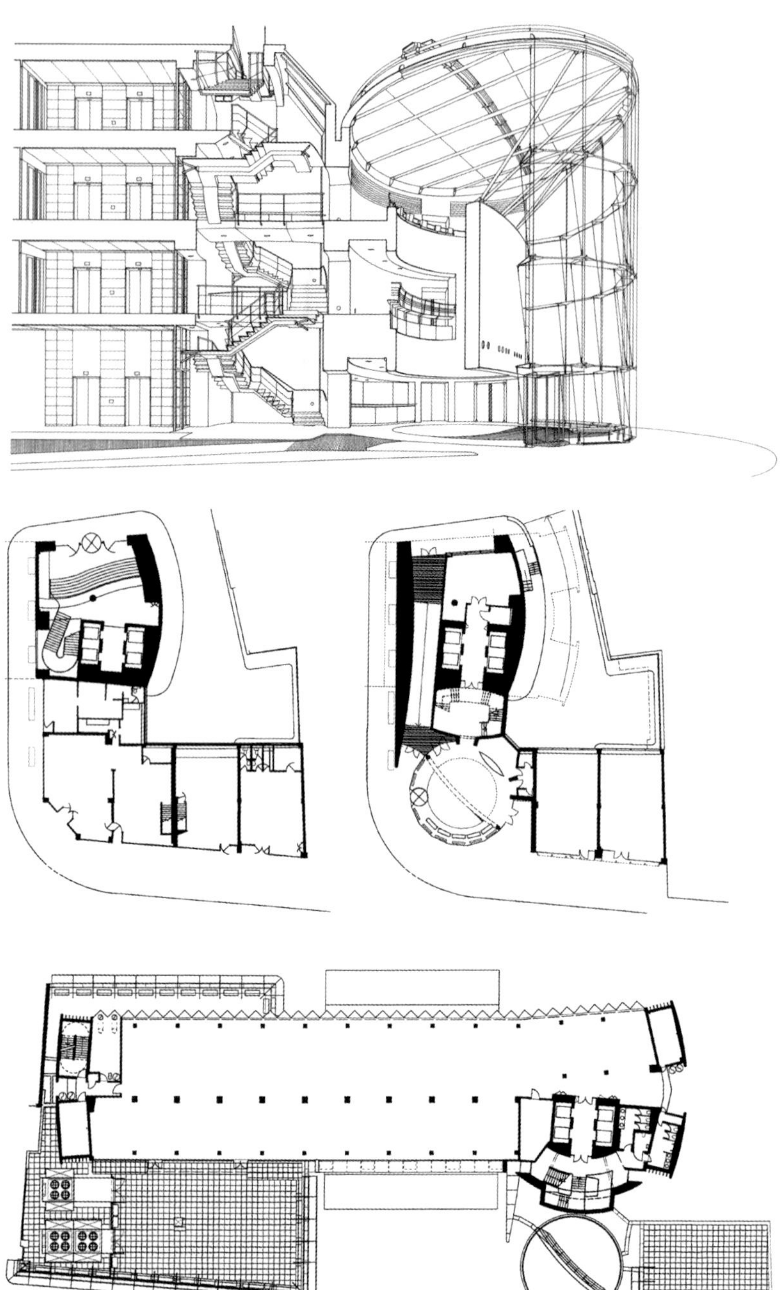

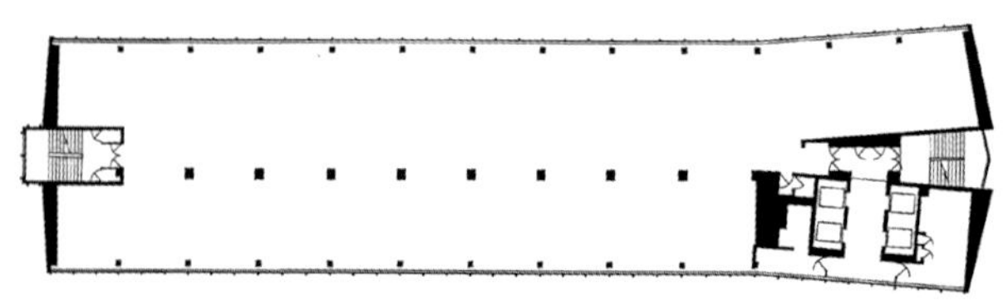

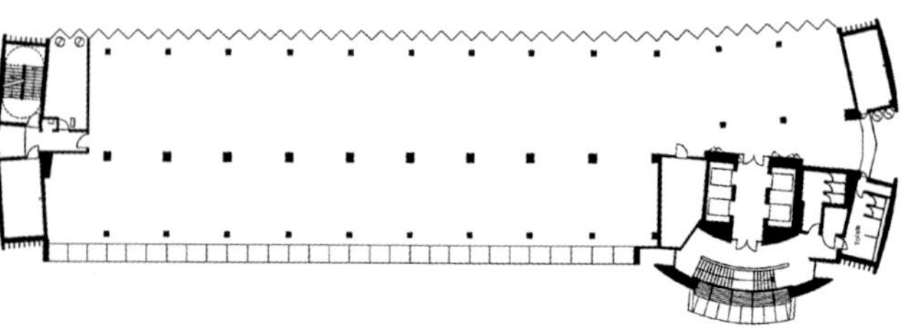

This Page
Top: Perspective section of the new foyer and main circulation core.
Upper middle: Main entrance; before (left) and after (right).
Lower middle: Third floor plan, after.
Bottom: Typical floor plan before (top) and after (bottom).

Opposite Page
Top left: The entrance foyer.
Top middle: St Ivo, Rome, Borromini.
Top right: San Stephano Rotundo; Rome.
Bottom: View up from the foyer.

Overleaf
(74,75) View from a typical floor with Westminster Cathedral (left) and Westminster Abbey and Big Ben (right).

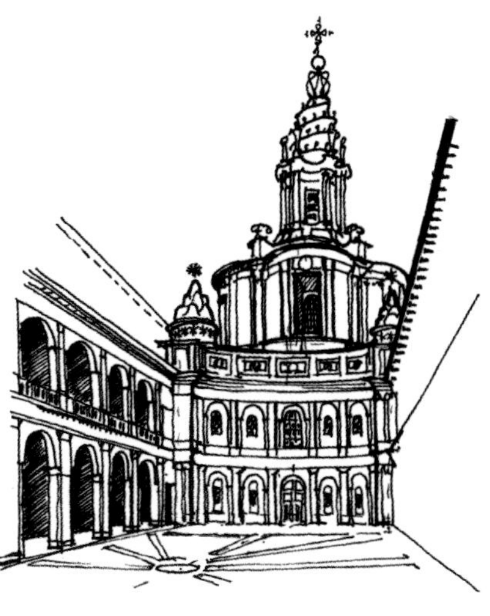

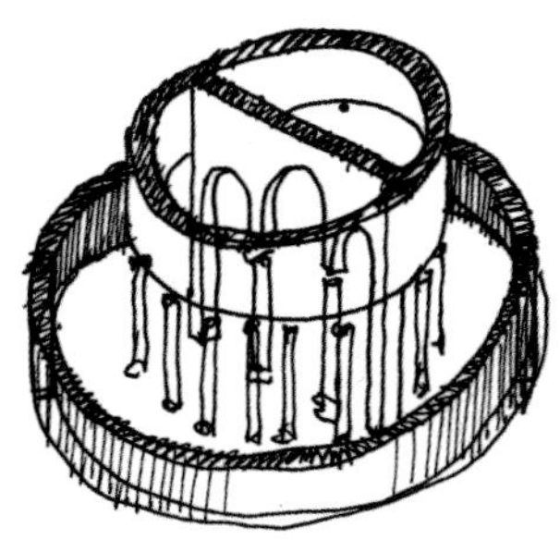

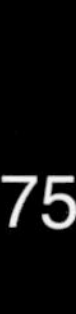

On the north side, where solar gain is not a problem, full height vertical glazing is used, drawing the eye outwards to the views over central London.

The additional top floor, unhampered by existing floor heights, recognises the unique nature of the space, providing a generous height under a sculpted roof structure with external terraces and spectacular views.

No. 1 Neathouse Place is an exemplary demonstration of the added value that intelligent design, coupled with the imagination to question perceived wisdom, can bring to seemingly intractable problems. The design has resulted in additional space for the building owner, an improved internal working environment, a dramatically enclosed visual and climatic environment where the building over-sails the road, and a dramatic focal point at what was a busy, but visually unsatisfactory, London interchange.

Perhaps the most telling evidence of its success is not the awards it has received, including the coveted Westminster Society Award and the British Council of Offices Award, but that it let within six weeks of being marketed at the highest rental in the area, and that the original multinational 'bluechip' tenant is still there.

Since No. 1 Neathouse Place, there have been many feasibility studies for significant sites such as the Swiss Centre, Leicester Square, 2000–2004 (pp. 154–155), and a proposal for a mixed use development in Kolkata, 2004–2005 (pp.166–167), which have continued to explore themes already established about mixed use adaptability, passive environmental controls, and the ordering of space through form, but disappointingly, with the exception of the Old Bailey project with the Sidell Gibson Partnership, (pp. 14–15, 172) the next major workspace building project has so far eluded the practice.

Within the changing landscape of architectural practice, Avery Associates has two faces. On one side it reflects the traditional model of the practice set up to support the interests and passions of the partners—what David Maister has typified as the practice-led business. However, on the other side of the coin is the embryo of a practice that could be a model for the future. As clients, with their concerns for certainty and managing risk, move towards a one-stop service integrating detailed design, production, delivery and ongoing maintenance, we may see the role of problem definition and conceptual design becoming an independent and valued offering. Over the last 30 years of practice, Bryan Avery has shown an intelligence and imagination to frame problems, bring order to complexity, and visualise opportunities through design. The time is right for such a service—and more importantly, for it to be rightly valued.

This Page
Top: No. 1 Neathouse Place after re-construction (Westminster Cathedral campanile middle right).
Middle and bottom: The principal staircase.

Opposite Page
Top left: The Eastern facade.
Top middle: The cafe interior.
Top right: Lower staircase levels.
Bottom: The Eastern facade showing the faceted window 'oriels'.

Chapter 5

Aspects of Innovation
by Matthew Teague

Most responses to a view of what life could be like in the future tend towards the extreme. Science-fiction writers and architects both share a pre-occupation with imagined future scenarios but whereas the output of writers can usually be categorised as either a dystopian vision of a technological hell (often a regressive, post apocalyptic slide into the past) or a future where technology is eulogised (or stigmatised) as a servant of its human masters, most architects would probably subscribe to the more optimistic 'future paradise' model.

That is not to say that there isn't also a nostalgic, backward-looking movement in architecture; a response to the city which turns away from the problem. Poundbury, the Prince of Wales' village in Dorset, built using 'traditional' practices and planning, (above) is a symptom of a mistrust in the abilities of architects to solve the problem of living in the city but is also, in its own way, another version of the 'paradise' model—a 'past paradise'.

However, in addition to the purveyors of the past, there is another resolutely technical school of building which seeks to showcase new technologies, but this can often appear merely fashionable and, as a result, can quickly become ironic and short-lived. It is a risky path to take.

Architecture's 'third way' is another, much rarer, philosophy that is more concerned with innovation and the use of technology as a considered answer to a particular problem. It is preoccupied with the production of technical solutions that are not subject to the whims of fashion, or even the latest advances in materials. It is a philosophy that is more interested in utilising the appropriate method or material in order to construct something better. The relevant solution might be non-standard, unusual or even counter-intuitive.

Bryan Avery's body of work falls squarely into this category, in fact it falls so neatly into this taxonomical artifice as to define it.

One example of this technical approach is his design for the Cellular Sedan 1987–1989 (opposite and p. 141). This is a modular car with a number of interchangeable body kits and panels. It not only uses the entirely sensible premise that, as most car interiors differ only slightly in size, this part should be standardised, but it also forms the platform for a wide ranging exploration of the vehicle's interaction with the countryside—which ultimately leads to a theory that allows for the essential nature of the wilderness to be preserved. Pivotal to the theory is the de-surfacing of roads in rural areas. This is discussed in more detail in Avery's polemic "Fragments of a Wilderness City" (Chapter 2).

This would at first glance appear to be a backward step, but the logic is irrefutable—cars with four-wheel drive would be perfectly capable of handling a rougher surface, albeit at reduced speeds. Arguably, safety would increase as the surface deteriorates. Thus whilst it would still be possible to access the countryside, it would be at reduced speeds on slower local roads—what the Italians might recognise as strada bianche. Access to the country would be more difficult (except for those who inhabit it) and would require a level of commitment and engagement not possible in an air-conditioned autobahn cruiser at 70 miles per hour (112km/hr). The Cellular Sedan and the later Scenic Saloon ideas of 2005 (p. 168) become the enabler for another, grander, scheme where the importance of distinguishing between the city's density, vibrancy and activity; and the countryside's space, openness and tranquillity is central.

This Page
Top: Poundbury, Dorset.

Opposite Page
Top left: Dirt road; Kenya.
Top right: The Cellular Sedan 1987–1989.
Middle: The Cellular Sedan, concept diagram.
Bottom: The Scenic Saloon 2005.

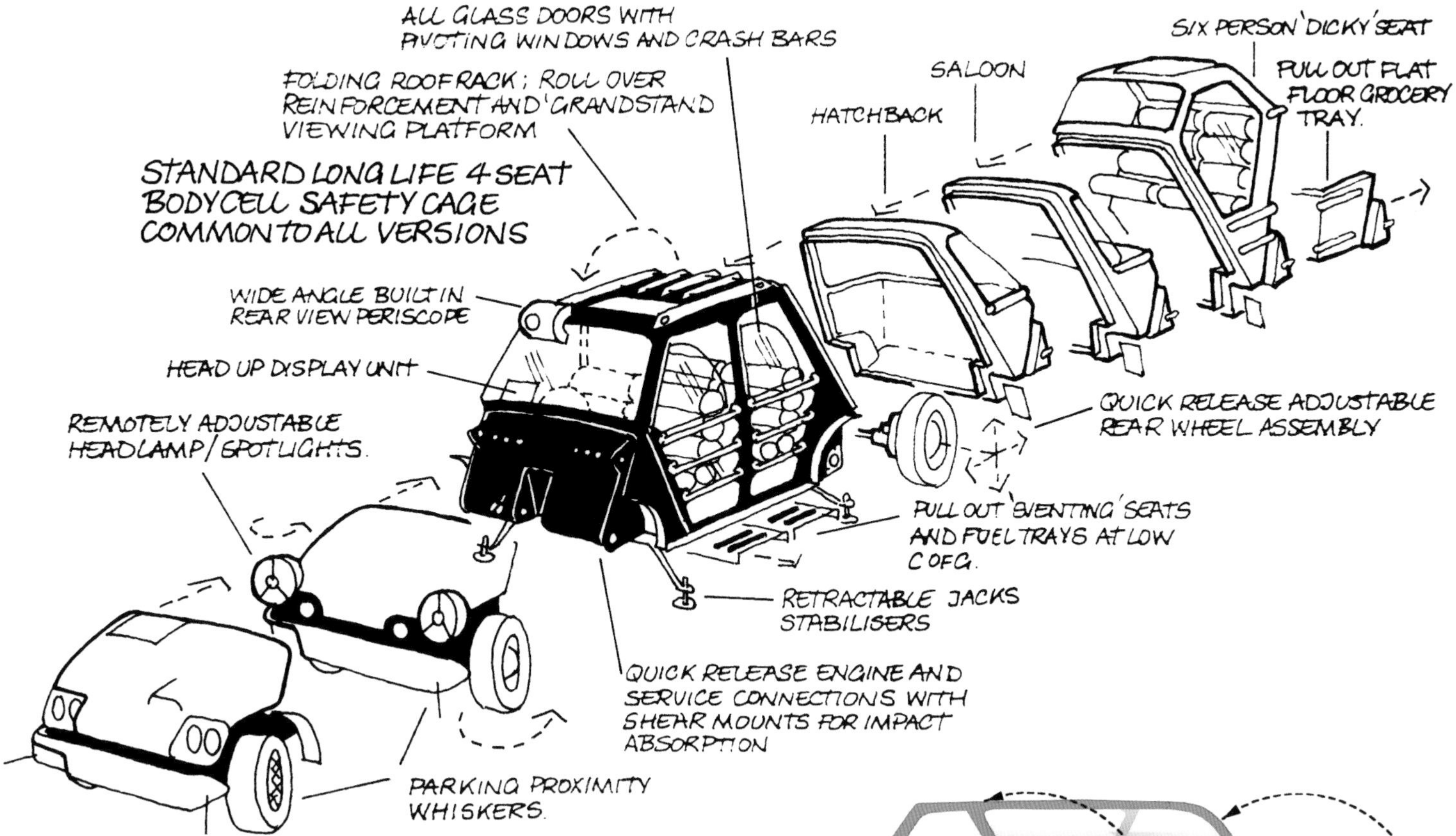

ALL GLASS DOORS WITH PIVOTING WINDOWS AND CRASH BARS

SIX PERSON 'DICKY' SEAT

SALOON

PULL OUT FLAT FLOOR GROCERY TRAY.

FOLDING ROOF RACK; ROLL OVER REINFORCEMENT AND 'GRANDSTAND VIEWING PLATFORM

HATCHBACK

STANDARD LONG LIFE 4 SEAT BODYCELL SAFETY CAGE COMMON TO ALL VERSIONS

WIDE ANGLE BUILT IN REAR VIEW PERISCOPE

HEAD UP DISPLAY UNIT

QUICK RELEASE ADJUSTABLE REAR WHEEL ASSEMBLY

REMOTELY ADJUSTABLE HEADLAMP/SPOTLIGHTS.

PULL OUT 'EVENTING' SEATS AND FUEL TRAYS AT LOW C OF G.

RETRACTABLE JACKS STABILISERS

QUICK RELEASE ENGINE AND SERVICE CONNECTIONS WITH SHEAR MOUNTS FOR IMPACT ABSORPTION

PARKING PROXIMITY WHISKERS.

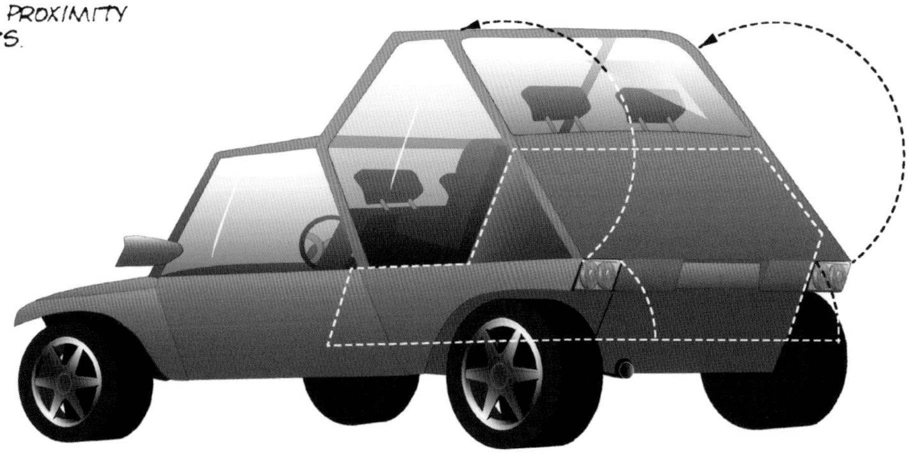

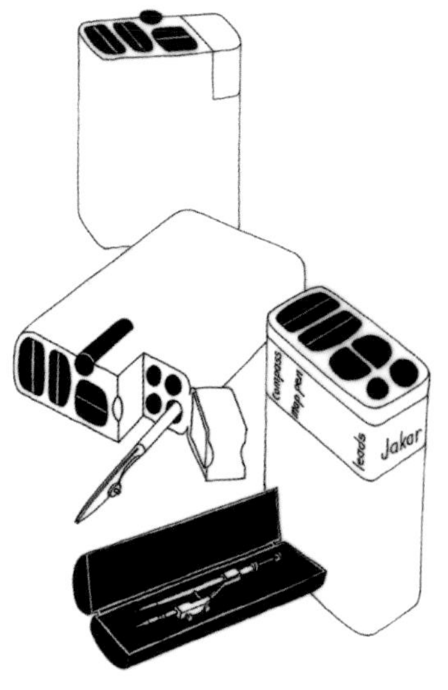

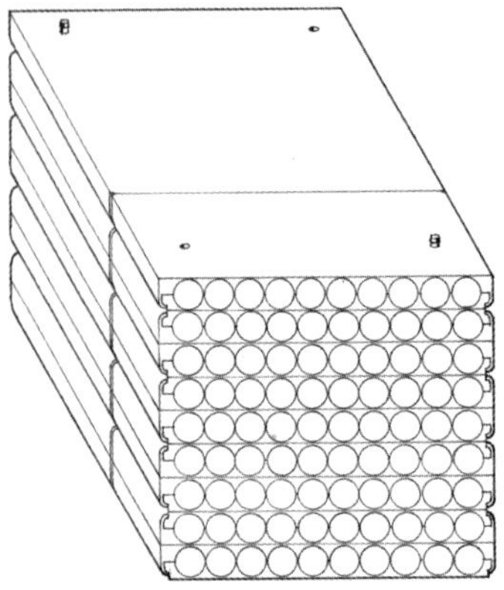

Bryan Avery started his career in product design, not in an architect's office. The product and industrial designer have an altogether more intimate relationship with the materials and processes used to manufacture artefacts. Early Avery projects include instrument cases for Jakar and a pressed steel coffer roof structure for British Steel. Other products, designed in the mid-eighties, include a plywood and metal chair and a range of downlighters.

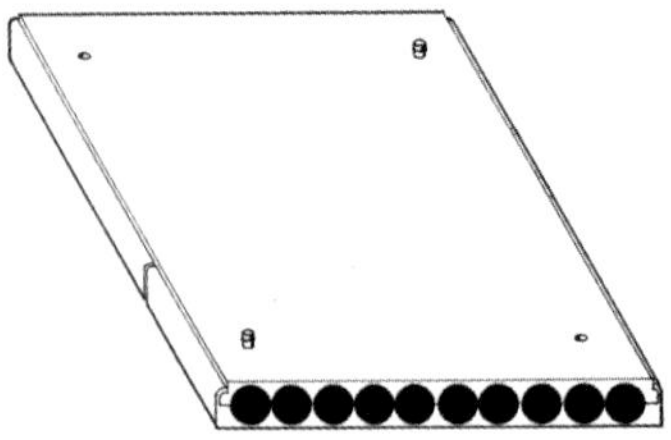

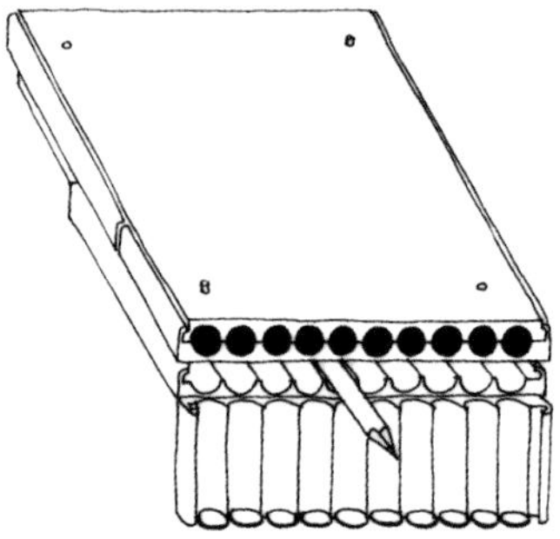

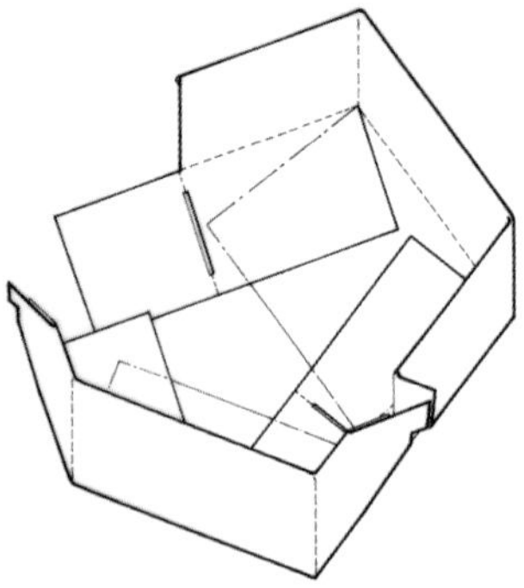

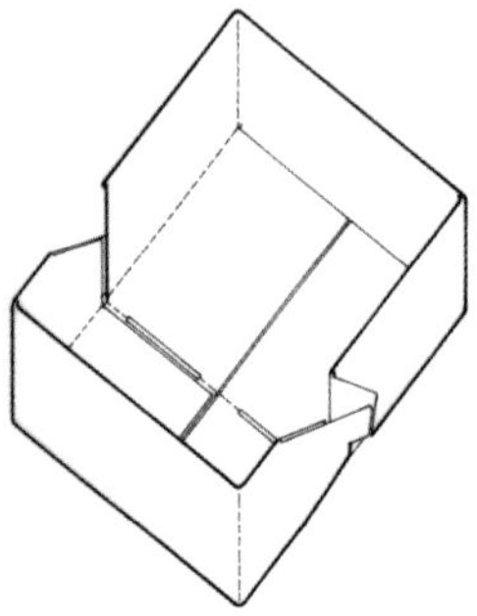

The chair in particular exhibits many of the recurring themes in Avery's built work—modularity, adaptability, and the appropriate use of materials. A simple perforated plywood spine supports a series of cantilevered armrests, seats and legs to suit a personalised specification. It is a million miles away from a formalised chair as design manifesto, yet it clearly exists to facilitate a technically better way of sitting. The family of products, distinguished by their shared backbone, presages some of the later residential projects and neatly displays a concern with an object being either multifunctional or customisable to suit an individual or use.

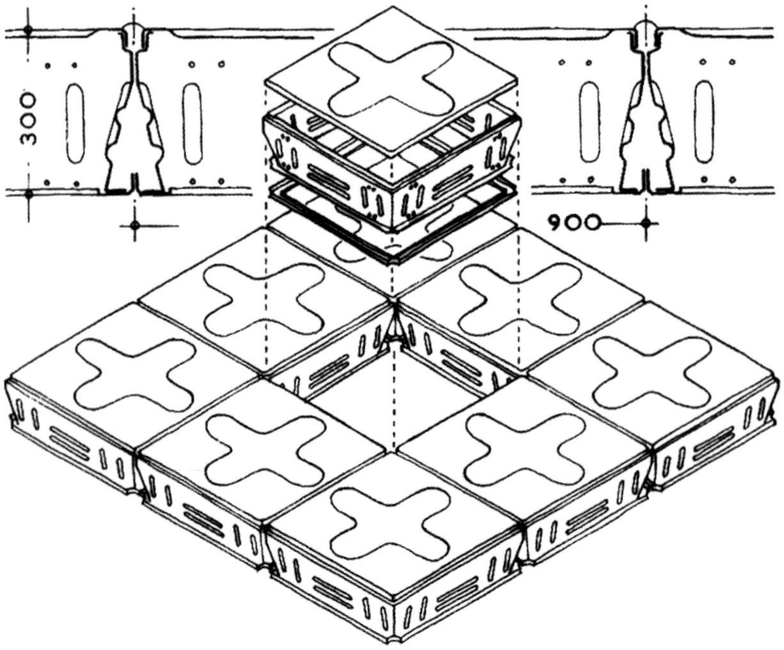

This Page
Top left: Drawing instrument case for Jakar Ltd 1969–1970.
Top middle and two down: Self-propping stackable plastic pencil case system 1969–1971.
Top right: Packaging for Jakar Ltd 1971.
Far right; middle: self closing cardboard package design (tray element) 1969–1971.
Bottom: Patented pre-fabricated metal roofing system for British Steel 1968–1969.

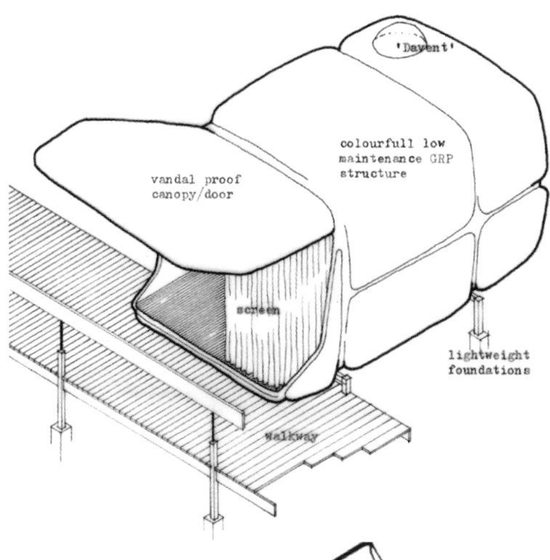

This Page
Far left: Pre-fabricated plastic beach hut, 1969.
Below right: The Plywood and Metal Chair 1987–1989.
Middle left and bottom left: Caravan; axonometric drawing and elevation (co-design with John Randall) 1969.
Bottom right: Skirting / trunking system adapted from a proprietary plastic guttering system 1971.

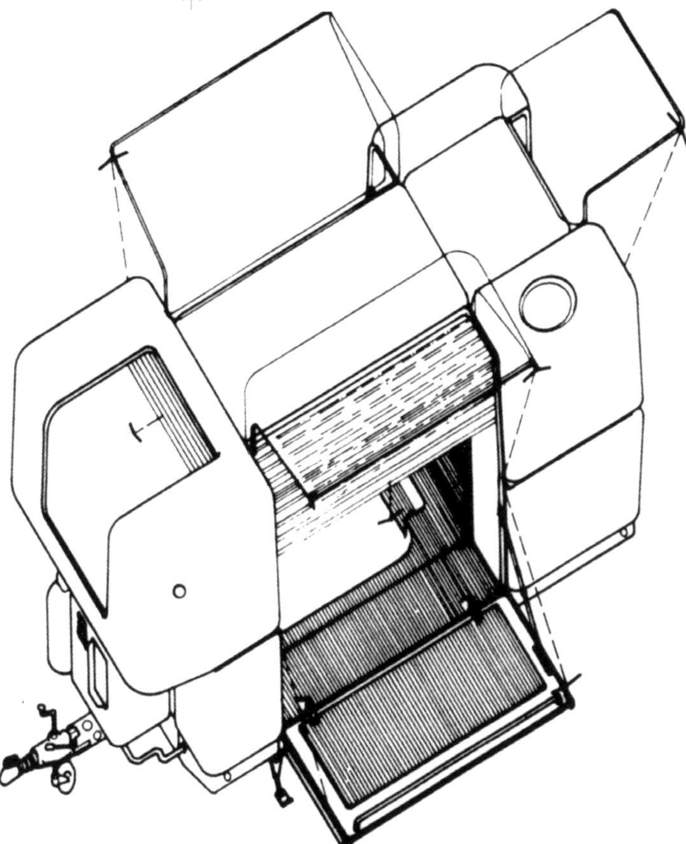

This Page
Far left: Cow Parsley.
Left and below: The Pavement Post 1999 (p. 151).

Opposite Page
Left from top down: Sketch and photograph of the office up/down lighter1982–1983; Assembly drawing of a direction sign at Plantation House; photograph of fire point at Plantation House
Middle from top down: Palm trunk glassware sketch; Telescopic tower design; MOMI 1985.
Bottom: Neon sign for MOMI 1984. Although unbuilt this this became the museum logo.
Far Right: Sketches of the seat design for the Jerwood Vanbrugh auditorium at RADA.

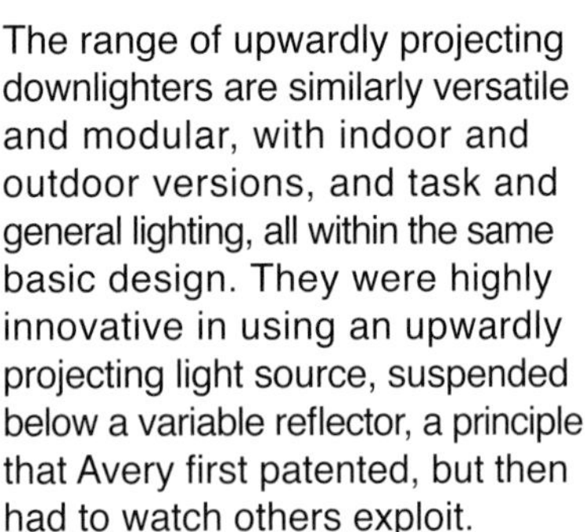

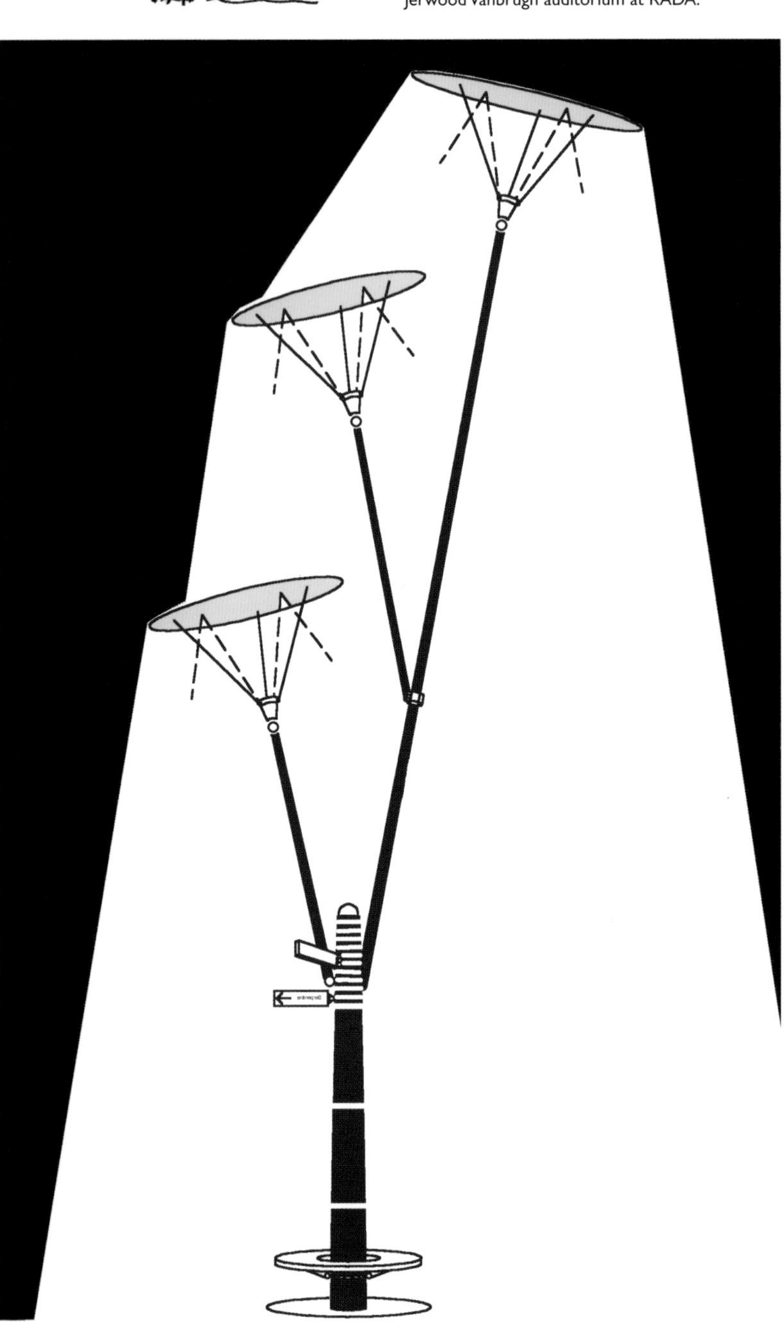

The range of upwardly projecting downlighters are similarly versatile and modular, with indoor and outdoor versions, and task and general lighting, all within the same basic design. They were highly innovative in using an upwardly projecting light source, suspended below a variable reflector, a principle that Avery first patented, but then had to watch others exploit.

Viewed as experiments in their own right, each Avery project is complete and well formed, and seen, against the backdrop of a larger, all-encompassing ethos of—dare one suggest—a utopian vision, each scheme and each product seems to reinforce elements of a way of living in which, to use Avery's own expression, "the poetry drives the technology".

Much of Bryan Avery's work can be distilled into a single detail or product that assumes an almost totemic role for the rest of the building.

One such example might be the telescopic sign at MOMI, an oildraulic telescopic billboard, complete with MOMI sign, lasers and TV cameras, which would pop up above the bridge viaduct at carefully timed intervals so as not to be visible for more than 28 days in any given year—thereby counting as a temporary structure. A more literal totem is Avery's EcoBeacon, a project

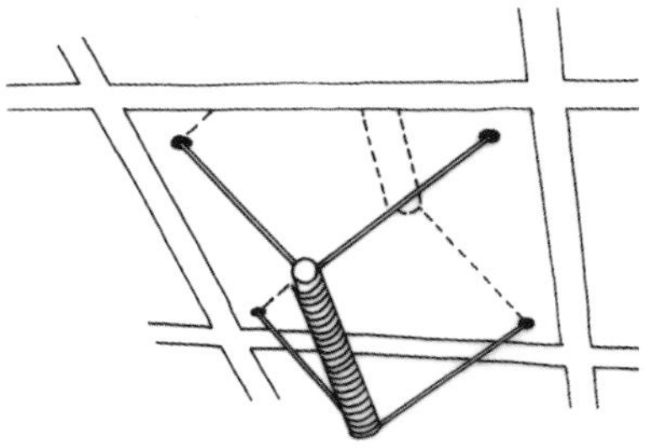

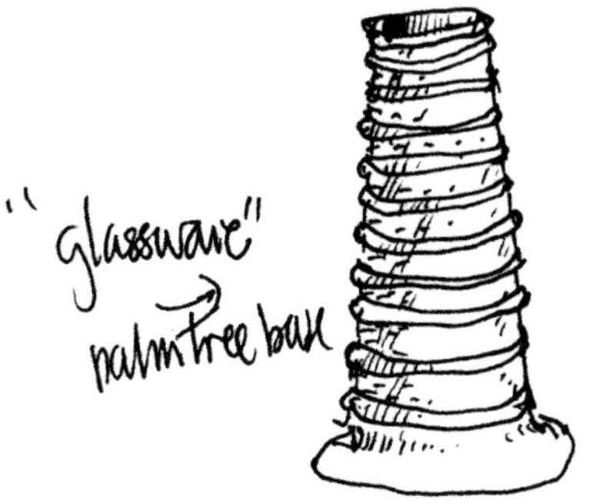
"glassware"
palm tree base

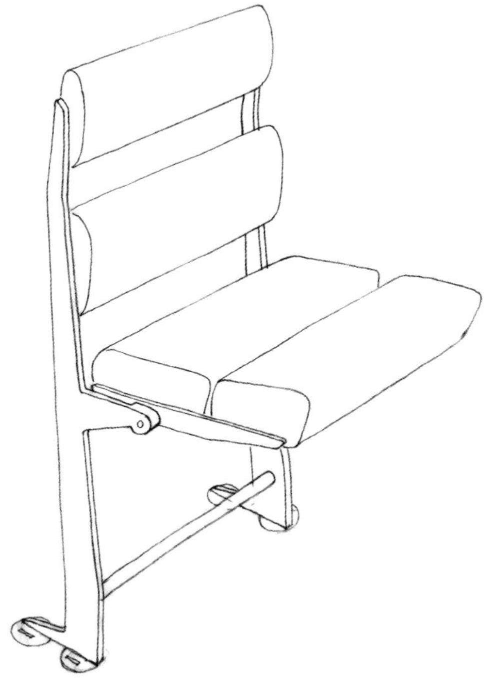

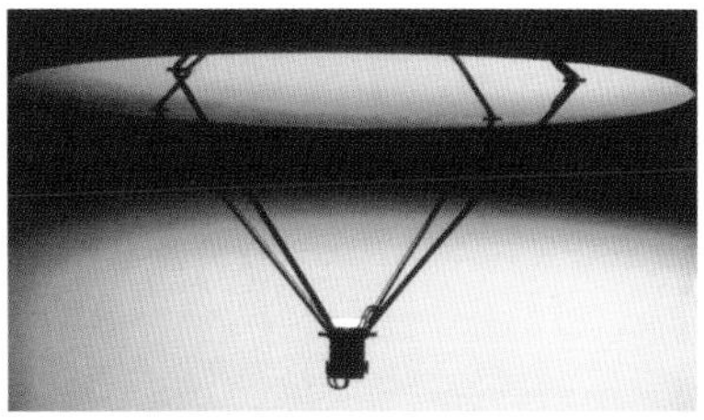

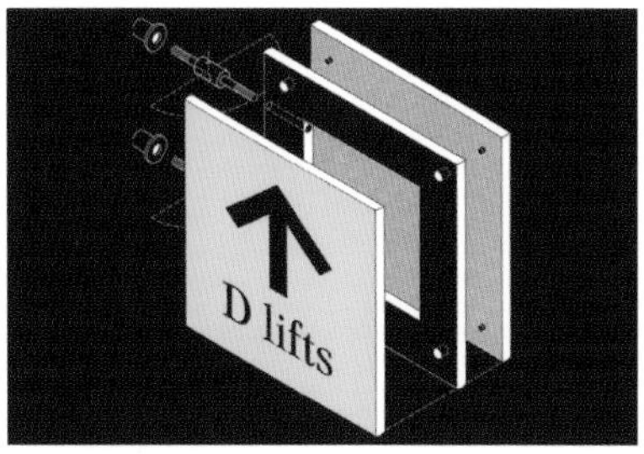
D lifts

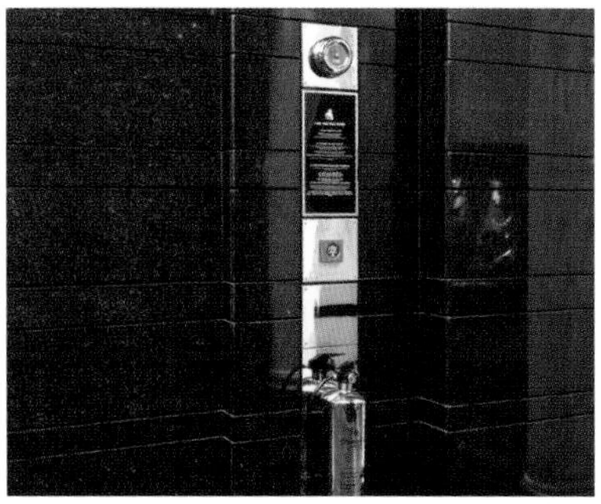

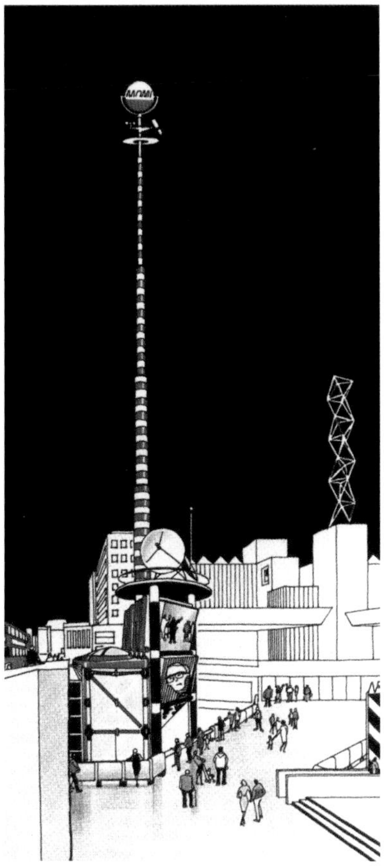

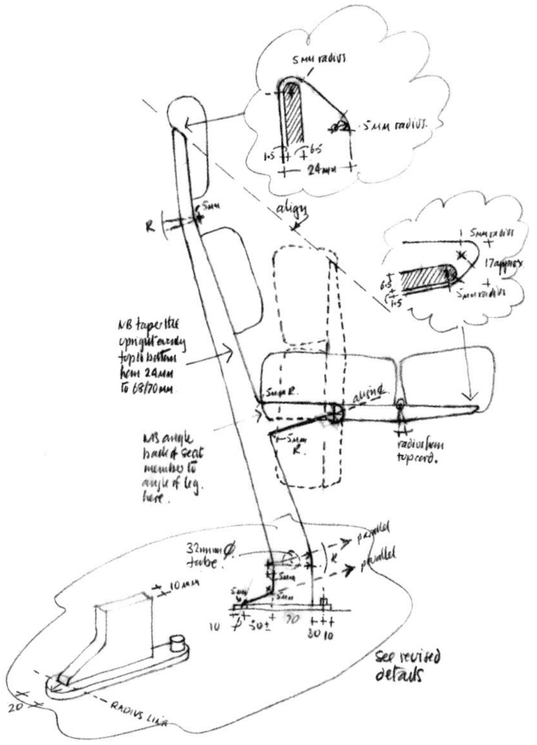
align
See revised details

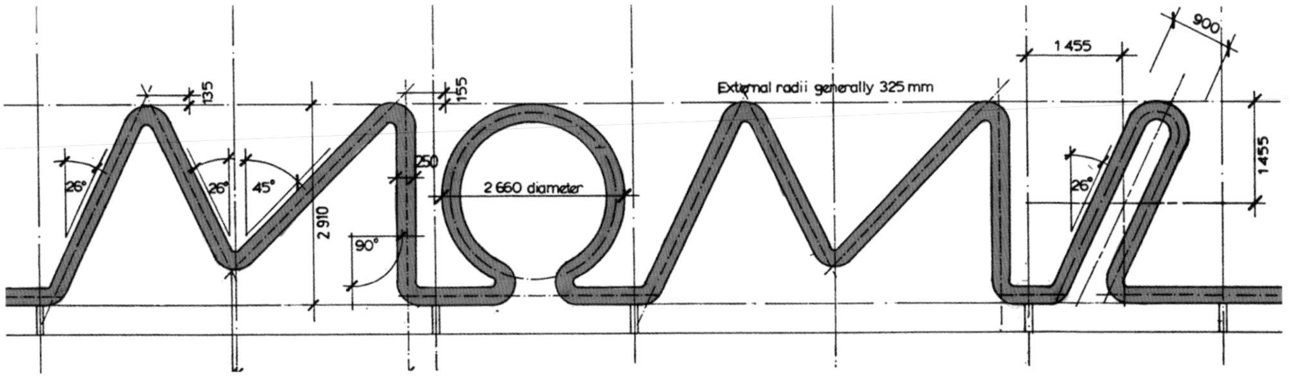
External radii generally 325 mm
2 660 diameter
1 455
900
135
155
250
2 910
26°
45°
90°

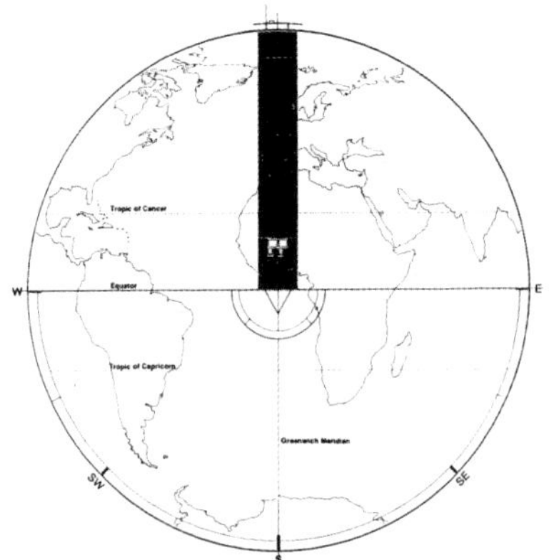

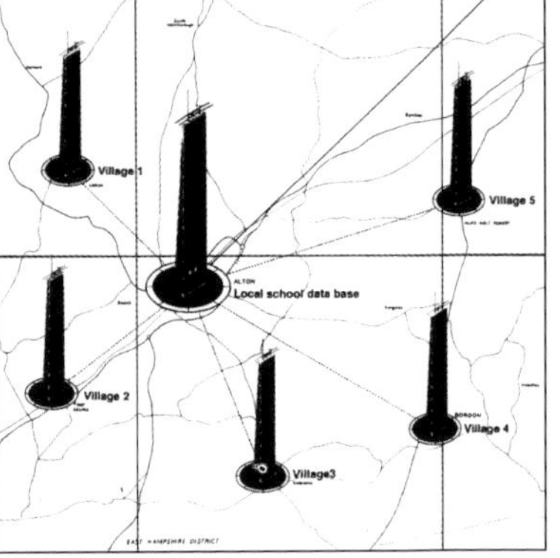

that was suggested as part of the millennium celebrations to establish a nationwide network of interlinked beacons that would be built in a standard form, but whose materials and particular function within the local community might be subtly different. In a village, for instance, the beacon might occupy the green and be fashioned in local stone or timber, whereas its city dwelling counterpart might be in stainless steel or concrete.

Each beacon contains within it access to both local and national information—whereby it could be possible to assess the environmental data for Tobermory from a beacon in Totnes.

The beacon is designed to a standard set of dimensions which relate to the planet. In plan, the beacon is an equilateral triangle, which tapers on two sides to a capping strip of stainless steel, which is slightly bowed to reflect the earth's curvature. The standard EcoBeacon is 9.27 metres in height, representing the distance from the earth's centre to its surface and the 15 millimetre strip of stainless steel at the top represents, in scale, all our inhabitable atmosphere, the biosphere.

An alternative reading is also possible, that if the 9.27 metres is taken as the total span of the planet's existence, then the 15 millimetre sliver of steel at the top is also proportional to mankind's time on earth. Our knife-edge of existence is expressed—as a knife-edge.

This use of a geometric design rationale reminds us of the Cenotaph and the hundreds of War Memorials in almost every village throughout the country—highly symbolic sentinels in remembrance of the human cost of war.

The EcoBeacon though, isn't commemorative, it is a more of an interactive warning device, drawing deeply upon the British race memory and the role that a chain of beacons had in preserving the Kingdom from invasion. This is as ingrained in the British mind (OK, the English) as the storming of the Bastille is in the French. Furthermore it was envisaged that, on the break of the new millennium, each beacon would 'activate' and become part of a nationwide celebration; beacons plugging into giant outdoor displays linked to each other all over the country, a UK live event which would be sustained not just on 1 January 2000, but well into the third millennium (for Avery's notes on this see p. 94).

This Page
Above: Beacon in Parliament Square, London.
Top left: Beacon at East Grinstead, Sussex.
Upper middle: The derivation of the form.
Lower middle: Beacon network.
Bottom: War memorial; Lymington, New Forest.

Opposite Page
Perspective of the Ecological Beacon.

If the EcoBeacon was a prescient response to a burgeoning global threat, the 'underbelly' at No. 1 Neathouse Place was a direct answer to a very localised environmental problem. Avery had been asked to look at the building because it presented a series of intractable problems for the developer. A large block was supported over a main road on a post-stressed beam which would make demolition extremely expensive and potentially dangerous. The building also caused a downdraft of such severity that it was capable of knocking people over. Avery's solution, designed in conjunction with an aeronautical engineer, was to fix a series of aerofoil baffles to the soffit of the building to collect the downdraft and channel it high above the pavement. The fact that this task is performed rather beautifully should not be dismissed as the blue-lit, slightly bowed stainless steel underside is a good example of what Avery actually means by 'the poetry driving the technology'.

This and Opposite Page
The windscoop and underbelly lighting at No 1 Neathouse Place 1994–1996.

To control the solar heat gain (an important factor in reducing the requirement for cooling) a raked, frameless glazing system was used, similar to the one Avery proposed for offices at Heathrow Airport some 30 years previously (p. 62). This achieved a slimmer air-conditioning duct, and thus a greater ceiling height—the key to the buildings re-usability.

On the north-eastern side, however, where there is much less need to control solar heat gain, another variation on the raked glazing is used; turned on its side (pp. 15, 74–76). This has two advantages; firstly, the serrated edge to the floor

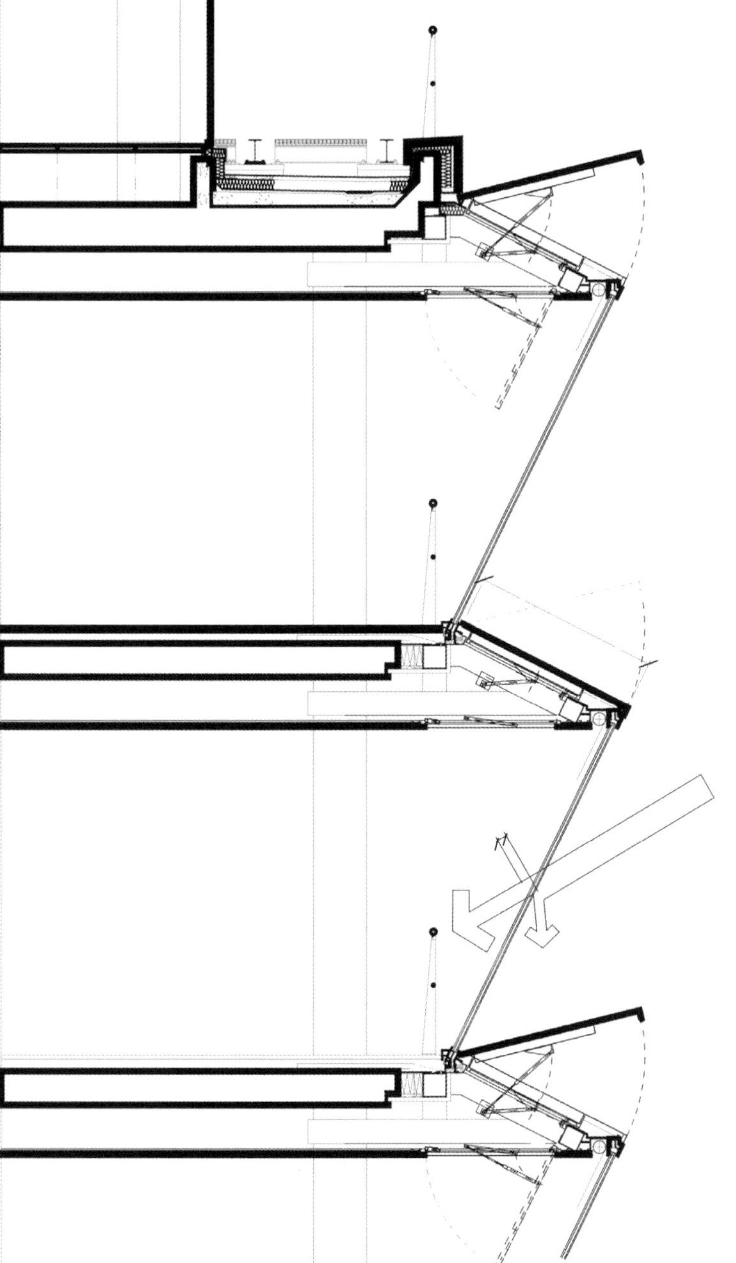

This Page
Top left and right: Internal views of the Western 'raked glazing' facade; *Below right:* Section. *Below:* Photograph through of the 'raked glazing' facade.

Opposite Page
Pavement reflections in the railed glazing facade

plate creates more valuable office area and secondly, the triangulated glazing also affords individualised oriel-like windows with views across London which help to turn the building into a much sought after location. By extending the floor-plate, moving circulation and services to either end, and controlling solar gain, this unglamorous 1960s block has been given a dramatic new lease of life.

No. 1 Neathouse Place's transformation has been likened to an ultra modern version of 1930s streamlining, but streamlining was always primarily concerned only with the wrapper; Lowey's railway engines and copying machines were not any different under the skin than their more lumpen counterparts, they just looked as if they were.

This building has undergone more than a facelift; what could be more sustainable than a concern for every aspect of the life and reuse of a structure? However, the resulting exemplar of clarity, as at No. 1 Neathouse Place, often belies the complexity of the Gordian knot that it has to unravel. Avery's concerns have always been more than merely skin deep. No. 1 Neathouse Place is patently not the same building with a new facade. The standard approach to a problem is not in Avery's repertoire, and this means that there can be no such thing as a typical Avery building or product, except that one would expect it to exhibit a high degree of ingenuity and that several others might have 'had a go' before and given up. In that sense, the continual analysis of a problem and its context, a phenomenological approach, the co-existence of 'big' (environment, culture and ideas) and 'small' (detail, application and materials) work together to give the distinct impression that this object or structure is at the nub of a particular set of questions: What is this building/object for? Who uses it? What do they need?

Of course, at one level, these are standard inquiries but the answers can sometimes surprise, as in Avery's thesis that everything is related and although architecture may be imbued with an identity of its own and the meanings that we as individuals may give it, we also have in common many deeper layers of understanding. There are ancient instinctual yearnings such as our connection with the land and seasons for example, that are part of the cause of the 'modern condition'—the retreat from nature, and the denial of the importance of place, which when exacerbated by misused technologies causes so much distress in our cities.

Avery's work has always been concerned with applying a technical solution to the problem of being disconnected from ourselves and our surroundings. It has to do with abstracted experiences of nature, alluding to the physical landscape without making obvious references to it, and allowing technology to facilitate the connection. In this sense, Avery's is a uniquely human approach which has at its heart another set of questions that might contain the following enquiries: What makes something beautiful? Why does looking at that landscape please us? How can a building or product have the same effect? What technology would make that work?

If architects and science fiction writers really are thinking about the same things, albeit sometimes on radically differing scales of time and location, then somewhere there must be a convergence of the two. Very few people ever occupy this space convincingly and, in doing so, they are often ultimately reclassified as 'innovative thinkers' or visionaries. Buckminster Fuller was one, so were Isaac Asimov and Arthur C Clarke. We should now add Bryan Avery to this list.

This Page
Above: The South Downs, Sussex with their savannah-like familiarity.

Opposite Page
Main picture and bottom right; the foyer at No. 1 Neathouse Place: *Middle right and top*; The Island Pavilion at Hadrian's Villa, a universal expression of 'island' but resonant too with the particular—the Isle of Wight.

Footnote to Chapter 5
The Ecological Beacons Project: 1994–1999

The United Kingdom was the first of the world's nations to industrialise, but the process which freed people from the dawn-to-dusk tyranny of the land and brought enormous prosperity to towns and villages alike, also brought with it a dangerous degradation of the environment.

With the rest of the world industrialising at an ever-increasing rate, and with commerce becoming increasingly international, the pressure on the world's natural resources is growing exponentially and the environmental consequences are no longer within the power of one nation to resolve. These issues are now set to become the world's foremost political problem of the twenty-first century.

However, having now industrialised to the point where 93 per cent of the population has been urbanised, and with only a relatively small and vulnerable natural environment still left untouched, the United Kingdom, more than most, urgently needs to develop an awareness and understanding of the ecological balance that must be achieved if we are to bring our industrialised society back into harmony with nature.

This was the purpose of the Ecological Beacon. The intention was to have built, by the year 2000, a nationwide chain of these modern monoliths, each based on a standard generic form for easy recognition but customised by local artists and craftspeople in a range of materials and sizes to suit the locale. The beacons would have had both a symbolic and a practical function. Symbolically, their form represents mankind's tenuous hold on the planet. They can therefore be used like ancient stone obelisks or war memorials to mark important public places—such as town squares, village greens or hilltop vantage points—thereby bequeathing to succeeding generations a permanent reminder of our end-of-century concerns. On a practical level, every beacon could also be fitted with one or more interactive visual display units, capable of giving local news and an A–Z street mapping service of the area for visitors, together with information on local noise and atmospheric conditions from its own built-in electronic sensors mounted on racks at the beacon's top.

The beacons would form part of a schools-based public awareness initiative to transform society's understanding of the issues and every beacon, in every village and in every town, would be interlinked one with another via the national telecommunications network to give immediate environmental read-outs.
(pp. 17, 061, 86–87, 148)

Chapter 6

Beauty is in the Eye of the Beholder

by Bryan Avery

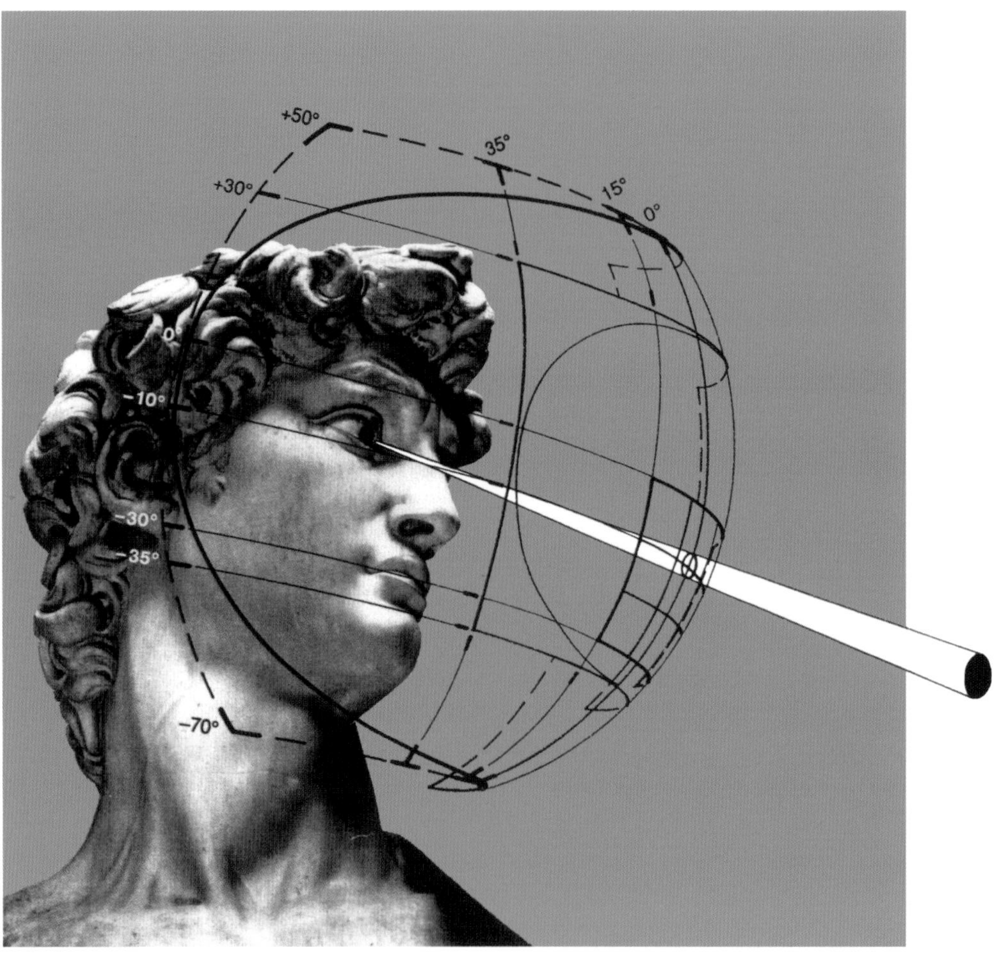
+50°
35°
+30°
15°
0°
–10°
–30°
–35°
–70°

The eye, the mind and the hand shape architecture and give it meaning. Sadly, however, we are today increasingly appealing only to the mind. We are more concerned that our work should be considered 'interesting' rather than 'beautiful', and in gratifying our mind we have so devalued the hand and the eye that only rarely now can we speak of them. They require an elusive and poetic language from which we have become estranged. If the hand, the tectonic one-third of our art, requires Heidegger to help us, little wonder that our interest in the eye has languished.

Giving pleasure to the eye is infinitely more difficult than to the hand or mind. There are no rules and no excuses. Most architects are silent on the matter. We seem tacitly to have accepted that aesthetics is a subjective discipline and if it pleases the mind we no longer need heed the eye.

And yet, for millennia, giving pleasure to the eye has been our predominant concern, and the quest for aesthetic perfection has been central to the philosophical debate. We face now an overwhelming global urgency to build more beautiful environments and our minds are active, but our eyes are closed.

Perhaps, in our search for a philosophy with which to explain everything, we have made it too difficult. If we contend instead that architecture is, for our public if not for ourselves, pre-eminently a visual discipline and, in the sense of non-monumental shaping of habitable space, it is principally conditioned by the pragmatic need to provide flat floors and more-or-less vertical walls, then, at the elemental level and before ever we introduce into it our accumulated cultural complexities, our art is essentially that of a geometer.

Given the all-pervasiveness of the horizontal and vertical in our work, both in the actuality of the experienced built space and, more significantly perhaps, in the visualisation of that space on paper or on screen, it should be our task to encourage the geometer in us to give meaning to these relationships and, ultimately, to make them pleasing.

Architects have long sought to understand what makes one shape more pleasing to the eye than another. The square, the double square and the golden rectangle have stubbornly re-surfaced in treatises of aesthetics from Plato to Corbu.

Perhaps this interest may be less surprising when we consider that the eye through which the ancients experienced the world was all but identical to the eye we use today. Indeed, it probably has not changed significantly since the dawn of man. It has a deep socket to shade and protect it, and a very wide visual field, unfocused and only in monochrome in the peripheral areas, but extraordinarily sensitive there to movement and light. Our tribal ancestors would have been acutely aware of this visual field, for out of it would have come both the predator and the prey.

To focus, however, the eye has only a surprisingly small area wherein the image is sharp. This is the 'foveal area' and it is directed almost instantaneously at everything that triggers its interest. The eye's tiny muscles are thus kept constantly in motion, adjusting and re-adjusting to stimuli, each eye passing information to the brain which measures the minuscule differences of angle between them in order to triangulate and calculate the distance. The eyes then are a geometer, and one of considerable accomplishment. With them, we can focus two foveal areas on the trajectory of a falling ball, giving the brain updated differential angles every millisecond of its passage, and then plot its projected angle and distance so that the hand can move to intercept it—a quite extraordinary feat.

This Page
Above right: Sketch of the The Acropolis; Athens.
Above left: Sketch of Santa Maria Novella: Alberti: Florence.

Opposite Page
Michelangelo's David.

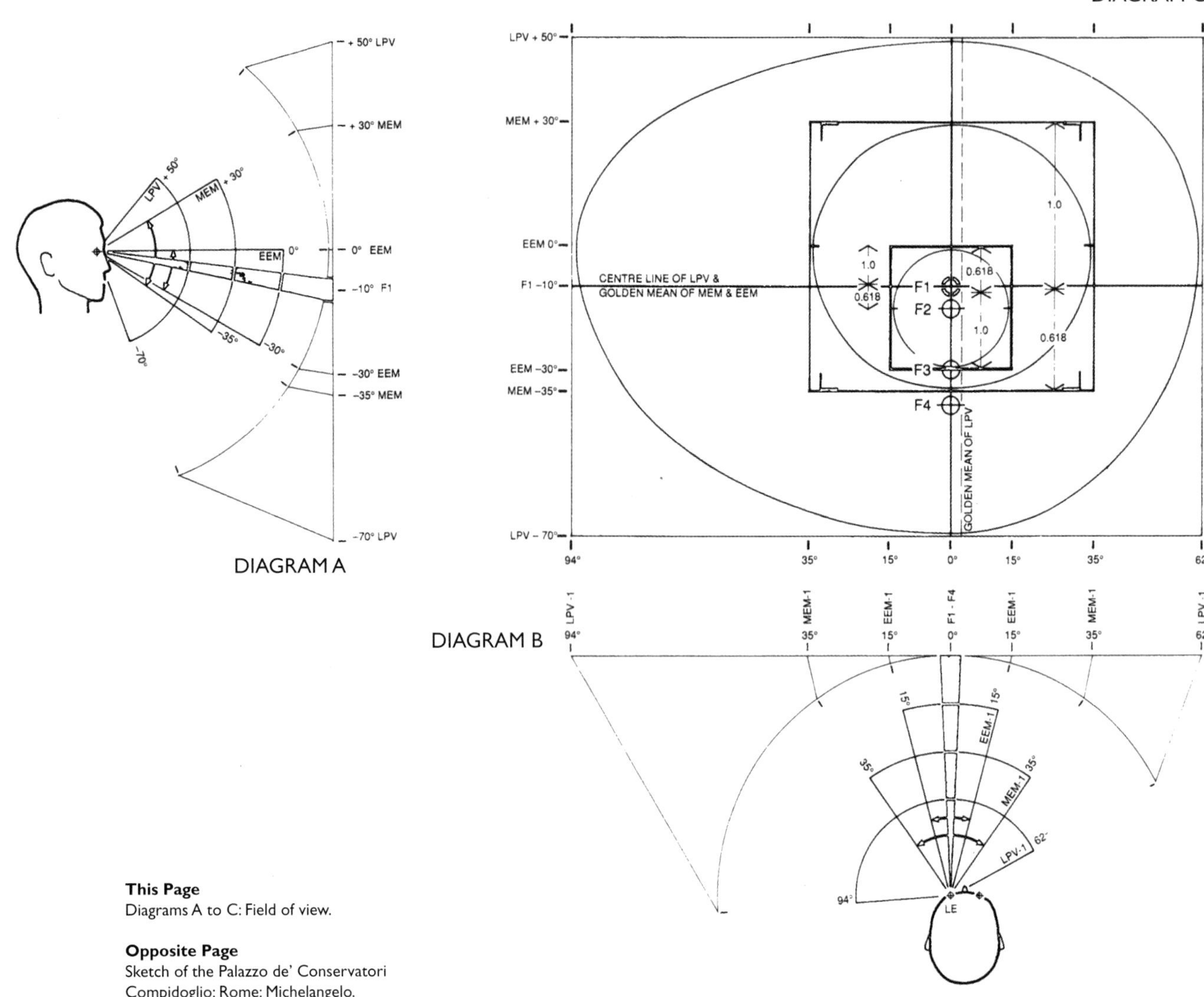

This Page
Diagrams A to C: Field of view.

Opposite Page
Sketch of the Palazzo de' Conservatori Compidoglio: Rome: Michelangelo.

*Humanscale-MIT Press 1974

Small wonder then that, with the need for such accurate triangulations, the eye has concentrated its movement to occur within a very small zone.

This is the 'easy eye movement' zone, and it coincides with the area of maximum acuity wherein the image is sharpest. The foveal area can be directed here faster than elsewhere, for outside it the muscles have to work harder and take longer to adjust, and beyond the 'maximum eye movement' zone the whole head has to be turned. Not unnaturally, what gives the eye most pleasure is not to have to move the head at all. Only then can the eye and mind be at rest.

Now, understanding that the eye is so structured and that it is so highly sensitive to angular relationships, it will be a little less surprising to learn that when the various zones are plotted graphically, some curious facts emerge.

Consider diagrams A, B and C shown above. These show the statistical standards* for the viewing angles of the eye in plan and elevation. If these same angular relationships are plotted on to a flat surface for clarity, visualised as if viewed from inside the eye looking out, they appear as in diagram C. This illustrates the left eye; the right eye is the same, but handed.

We are not so concerned here with the elliptical shape given by the cut-off from the eyebrows, nose and cheeks, more with the vertical and horizontal extents. These reflect the alignment of the two eyes horizontally and symmetrically about the vertical axis of the body, a key component of vision, and of architecture too.

The intriguing result of this is that when we look out on the world,

our view is framed by the overall limits of our peripheral vision, and the centre-line of the eye in its vertical axis is set almost exactly on its 'golden mean'.

The golden mean, or the golden section, is the point at which a line may be cut so that the smaller part is to the greater as the greater is to the whole. The ratio is 1:0.618 and the golden rectangle, so fascinating to the ancients, is a rectangle with the same ratio between its two sides.

Even more interestingly, the horizontal axis cuts the maximum eye movement zone again on its golden mean (if we take the horizontal axis to be the centre-line between the upper and lower limits of our peripheral vision, that is, the centre-line of our overall field of view which, coincidentally, is the normal declination of the fovea when sitting 'attentive'). Furthermore, not only is the easy eye movement zone similarly disposed, but so too is the declination of the fovea when sitting 'attentive'. All cut the centre-line at the golden mean.

Of course, all of this could just be coincidence, but there does appear to be a geometrical relationship within the very structure of the eye, much deserving of our attention. It is not that we necessarily 'see' these relationships, it is more likely that the eye finds them the easiest to accommodate and the mind, therefore, recognises them as familiar.

If we then go one stage further and plot the angular relationship of both eyes, as in binocular vision, and project them to infinity as in diagrams D and E (next page)—ignoring for the moment that the two eyes are set very slightly apart—then the overall field of vision, which is the context within which our view of the world is framed, is itself a golden rectangle, and the maximum and easy eye movement zones are both very close to being circles inscribing squares which are again set in a relationship to the horizontal centre-line by the golden mean.

Naturally, not all of the relationships are exact to the millimetre, nor could one expect it from the average angular data deriving from ergonomic studies, but they are all so extraordinarily close—well within accepted perceptual tolerances—that it is very difficult to ignore them.

The evidence does not stop there. If, as in diagrams F and G, we then introduce the distance apart of the eyes—which at, say, 65mm appears so small as to be negligible except for very close visual tasks—and plot the effect at an average reading distance of 500mm, our overall view of the world is still framed by the proportion of the golden rectangle and the maximum eye movement zone comes closer still to a circle inscribing a square. The easy eye movement zone, however, or more accurately that part of it within which both eyes can be brought to a binocular focus, is changed from a square to a portrait format with an overall proportion of 4:3.

This Page
Right: Sketch of the Millowner's Association Building; Le Corbusier; Ahemedabad: India.
Bottom: Diagrams D and E

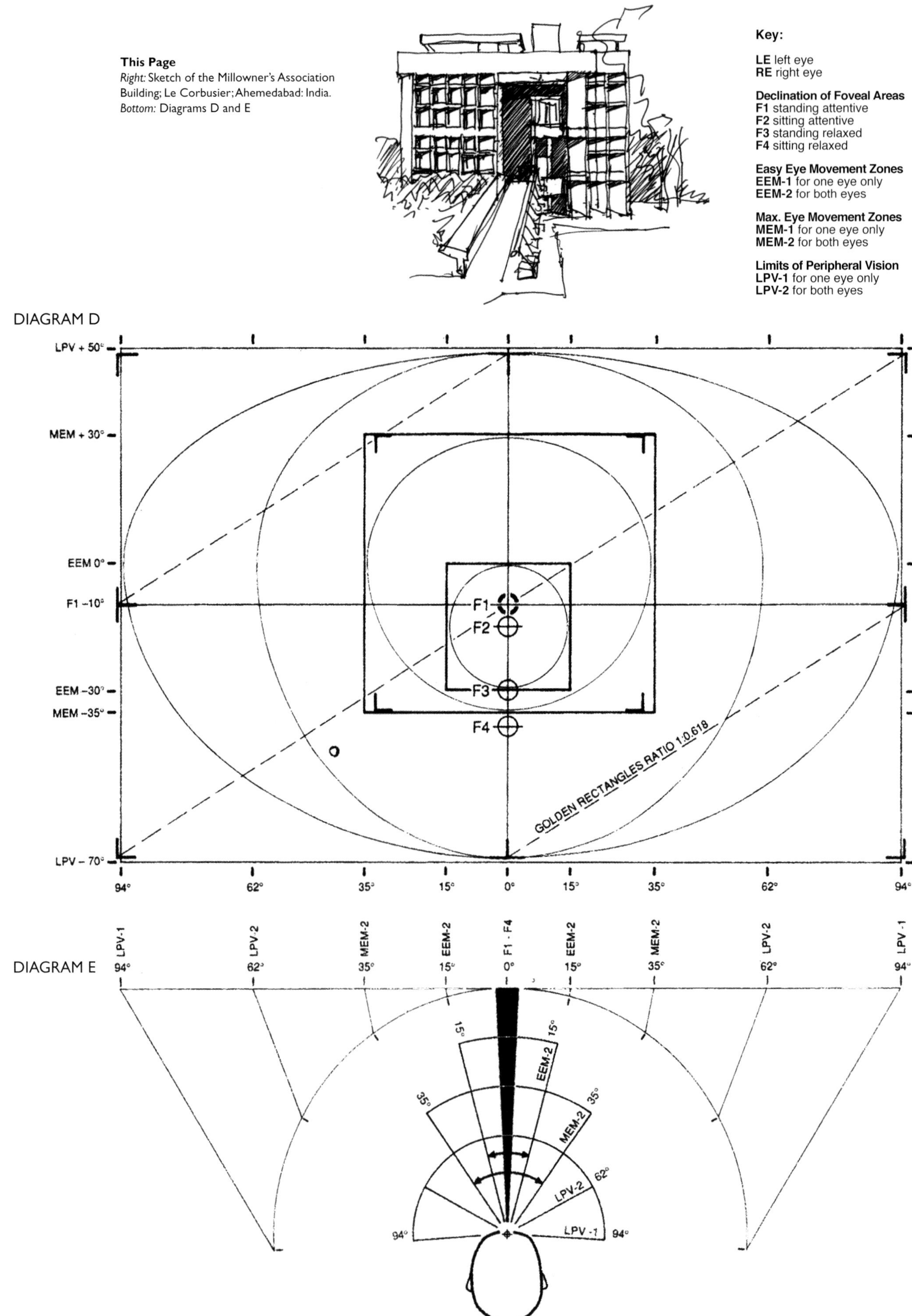

It may again be a coincidence, but this is the proportion of a typical Georgian window and many magazines and books use something close to this too. Is this perhaps why they are so pleasing to the eye? I have put forward these observations out of curiosity and it will be apparent that I have purposefully not tried to extrapolate too much from the angular relationships within the eye itself to the projected effect of these upon the composition of works of art or architecture, for that would be a considerable undertaking. However, I believe if this were to be done we might well discover some interesting new facts about ourselves and why, if we were to try through the geometry of our structures to give pleasure to the eye, we might quite literally be doing just that. Beauty may indeed be in the eye of the beholder.

A version of this article was first published in July 1992 in *The Architectural Review*.

This Page
Diagrams F and G.

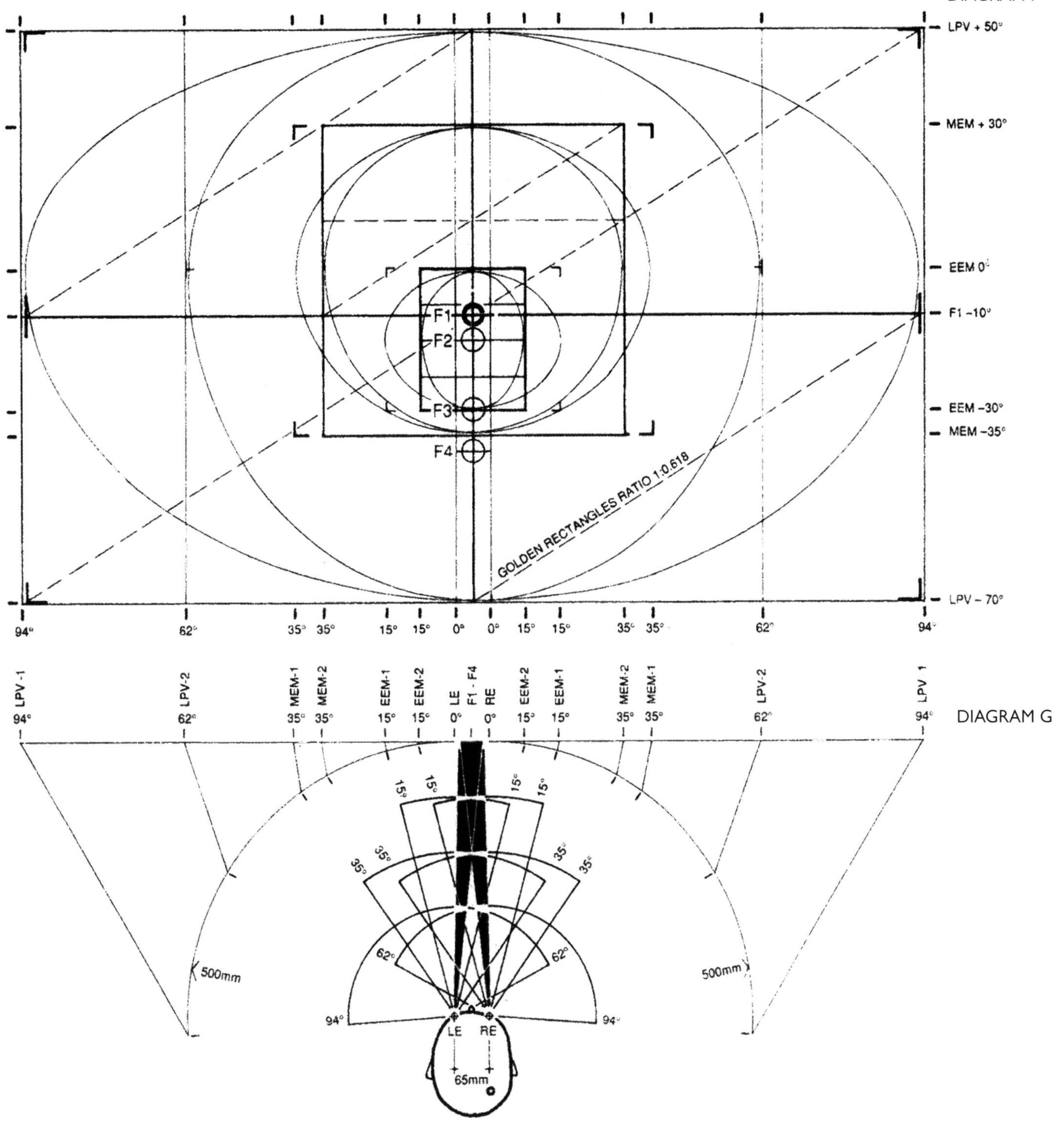

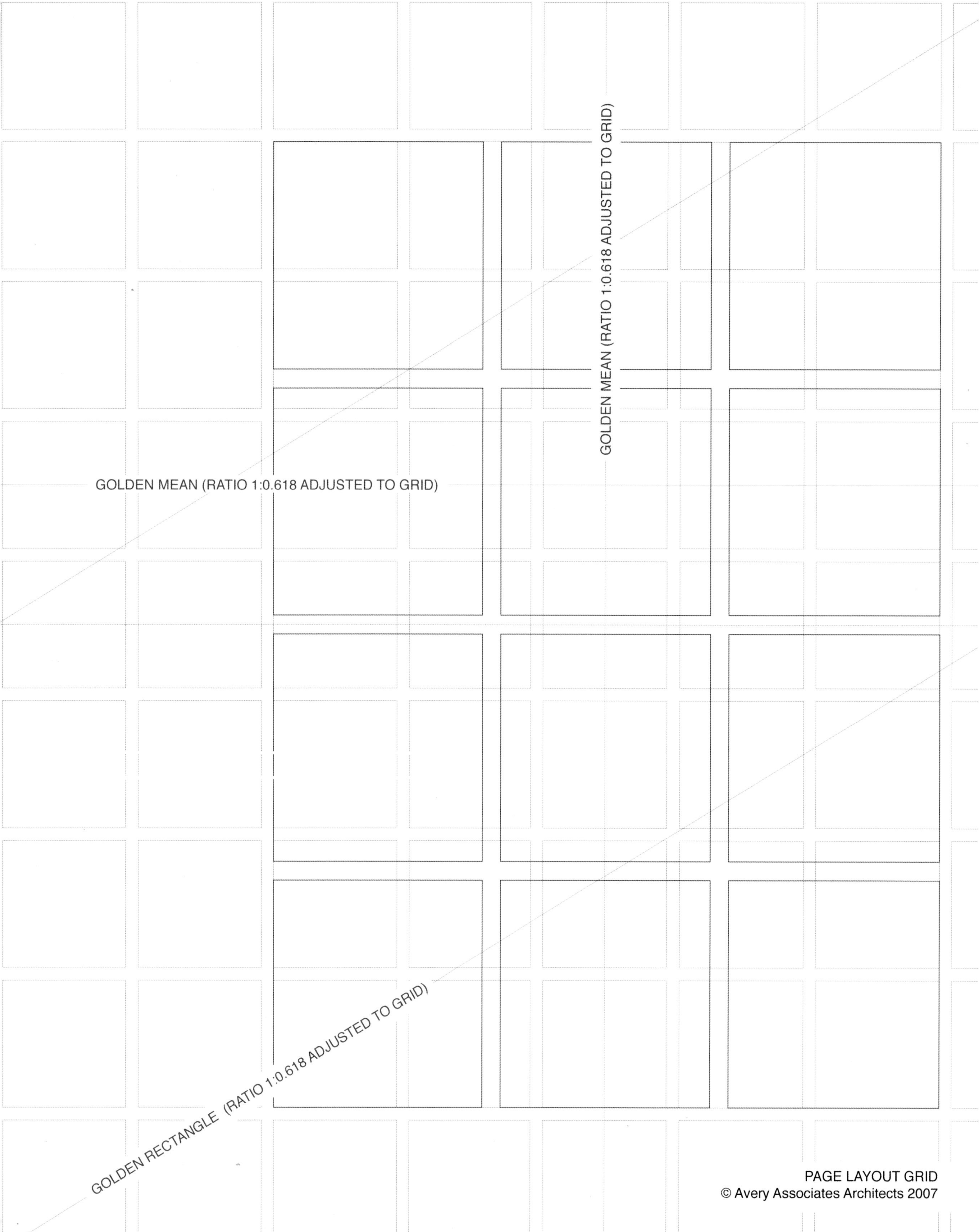
GOLDEN MEAN (RATIO 1:0.618 ADJUSTED TO GRID)
GOLDEN MEAN (RATIO 1:0.618 ADJUSTED TO GRID)
GOLDEN RECTANGLE (RATIO 1:0.618 ADJUSTED TO GRID)
PAGE LAYOUT GRID
© Avery Associates Architects 2007

Chapter 7

The Cultural Dimension

by Edwin Heathcote

London's culture of building for culture tends towards the slotting in of linking buildings, of new bits of the city delicately inserted into a robust working model, scraps filling out the collage city. Of course there is the tradition of the grand institution, from the British Museum to the National Gallery but largely, from our operas to our cinemas, galleries to theatres, the city's cultural fabric is knitted tightly into a commercial streetscape, always conscious of cost and land, smartly addressing every square inch. This is not the tradition of Paris or Vienna, of stand-alone grandeur, of architectural pomp and space guzzling self-confidence, rather a frank realisation of commercial reality and a reliance on spatial invention and quirky eccentricity, more Sir John Soane's Museum than the Louvre.

Bryan Avery's architecture has proved an eloquent attenuation of that particular tradition. From the city's first IMAX, its gasometer drum extruded from one of the city's least pleasurable roundabouts, to the intimacy of the RADA Theatre, from the insertion of the nearby and now defunct MOMI beneath the South Bank's concrete layers to the skilful reworking of Covent Garden's Transport Museum, Avery's cultural buildings have almost all revolved around the ingenious use of left-over space, the creation of something from nothing, or at least from very little. The other thing they have in common as a genre is a particular sense of movement, as if it were possible to sense the nature of a city under constant transformation through the architectural and structural language the buildings employ. All the structures share a vocabulary gleaned from a particularly British vein which melds expressed engineering with contemporary architectural dynamics to give an architecture full of motion and expression, alive with their own internal spatial and structural dynamics. It is a very particular oeuvre and one which has served the city well and established Avery as a significant and consistent contributor to the city of movement and perpetual change.

Among the main characteristics of Bryan Avery's architecture has been an expedient expansion of internal space, a kind of Alice in Wonderland explosion of interior space so that a series of complex, functional volumes are embedded into an urban fabric hardly dense enough to contain them. Standing in front of the RADA Theatre in the uniformly terraced rigour of Malet Street in London's Bloomsbury, it is hard to imagine the scale and ambition of the building behind this polite, gently theatrical elevation. This is even more the case from the Gower Street side, where the vaguely Deco stylings of the original facade are retained in an effort to maintain the famous brand and preserve its presence in the city's most established further-educational streetscape. Yet this self-effacing corridor through the urban block contains one of the city's most intensely theatrical spaces, an auditorium inspired by an unrealised design by Inigo Jones for William Davenant from 1638. Achieving a success in all adaptations of stage from courtyard and proscenium (with or without pit) through in-the-round, the intimate auditorium embraces all variations of performance with extraordinary success.

Nestling in its faux Georgian setting, the RADA Theatre is a slice of the city, more ambitious in its surprisingly stretched ten-storey sections than in its slender plan. A fissure at the heart of the building allows light to be sucked down into the lowest levels of workshops whilst the jacking up of the auditorium and stage create a clear passage through the site at ground level and make for easy orientation both horizontally and vertically through the structure. The gentle curve of the glazing on the elevation subtly suggests the barrel vault above the theatre space and the auditorium itself, as if the power of the drama were gently buckling a structure barely able to contain it.

Avery compared the task to 'Swiss watchmaking', a feat of cramming a hugely complex set of gears and components into a seemingly impossibly confined casing. The theatre has settled seamlessly into the London tradition of performance spaces shoe-horned into unpromising sites, to become one of its most successful theatrical and public places in a field in which architects' efforts are so often merely hit and miss, and where they have so often noticeably failed (for Avery's notes on this see p. 132).

RADA has been compared, in its tectonic language at least, to a building for cinema. Avery himself admits the curved frontage recalls the brasher commerciality and self-conscious modern streamlining of theatre's sister oeuvre but perhaps our perception has been tainted by Avery's extensive role in defining the new genres of cinema architecture which have sprung up in a post-TV age. One of his early successes was the building for the Museum of the Moving Image,1984–1988 (pp. 2–3, 61, 84–85, 140), which itself grew out of the architect's work at the National Film Theatre, notably the superb bookshop. Now sadly defunct, this surprising

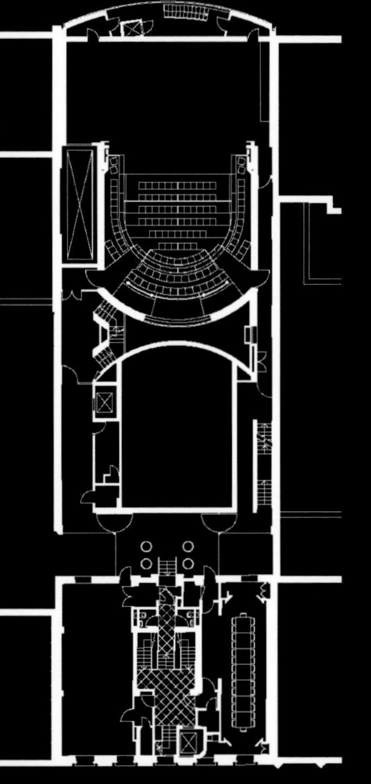

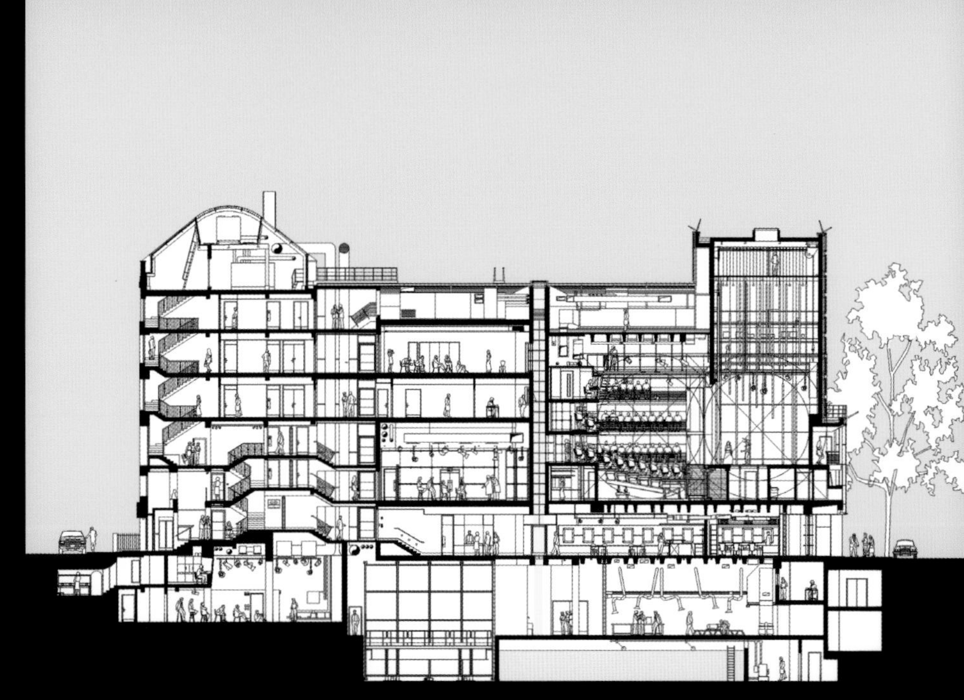

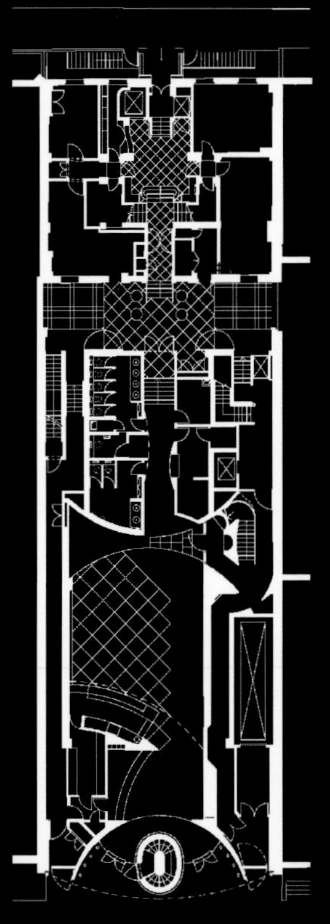

This Page
Above: Ground floor plan, 1994–2000.
Above top: Second floor plan.
Right: long section (top) and cross-section (bottom).

Opposite Page
RADA: The Gower Street Entrance.

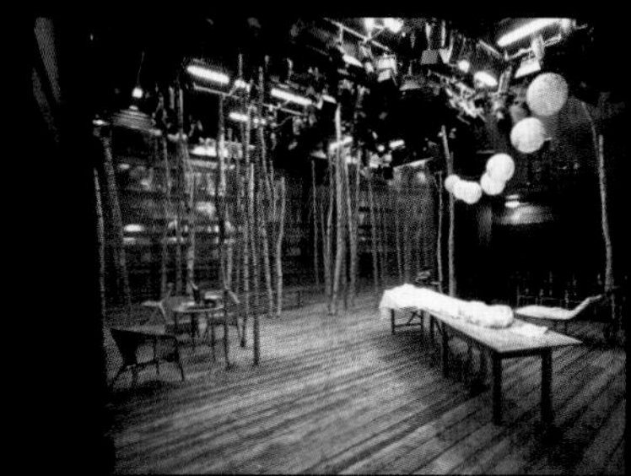

This Page
Above: The 'Cleft'; RADA.
Top right: The Malet Street public entrance.
Upper middle: The bar.
Middle: George Bernard Shaw Theatre.
Lower middle: The Gielgud Theatre.
Bottom: Acting room.

Opposite Page
Main image: The Cleft;
Smaller images from top down: George Bernard Shaw at RADA (second from right): Study windows within the Cleft: The Barrel Vault roof looking East and West.

This Page
Main image and top two images (left) above: The Jerwood Vanbrugh Auditorium in classical 'end stage' and 'proscenium' formats.
Middle above: Anthropomorphic balcony front 'sitting attentive'. The seats were all purpose-designed for RADA by Bryan Avery to make use of a cheap seat swab and back rest from a proprietary manufacturer (p. 85).
Right: Sketch of Inigo Jones' plan for a theatre 1638

This Page

Main image: The Jerwood Vanbrugh Theatre with the floor raised for an 'in-the-round" production:
Top left: The geometry that creates the Vesica Piscis over the forestage area;
Left: Some of the options possible with prosc-flaps; adjustable flooring and removable seating.

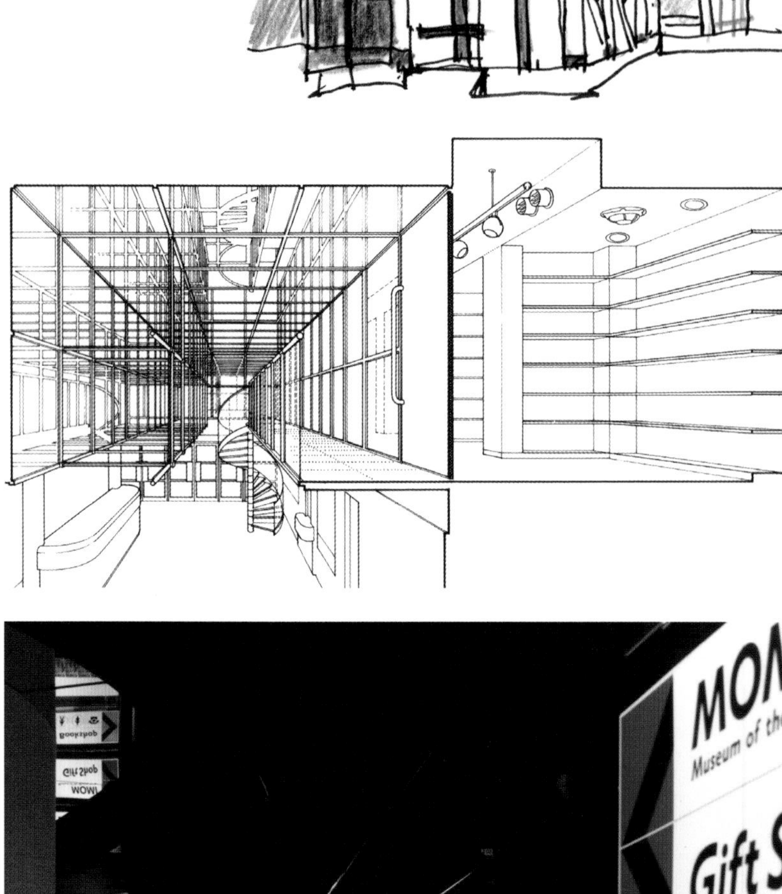

intervention became one of the first and most successful instances of the High-Tech architecture that Britain was becoming famous for but that had remained primarily an export product. From the Centre Pompidou to the Hong Kong and Shanghai Bank, London seemed, at the time, destined to do without the style which its city and its architects had fostered, nurtured and consistently developed from the Crystal Palace and the great railway termini to the fantastical buildings of the Festival of Britain. In fact, it was on the edge of the site of the latter that the building emerged.

The sophisticated blend of Pop Art imagery, High-Tech vocabulary and striking Meccano members was an influential and entertaining intervention in a period in which the architecture of London was in a notable lull. Squeezed between the car park of the Hayward Gallery and the underside of the approach ramp to Waterloo Bridge, it represented the beginning of a move to address some of the problems created by the Brutalist planning and tectonics of the South Bank, which remains an ongoing theme and one which has not since been handled with this kind of verve.

This Page
Top: Early Sketch; MOMI 1984.
Middle: The first bookshop project for the British Film Institute at the National Film Theatre 1982.
Bottom: The National Film Theatre Foyers 1992–1993.

Opposite Page
The third bookshop project for the British Film Institute 1992–1993.

New Titles
Now Showing
Biography
World Cinema
CINECITTÀ
FELLINI
GREAT HOLLYWOOD MOVIES

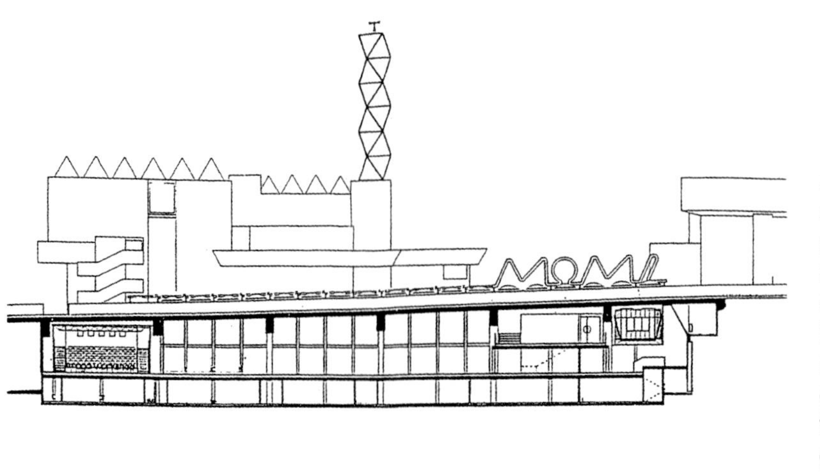

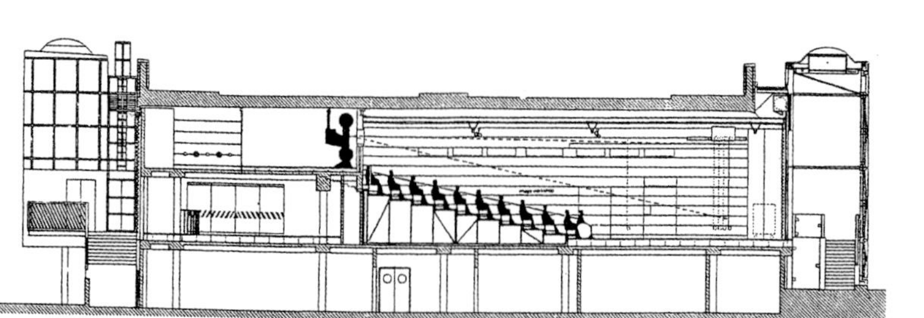

Avery's MOMI, then the most successful museum of its kind, presented a journey through the building as a filmic, chronological sequence, taking in the whole history of the moving image from shadow plays to film and TV. Its glazed facade became a trailer for the main feature, a glazed screen giving onto a world of images, flashes of image and movement which typify Avery's persistently dynamic approach to building and intervention.

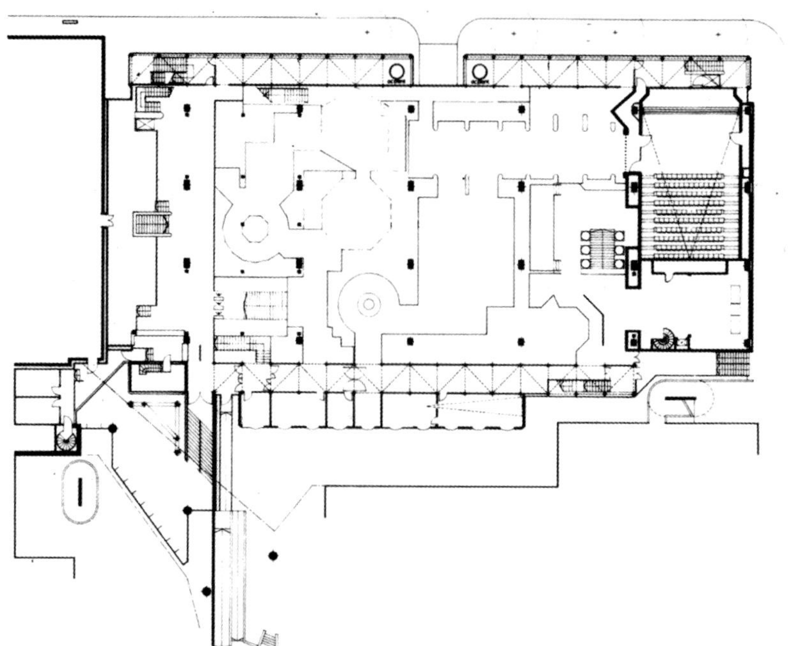

This Page
Top left: The Museum of the Moving Image, MOMI; long section (top); cross-section (below).
Left: Principal floor plan.
Bottom left: Aerial view.
Below: The site plan; Waterloo Bridge, London.
Below bottom: The eye and lens roof lights.

Opposite Page
Main image: The original foyer design; MOMI, axonometric.
Bottom from left: The Agitprop train; Hollywood studio (Designer Neal Potter); Bart and Ernie (Muppets).

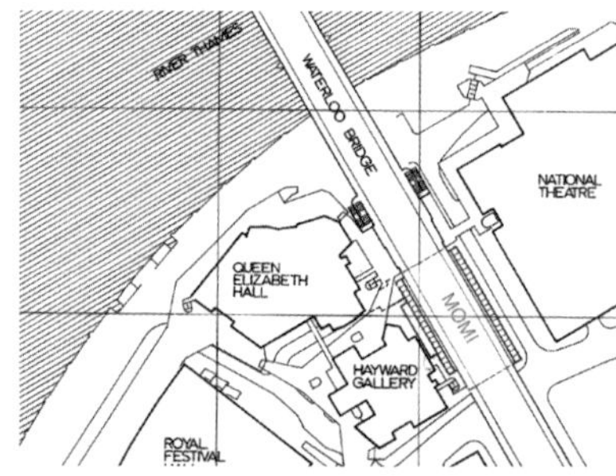

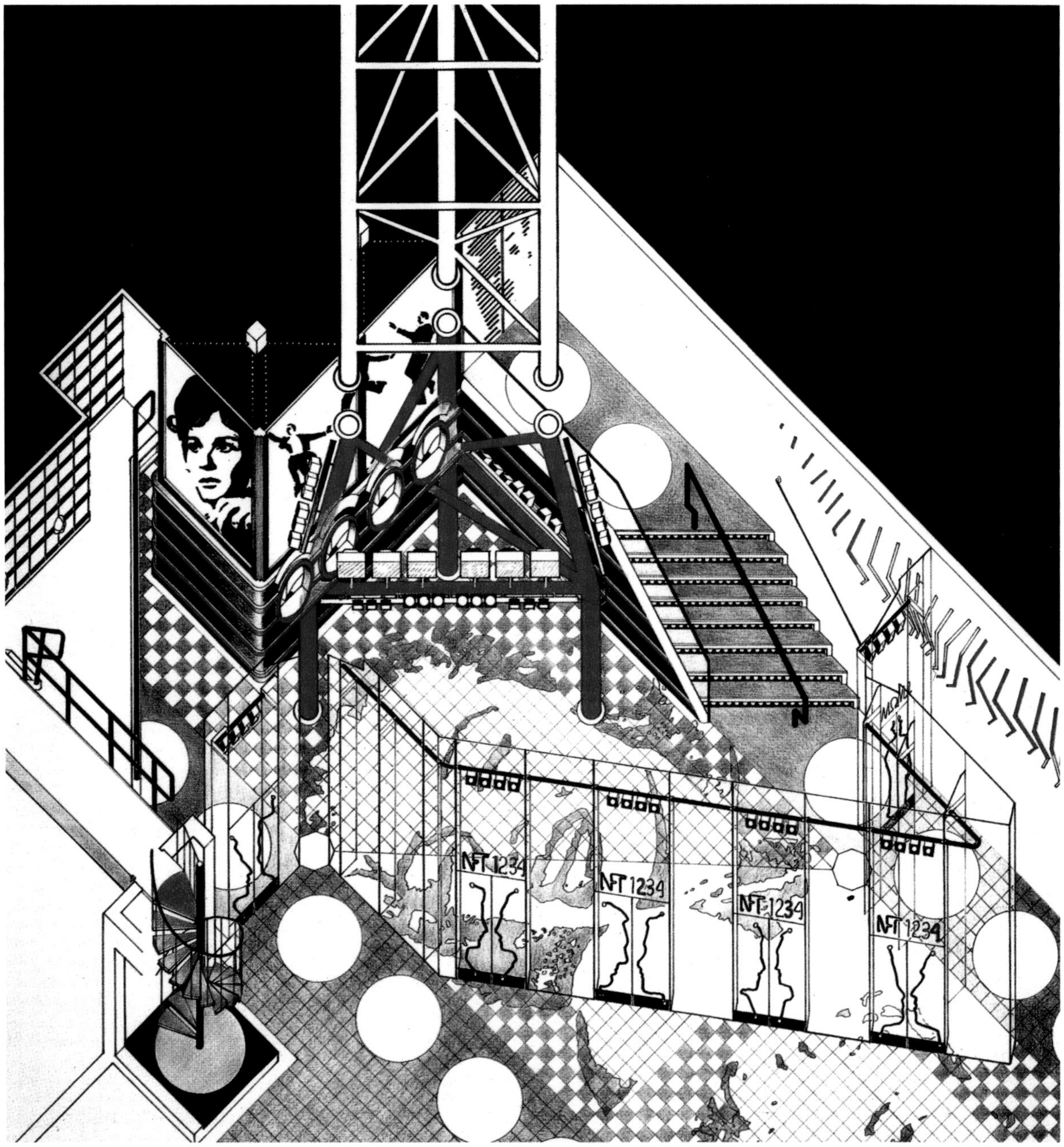
NFT 1234
NFT 1234
NFT 1234
NFT 1234

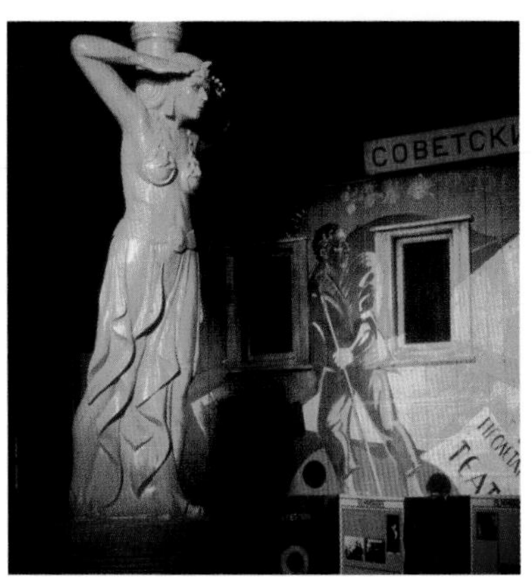

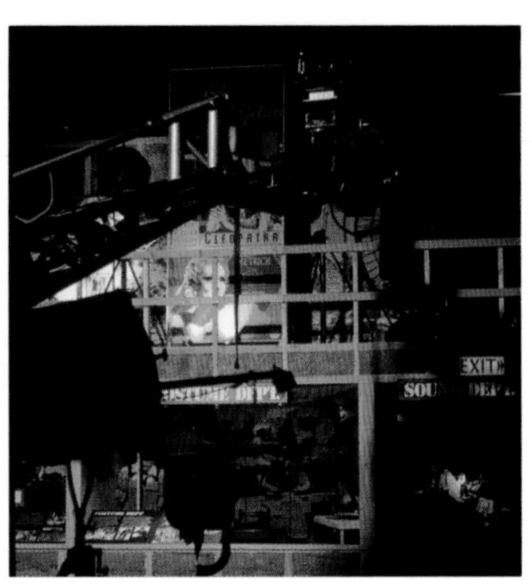

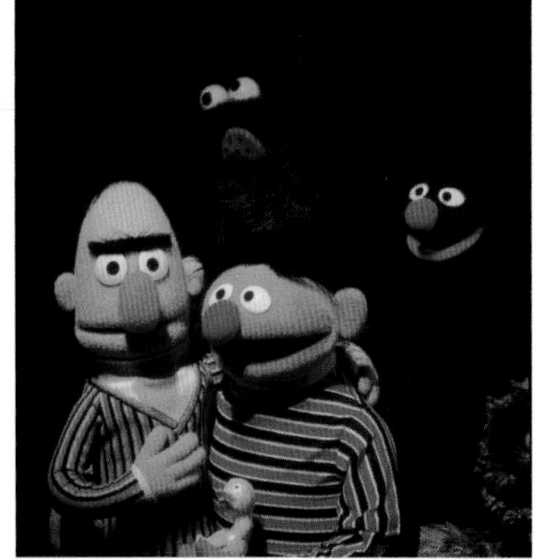

The building's exo-skeletal tectonic language, with its vocabulary of diagonal struts and illuminated signage, chimed with the Hayward Gallery's beacon-like kinetic sculpture whilst rebelling against the monolithic concrete of its host structure.

The building, buried as it was in the concrete underbelly of the city, was to be announced, like the Hayward, by a towering neon sign, a powerful reference to the illuminations which were cinema's contribution to the city of darkness but this, like so many opportunities in London's alternative architectural history, was lost. In the roof's futuristic bubble skylights, lurking mysteriously beside the clogged bridge approach there is an element of JG Ballard's concrete islands here, a future city simultaneously hypnotically intriguing and sinisterly subterranean, the perfect metaphor for film. This was an innovative, intelligent intervention, a building which developed an internal typology for a new kind of institution which bafflingly failed to take advantage of what it had succeeded in developing. A version of this High-Tech gridded facade with a blend of projection and filmic imagery was also, intriguingly, proposed for Bankside in what could have been a fascinating potential future for the Tate Modern site.

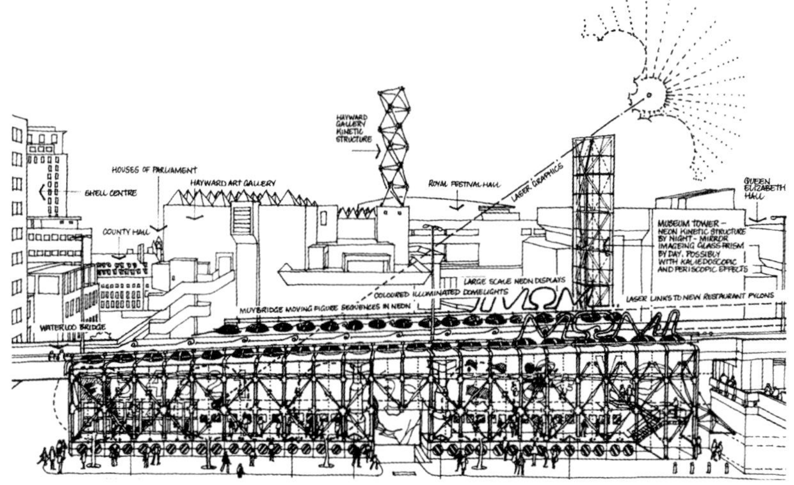

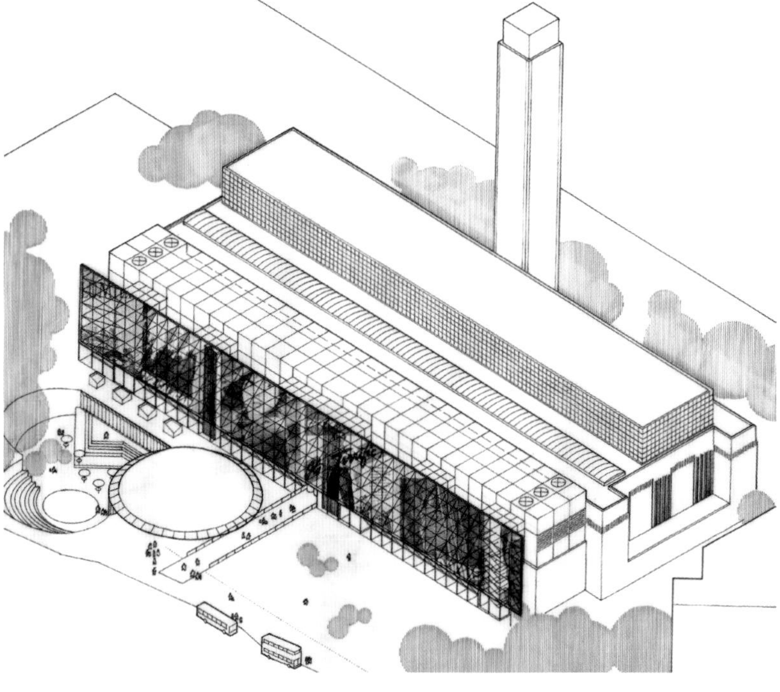

This Page
Top right: Conceptual drawing; MOMI 1984.
Middle right: MOMI and 'Electric Avenue'—the National Theatre covered link proposal.
Right: The British Film Institute; Tate Modern, Bankside Project 1995.

Opposite Page
Facade detail; Comedy and Tragedy at the Museum of the Moving Image; MOMI.

Another modern landmark seemingly perennially under threat (though now more than ever), Kensington's Commonwealth Institute, was conceived as a forum for the arts and culture of the Commonwealth (pp. 152, 157).

The whiff of colonialism, however, seemed to hang around it whilst it was allowed to fall into a kind of semi-municipal decline. Designed in 1962 by Sir Robert Matthew's RMJM, the Commonwealth Institute was one of the city's few important public buildings from this era, caught between the enthusiasm of post-war construction and the controversial delights of the South Bank's chunks of Brutalism. Avery's restoration of the building was noted chiefly for its tackling of one of the city's most notoriously unsuccessful roofs, a neo-expressionist saddle famous as much for the water it let through as for its extravagant and inventive form. The works transformed the structure into a fully functioning space, much in demand for trade fairs and shows, although, due to the huge value of its Kensington site and government reluctance to protect contemporary architecture, its future looks uncertain.

Another roof causing problems on one of London's more visible and visited public buildings was that over the London Transport Museum in Covent Garden (p. 157). Originally designed as a market hall, the greenhouse effect of its roofs led to severe solar gain and was threatening

This page
Top: Sketch of the Spitfire;
Left, top and bottom: The Commonwealth Institute 1999–2003:
Below: The new entrance to the London Transport Museum 2001–2007.

Opposite Page
Main image: The 'Spitfire Wing' 2006–2008;
Top left: Sketch of tanker in Southampton Docks.

B12
OPTARE
Live traffic congestion
LIVERPOOL St
BRYMAY
SAFETY MATCHES
STRATFORD
LA 9928

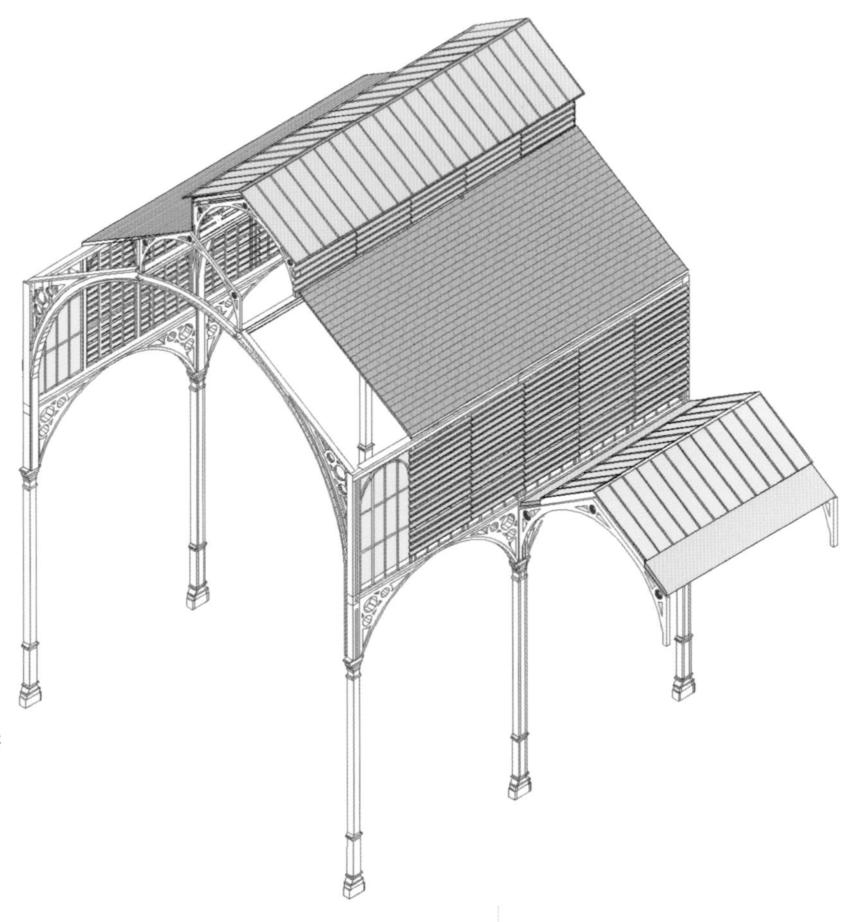

This Page
Right: Roof bay structure; the London Transport Museum 2001–2007.
Below: New and existing structure juxtaposed.
Below right: Second floor plan (top) and ground floor plan (bottom).

Opposite Page
The main hall; London Transport Museum.

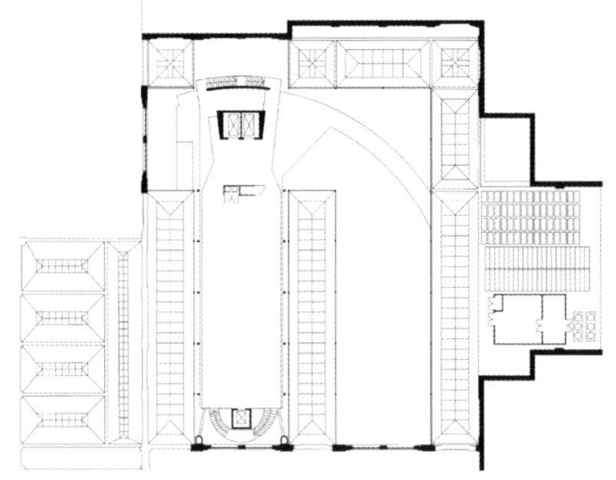

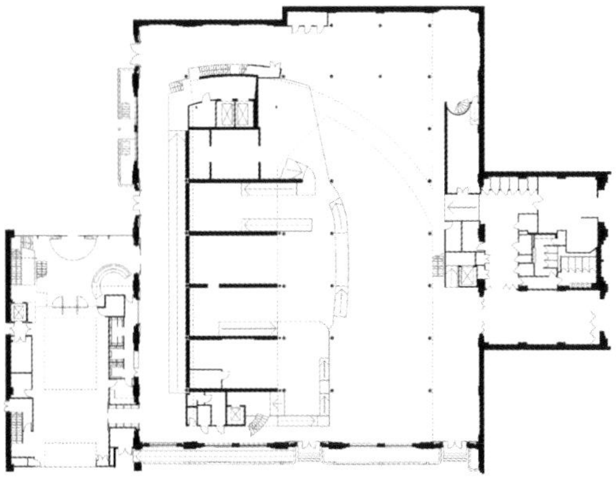

Key:

1 New Victorian Gallery
2 Train Table
3 Vehicle Hall
4 World City
5 Museum Shop
6 New Mezzanine Café
7 New lecture Theatre
8 New Café Store Room
9 Cloak Room
10 New Entrance Foyer
11 Theatre Museum
12 Study Rooms
13 Offices
14 Activities Studio

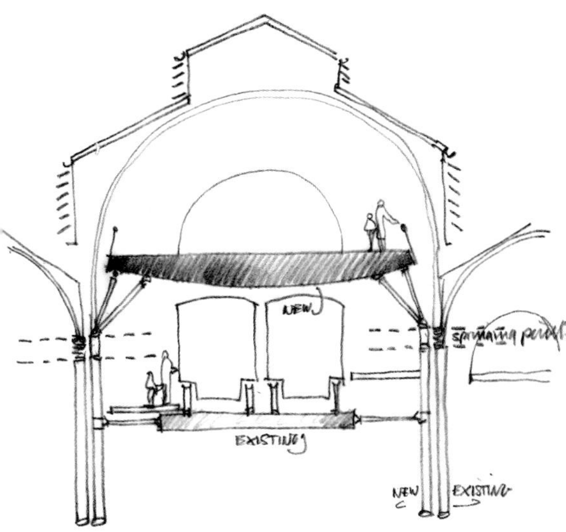

the survival of the exhibits. As well as sorting out the environmental issues, the scheme comprises a significant internal expansion to incorporate a new lecture theatre and temporary exhibition spaces.

The Victorian version of High-Tech employed to design the original halls seems the perfect partner to Avery's gently (and self-effacingly) futuristic designs. Indeed, a glimpse of the No. 1 Neathouse Place development opposite his Victoria offices (pp. 14–15, 48, 70–77, 88–92, 147) seems to suggest the same kind of quest for transparency and structural lightness and rationale.

Neathouse Place, a particularly dim piece of 1960s commercial architecture, was transformed into a highly desirable piece of commercial real estate. The astonishing urban panoramas from within are balanced by an articulate and architecturally sophisticated set of elevations which draw on Modernist and High Tech traditions, book-ending the formal expressions of the twentieth century.

The architecture which emerges from the office of Avery Associates is all, in its way, cultural architecture. Each task is given the same consideration and weight and there is none of the common phenomenon where offices concentrate more fully on cultural landmarks as useful PR whilst churning out commercial behemoths on the basis of pure square foot calculations.

From the earliest output, embracing innovative urban schemes for Trafalgar Square and the South Bank (p. 136, 137) and a raised traffic flow system for Oxford Street (p. 137) (allowing tree-lined pedestrian routes below, funded by extra retail space), Avery's office has continued to question urban norms and propose new typologies whilst never retreating from the awkward problems posed by the exigencies of the city's least successful spaces. It has been a consistently humane approach, accepting the faults of the urban fabric and proposing mechanisms to heal rifts and stitch together the fissures, holes and ragged edges left at the interstices.

Avery's recent essays and designs for the Wilderness City reflect these same concerns (Chapter 2). His is a utopianism which recognises the density, grit and imperfection of the city (as well as the existential and spiritual importance of its counterbalance, the dark primitivism of the wilderness) and is profoundly concerned with what happens at the edges.

His is an architecture prepared to address the city, the wider social implications of a site and issues far beyond it. Unconcerned with the single statement building which has reduced much recent architectural debate to simplistic formal gesturalism, Avery continues to plough a generous and urbane furrow, a route very much his own, which is nevertheless tied in to contemporary culture and the elements it lacks, from our relationship with the landscape, the skies and the cosmos, to our proximity to the myriad failures of the urban environment and the increasingly suburbanised landscape of our countryside. His architectural oeuvre comprises a series of physical, concrete lectures which begin to illuminate the problems but also eloquently illustrate some of the more elegant and intelligent of the solutions.

This Page
Above: The original sketch for the new Victorian gallery; London Transport Museum.

Opposite Page
Section and photomontage; London Transport Museum.

Footnotes to Chapter 7
The Royal Academy of Dramatic Art (RADA): 1994–2000 Notes of the principle design elements:

6.1 The Foyer: The foyer is a quite complicated multi-functioning element. It has to be a comfortable space for students to call their own but it has also to dress up for audiences and work as an exhibition space, a meeting room, a bar, a performance space —and as a foyer.

At 12 minutes to 12 on 21 June—the day when the druids gather at Stonehenge to celebrate the midsummer solstice—another spectacle unfolds at RADA. On that day, at that time, the sun reaches down into the foyer to the base of the cleft and touches a bust there by Epstein of George Bernard Shaw—arguably the most influential of all RADA's principals and patrons.

6.2 The GBS Theatre: The GBS (George Bernard Shaw) theatre was retained from the original building as a valuable historical reference for the new academy. It's fly-tower was truncated to create a through-route across the site and it has been given a flat floor and technical teaching rooms, but its essential character, with all its historical resonances, remains.

6.3 The Malet Street Facade: The site is only 15.5 metres (51 feet) wide yet it had to provide for four public escape routes, a service access to the kitchen and bar, a get-in for the three theatres (sufficient for a fork-lift truck) and a public (audience) entrance. Above the entrance are the dressing rooms, ladies one side, men the other, and they each have a bay-window with a window seat where they can come out and greet members of their audience.

Above that is the back stage cross-over which, being made of white glass, works like a shadow-play, and above that is the fly-tower, with large terra-cotta panels, a reference to the brickwork of the adjacent buildings.

6.4 The Gielgud Theatre: There used to be a very flexible and particularly intimate small studio space in the old RADA building called Room 14. It was technically and environmentally flawed but it had a particular size and proportion that made it very much loved. The new space recreates this but is now fully equipped for rehearsals, television work and public performances. A particular feature of the space is the use of "Halfen" channels built into the wall to provide a very fast and flexible fixing system for scenery, props and lighting.

6.5 The Roof: The barrel vault was designed to maximise the internal volume whilst minimising the over-shadowing of adjacent sites. Plant rooms occupy the bulk of the vault, separated by the glazing over the cleft light well. The plan was to have a 'contemplative' garden on the fly tower roof where students could escape the pressure of the academy and enjoy the fresh air and views, but unfortunately due to the cost of access this had to be abandoned.

6.6 The Jerwood Vanbrugh Theatre: The three key innovations in the plan are: the tension wire grid (an indispensable teaching aid with up to eight students able to work on it at any one time) the powered floor mechanism (which enables an orchestra pit, raked stalls or flat floor to be created in seconds) and the adjustable prosc-flaps. These consist of two, double-hinged proscenium wing panels on each side that can be folded out to form proscenium frames at either the front or back of the forestage area. They can also be used together to create a juliet balcony, or folded away to create a courtyard theatre, an end-stage, an in-the-round space, etc.. These transformations take less than 30 minutes, completly belying the notion that the only flexible theatre is a black box with bleacher seating.

The Jerwood Vanbrugh plan follows the ancient tradition of theatre design with the two realms of the actors and of the audience represented as two spheres intersecting in a 'vesica piscis', considered the point where the actor can have the most intimate relationship with the audience.

The challenge was to make this small space, seating just over 200, play 'big' so that the students would learn to project their voices. The first part of the answer was to read the space to the side walls, not to the balcony fronts, which required that the balconies be as open as possible. The second part was to persuade the eye that the space was larger than it actually is, achieved by adhering to the proportional spherical geometry of the plan which generated floor to floor heights of just 2.25 metres (7 feet-4.5 inches) and ceiling heights of 2.1 of metres (6 feet-10.5 inches).

The balcony fronts are angled forward, in part to reduce their visual height, thereby to increase the scale of the room, and in part to evoke an empathetic postural response from the audience that it should sit attentive, knees bent, leaning forward—the reaction the actor hopes for. The materials are in a new-old dialogue, the stainless steel of the twenty-first century in counterpoint to the 'ancient' bleached, stained, maple.

6.7 The Cleft: Given that over most of the building light and air can only get in from above, the cleft is both a critical functional element in the design and a key symbolic element at the heart of RADA.

It sits at the pivotal point between the four RADA 'realms'. The realms (in plan) of the public (audience) and private (Academy staff and students) and the realms (in section) of the acting students above in the 'gods'; and of the technical students below in the 'pits'.

The function of the cleft is to unite these four realms thus, looking down, the glass floor in the foyer not only brings valuable daylight into the below-ground workshop areas, but symbolises the strong connection that the technical students must have with their audience, a facet of the academy's life not often formally expressed;

The windows in the Cleft refer to those in Soane's house in Lincoln Inn Fields. There they are used with mirrored panes to direct light into spaces at the bottom of a well, but here they are used to afford views down. The windows at the back of the Cleft are in a quiet 'student' area and have window seats for those who might wish to study whilst keeping in touch with academy life and, looking up, the backs of the Jerwood Vanbrugh and Gielgud Theatres almost, but not quite, touch across the space in a gesture of creative tension.

Chapter 8

Chronology of Principal Projects

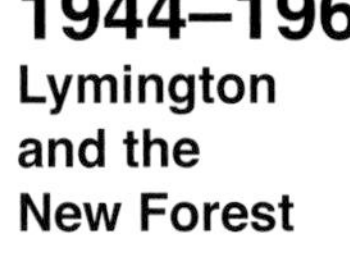

1944–1962
Lymington and the New Forest

Lymington (top and left) is a small Georgian market town and yacht building centre in the New Forest, Hampshire. The famous local author Dennis Wheatley commissioned Avery to paint a zodiac freeze for his home – the brickwork walls of which (middle above) were 'wavy'—a local tradition used to stiffen them (See Expo 2010 project p. 21). Avery also painted local landscapes, one of which was exhibited in Southampton Art Gallery (p. 5). He was awarded an RAF Flying Scholarship and taught to fly at Southampton (Eastleigh) airport (Avery standing at right in picture above). His flying instructor, John Fairey owned a spitfire (See Spitfire Wing Project for Southampton p. 126).

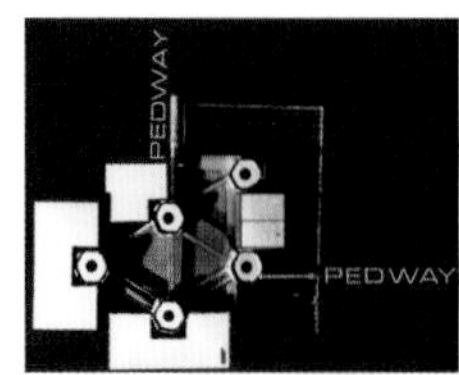

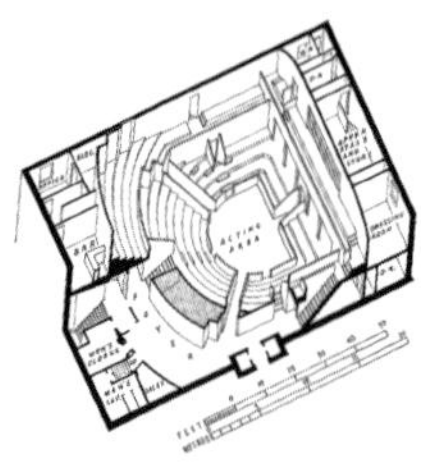

1962–1968
Leicester School of Architecture.

Undergraduate Year Master was Richard Leacroft, author of 'Theatre and Playhouse'. He was noted for the use of cut-away isometric projections to depict architectural space (second from top above). The final year Master was David Greene, member of the Archigram Group. Avery's final thesis was on 'Understanding the Industrialisation of Building' and the final design project was a new school of architecture (above top and p. 178): Above (bottom two) Stirling and Gowan's Engineering Building at Leicester 1959–1963

1964
Travel Award and Essay; Switzerland

Intended as the second of a trilogy of essays on the sense of time, place and function in architecture, the Award Essay focused on two regions of Switzerland—the Valais (middle above) and the Oberland (bottom above) and sought to demonstrate how, from within two very similar environmental contexts, two completely different but hugely evocative visual expressions could be developed. This led ultimately to the notion of 'contiguity', a contextual phenomenon of the proximity of stimulus and response causing their association in the mind (pp. 6–7). This was the opportunity also for the first visit to Italy which was to have a profound influence upon later work. Above top, watercolour of the Doges Palace Venice from San Giorgio Maggiore 1964.

1965
USA

In the course of travelling through North America to experience the works of Frank Lloyd Wright (above, from bottom: Taliesin West; Johnson Wax; Falling Water) Avery designed a rationalised system of residential timber construction for a contractor in Rocky Mount, North Carolina. The first house using this system was designed, built and sold in six weeks. In all 300 houses of this type were completed (top).

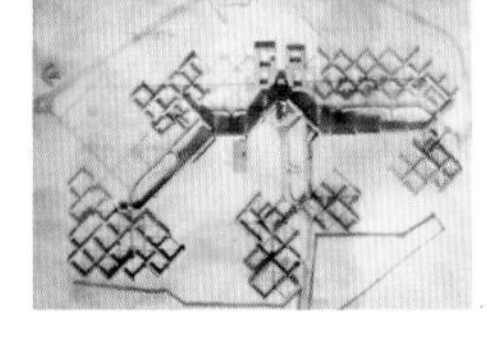

1966–1967
The Greater London Council

In the then much revered housing division of the GLC, Avery developed this masterplan for the Hendon Aerodrome Redevelopment Project (above, bottom) and worked on the innovatory SFI plastic clad pre-fabricated housing system in which the outer structural frame came to site with three stories of cladding already in place (above, top).

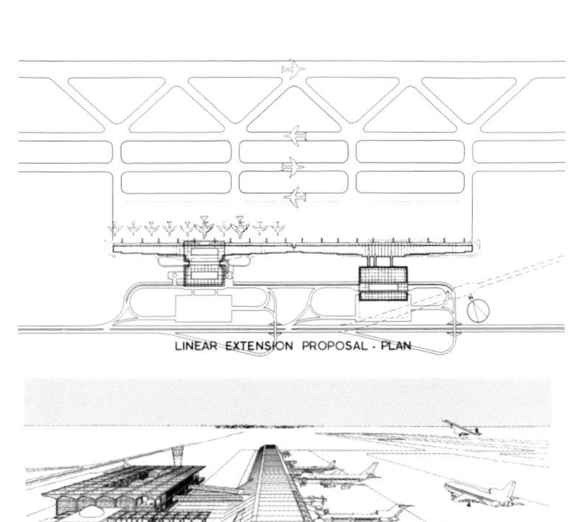

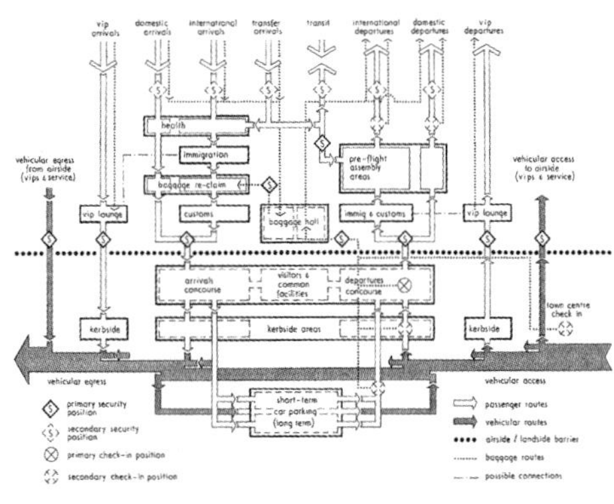

1968–1969 Component Development Consultancy

Instead of joining an architectural practice after graduating, Avery joined Anthony Williams and Burles, a Component Development Consultancy. The firm was a pioneer in the field working primarily on the IBIS (Industrialised Building in Steel) programme (above/bottom). Avery designed a number of building products for the firm including partitioning and shelving systems and a patented pre-fabricated modular roofing system (above; top and p. 82)

1969–1970 Essex University

As a corrective to the narrow focus of the technology specialism, Avery took a masters degree in the History and Theory of Architecture at the Faculty of Art, Essex University.

The course was run by Joseph Rykwert and Dalibor Vesely, both of whom were to become internationally famous for their teaching and scholarship. The Legacy of this for Avery was considerable. It provided an introduction to the work of Heidegger and the Phenomenologists, and led to the development of a personal architectural theory that helped shape every subsequent project.

1972–1975 Raymond J. Cecil and Partners

In the building boom of the early 1970's the RJC practice was unusually experimental and created the opportunity for several important projects. The block of flats and the service core (above) reflect the FLW legacy, as do the Heathrow Offices (pp. 8, 62) and the Spiral Building (p. 63)—these later two also pre-figured many later projects.

1975–1976 Dubai International Airport

The practice at Page and Broughton had designed the existing terminal building some years earlier and Avery was brought in to add a very substantial increase to its capacity. Several configurations were explored including satellite terminals (above second from bottom); a (then) innovative linear terminal (above, top left and right) and a completely new terminal located between a new second runway (above, bottom). Thirty years later, the latter two were eventually implemented.

1976–1977 Architects Journal, Metric Handbook

The Gollins Melvin and Ward (GMW) practice was then one of the leading UK specialists in airport design. Avery was asked to research and write the Handbook Guide to Airport Terminal design. The diagram above, still in use today, distilled the essence of the security and circulation systems and can be seen manifested in terminals such as London Stansted Airport.

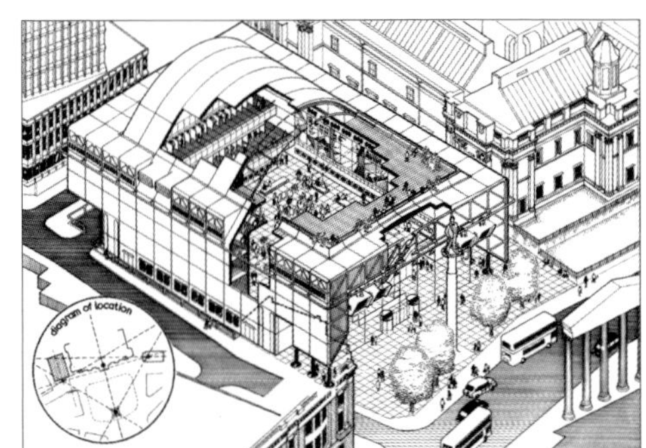

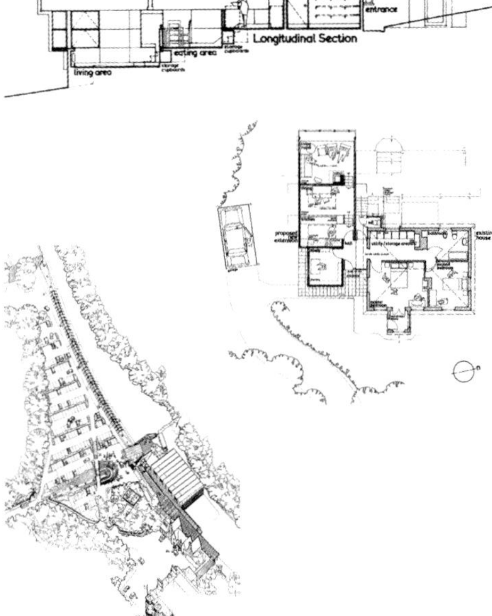

1976–1978
The British Carpet Trade Centre; London

This was the practice's first built project and the first attempt to create a Concinnity, a 'harmony of the parts' (pp. 18–19). The key to the design was a 600 x 600 mm planning grid, in both plan and section, which generated 1:1 and 2:1 cubic proportions throughout the interior. At 2.4 metres, the ceilings were purposefully kept low, except in the main 'square' where reflections produced by chromed aluminium ceiling slats set 3 metres above the floor created an illusory space 6 metres high. The resultant intimacy of small 'real' spaces set against a grander 'virtual' space is an approach much used in subsequent projects. The executive architects were Greenbourne Associates.

1979–1983
Electro-Tech Project No. 1; Trafalgar Sq; London

Heidegger wrote in The Question Concerning Technology, "Technology is no mere means. Technology is a way of revealing. If we give heed to this, then another whole realm will open itself up to us. It is the world of revealing, of truth."

The Electro-Tech projects were a series of proposals which sought to forge a rapprochement between people and the then newly emerging electronics technologies.

Through the use of these technologies as cultural, museological and entertainment aids, it was hoped that their benefits and potential uses might be better understood.

Such buildings were later made particularly popular in France where they became known as 'mediatheques' or 'videotheques'.

The architectural language of all three projects was the result of a quest to find a metalwork equivalent of the elements of the classical language, specifically, the portico, vault and dome.

The format of this first project was heavily influenced by Lord Norman Foster's Sainsbury gallery in Ipswich but defers also to the National Gallery and the Buildings around Trafalgar Square

1980
Repertory Theatre; Keswick; Cumbria

The site was hard against the hills, a derelict railway station with an abandoned platform hemmed in by trees; dark, dense and mysterious.

The theatre hovers at one end of the platform, set back from the edge, its black glass impenetrable, its finely swaged stainless-steel skin glinting, its air-handling units humming, the condensers steaming.

Thus the project sought to express the complex and contradictory themes generated by the content of the building and its relationship to its historic and geographical setting—its Contiguity—ideas explored in many subsequent projects (pp. 48–49).

1980
Zoller House; Surrey

An early stepped-section project (above plan and section). See also the Electro-Tech Projects No. 1 (p. 136) and No. 3 (p. 139); The RMCS Library (p. 139); the NFT Restaurant (p. 139); Kolkata (p. 167); Southend Museum (pp. 179–181) and the Grand Cascade (pp. 182–183).

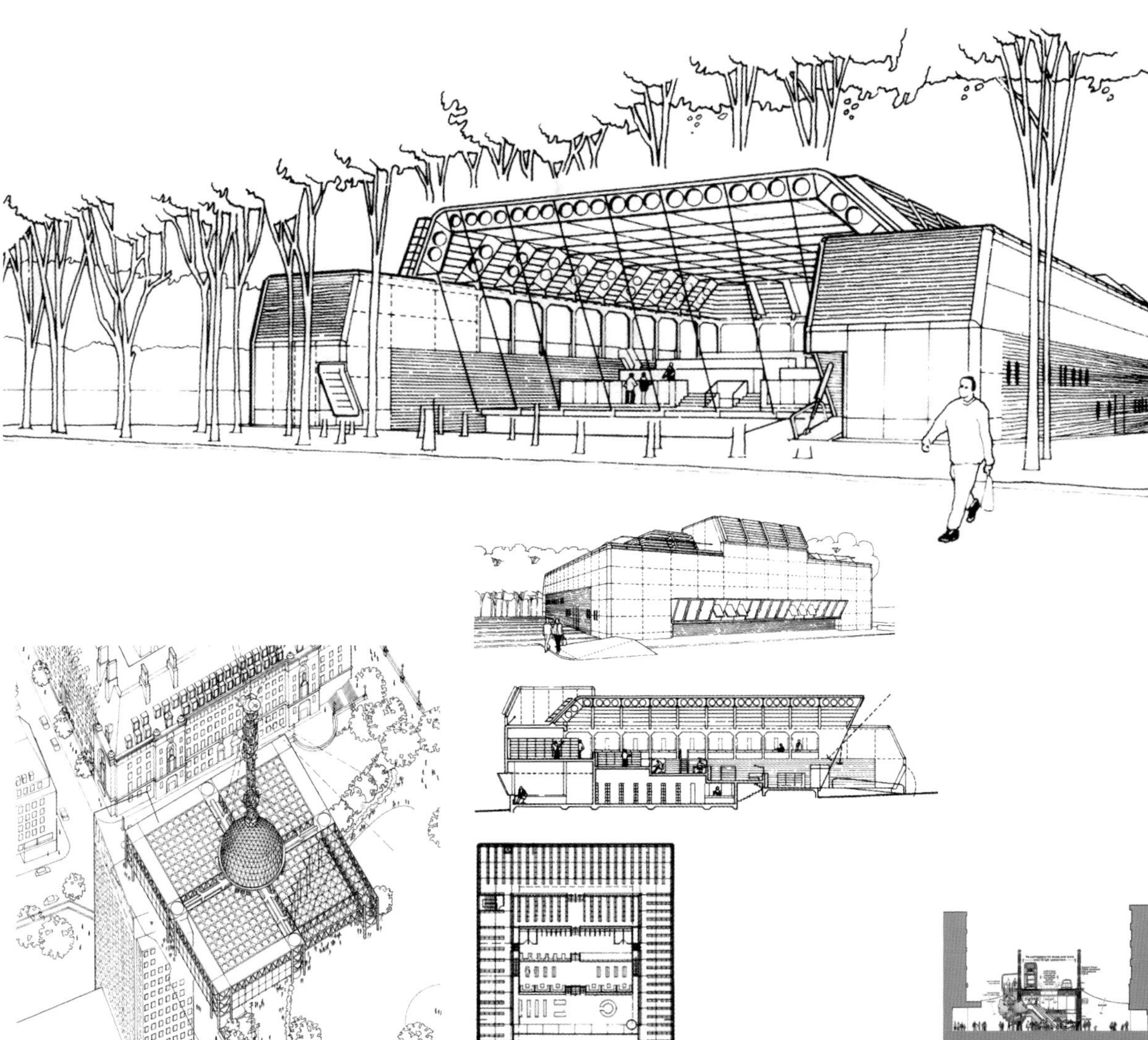

1981
Electro-Tech Project No. 2; South Bank; London

The second of the three projects, this responded to its site adjacent to County Hall by focusing upon conferences, events and trade expositions to promote the newly emerging electronics industries.

The building's form sought a dialogue with County Hall and with the still extant resonances of the structures of the 1951 Festival of Britain.

1981
The Royal Military College of Science Library; Shrivenham; Wiltshire

The clarity of the extruded section had become almost a cliché of 1970s high-tec architecture, but its explicit evocation of construction rigour was often to the detriment of other concerns.

The aim here was to express the nature of lightweight metal technologies whilst also allowing for dissimilarities, terminations and a variety of orientations, that is, a less self-referential architecture with a more responsive technical and aesthetic vocabulary that would allow the content and contiguity of the building to be fully expressed.

The resultant form drew more upon military vehicles and the fabrication techniques of the transport industries than upon architecture. The library interior could, therefore, defer to the axial galleried layout of traditional libraries, whilst allowing the whole a greater dynamic of movement and presence more in keeping with its purpose and location.

1981–1983
The Oxford Street Pedestrianisation Project; London

Once a special treat for families, the street in 1981 was fighting for tough young bargain-hunters and tourists. Going 'up West' to shop was no longer a pleasurable experience.

Consider, though, if the buses and taxis could be whisked away on an aerial artery, then the street below could be pedestrianised, made safe and sheltered against the rain.

Perhaps then it would regain some joy and become a great city street, a place of character as well as commerce, a place for promenading as well as purchasing (pp. 50–51).

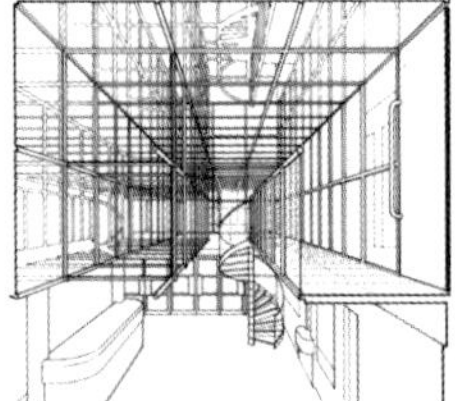

1982
The National Film Theatre Bookshop; Project No. 1; London

A planned refurbishment of the foyer to the NFT created an opportunity to use the double-height above the ceiling to provide a new bookshop. The aim was to integrate the new bookshop into the ceiling using a three dimensional grid of mirrors and coloured cold cathode tubes. The result was a kaleidoscopic tableau through which the customers would pass and thereby generate a moving image experience for those below (p. 112).

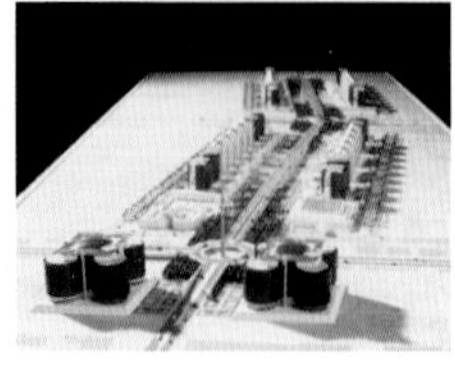

1982
The Avenue of the Emirates; Abu Dhabi

A development of the Oxford Street project with its viaduct 'highway' (pp. 137, 50–51), this proposed masterplan for Abu Dhabi, the Avenue of the Emirates, covered a total area 2.25 kilometres long and 0.5 kilometres wide and was based on a series of autonomous city blocks, each 120 meters square (pp. 50–51). The proportional subdivision of these blocks into ever smaller squares and double-squares generated a Concinnity—a harmonious arrangement of the parts—which was to reappear later on projects such as that for Rank Xerox (pp. 145, 64–65).

1982–1983
Capsule Hotel Tower; London

The brief for this mixed-use development on the corner of Tottenham Court Road and Oxford Street called for three levels of shops and restaurants to be linked into a new underground station with offices and hotel above. Based on Japanese 'capsule' hotels, the hotel tower was envisaged as a sophisticated, well serviced 'crash-pad' offering overnight accommodation in the heart of central London for out-of-town theatre-goers and itinerant or late-working business people.

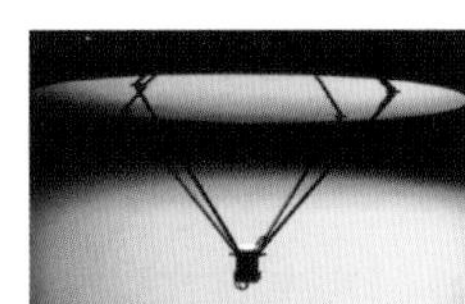

1982–1983
The Up-Downlighter Lighting Range

Patented in 1984, and now commonplace in various guises, the original reflector downlighter was designed as a whole family of fittings to include both interior and exterior lights, as well as an integrated ceiling lighting system that would remove the problem of switching, wiring and relamping from the suspended ceiling zone (pp. 18, 84).

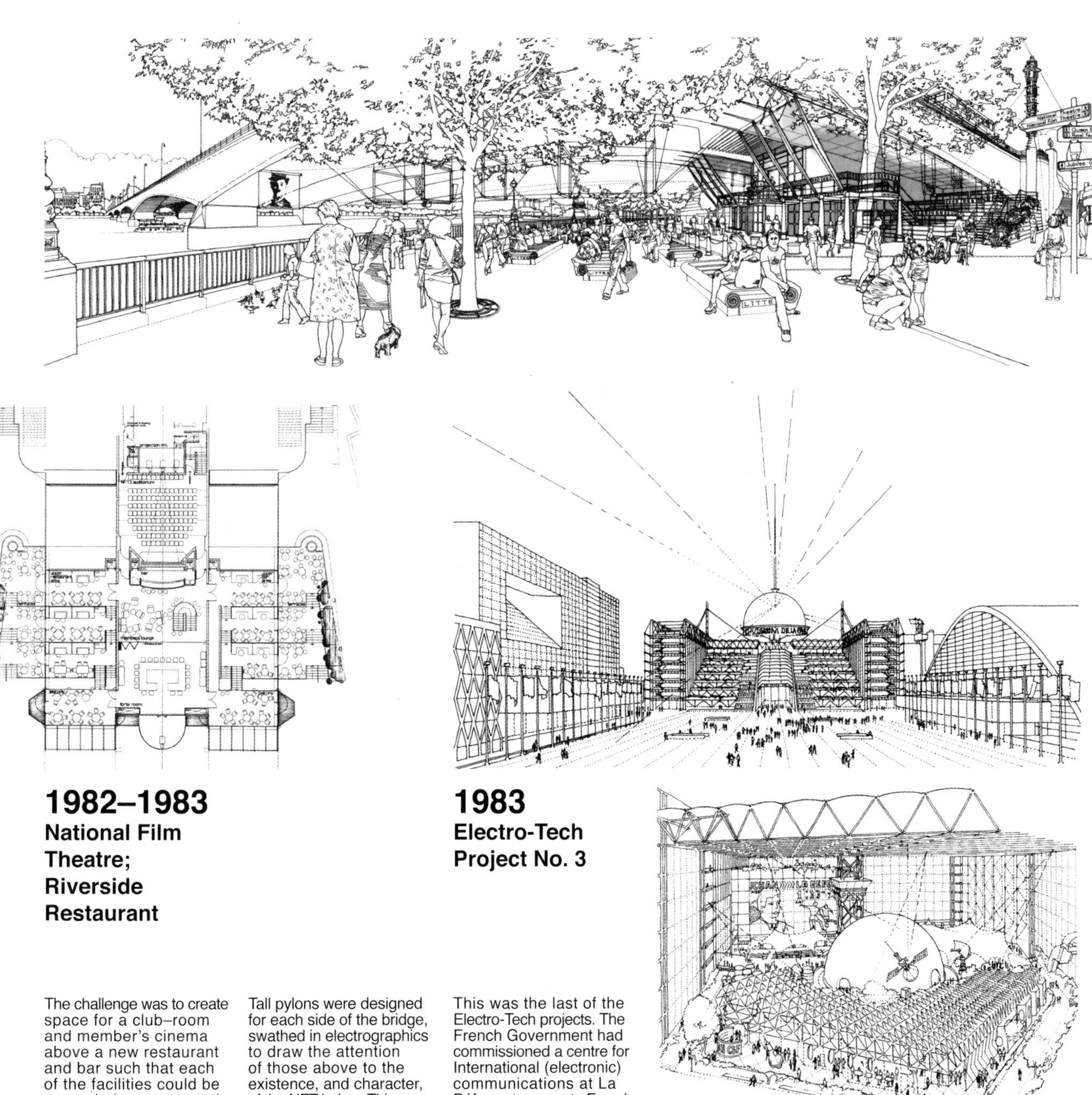

1982–1983
National Film Theatre; Riverside Restaurant

The challenge was to create space for a club–room and member's cinema above a new restaurant and bar such that each of the facilities could be expanded or contracted as the occasion required. This was resolved by linking the private areas, located on the first floor, with the public areas on the ground floor by stepped platforms so that any of the functions could expand up or down.

The result was a pair of highly flexible 'tiered' interiors—like auditoria—that nestled under the protective arch of Waterloo Bridge and looked down onto the 'stage-set' of the riverside promenade.

Tall pylons were designed for each side of the bridge, swathed in electrographics to draw the attention of those above to the existence, and character, of the NFT below. This was to have been further enhanced with the addition of coloured 'freeze-frame' lighting over the riverside promenade and a large outdoor screen suspended beneath the bridge, on which young movie-makers would be invited to preview their productions.

Above, First floor plan; top, perspective.

1983
Electro-Tech Project No. 3

This was the last of the Electro-Tech projects. The French Government had commissioned a centre for International (electronic) communications at La Défense to promote French language and culture but it proved too ambitious—the result being the ministry building, now known as the Grande Arche.

The Architectural response here was to extend the sidewalls that define the grand axis from the Louvre; to raise up the floor plane to afford views back to Paris; and then to terminate the axis with a dome surmounting a huge exhibition space below.

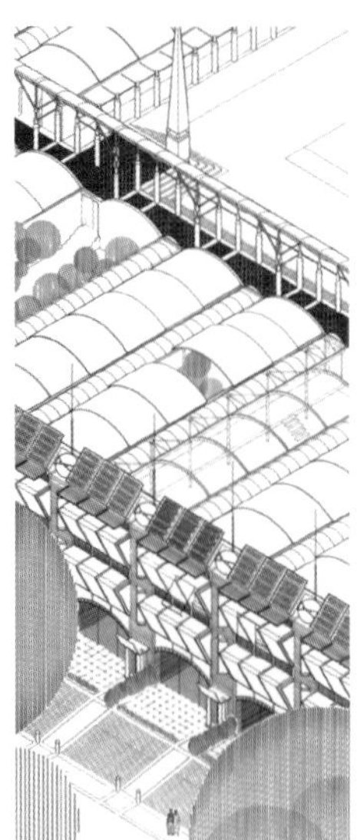

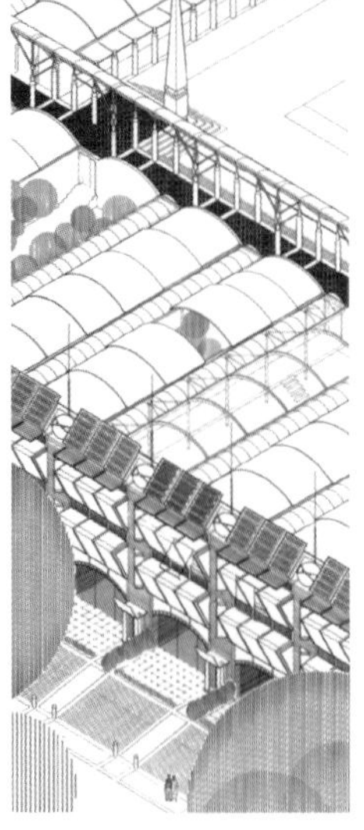

1984–1985
The Advanced Technology Housing Projects

The first ATH project was a proposition on the future of the suburbs (image above, bottom); the second looked at the future of the city using a minimum footprint 'back-to-back' house type (image above, top) (pp. 38–39, 54–55) and the third (image, left) looked at the future of the countryside. This was the beginning of the Wilderness city project (Chapter 2 and pp. 4–5, 56–57, 80).

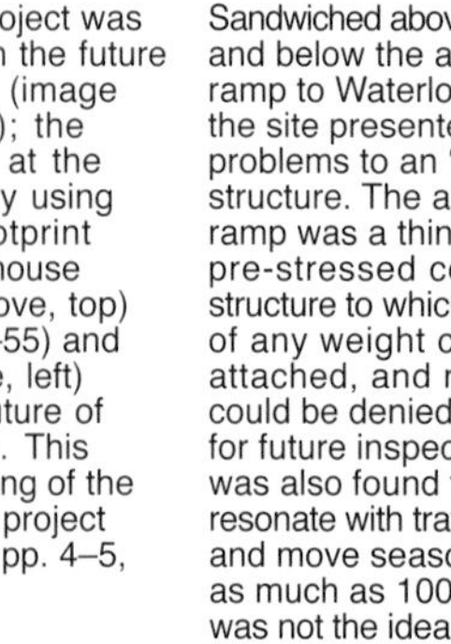

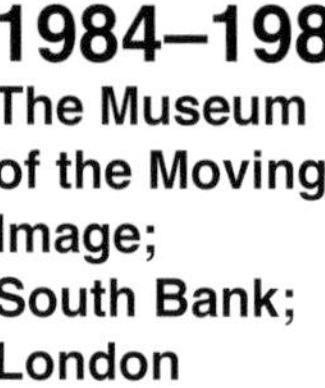

1984–1988
The Museum of the Moving Image; South Bank; London

Sandwiched above a carpark and below the approach ramp to Waterloo bridge, the site presented similar problems to an 'air rights' structure. The approach ramp was a thin, sloping, pre-stressed concrete structure to which nothing of any weight could be attached, and no part could be denied access for future inspection. It was also found to leak, resonate with traffic noise and move seasonally by as much as 100mm. It was not the ideal context for a new museum (pp. 2–3, 61, 84–85, 112–117).

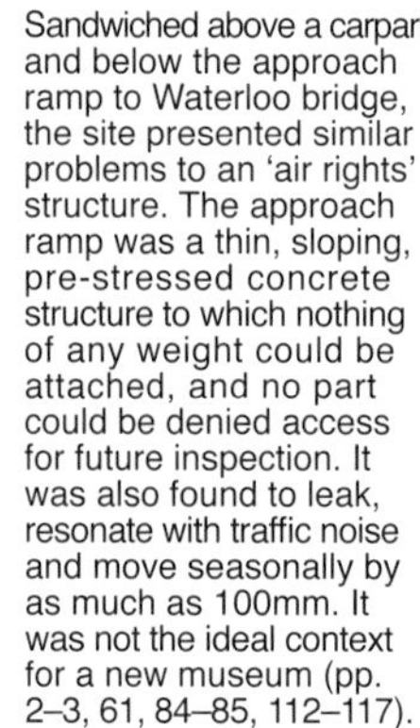

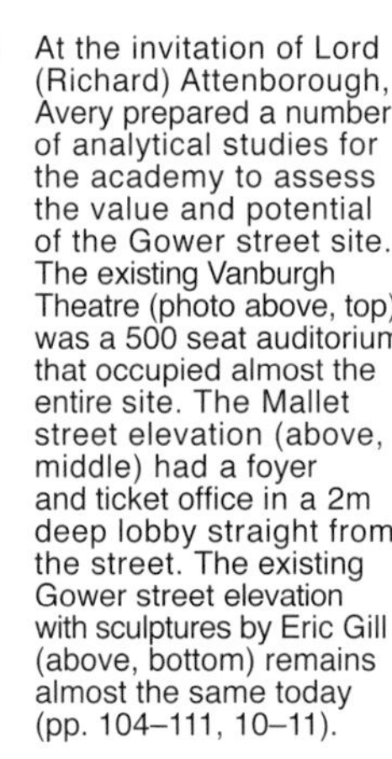

1984–1986
The Royal Academy of Dramatic Art; First Project

At the invitation of Lord (Richard) Attenborough, Avery prepared a number of analytical studies for the academy to assess the value and potential of the Gower street site. The existing Vanburgh Theatre (photo above, top), was a 500 seat auditorium that occupied almost the entire site. The Mallet street elevation (above, middle) had a foyer and ticket office in a 2m deep lobby straight from the street. The existing Gower street elevation with sculptures by Eric Gill (above, bottom) remains almost the same today (pp. 104–111, 10–11).

1985–1991
Plantation House; Fenchurch St; City of London

With it's imposing eight-storey Neo Classical facade, Plantation House in Fenchurch Street was one of the best known buildings in the City of London. Owned by the British Land Company, it consisted of 32,500m^2 (350,000ft^2) of multi tenanted space and the refurbishment involved renovating some 30 office suites to commercial standards and a complete transformation of the internal public environment.

This entailed working with the existing proportions and details whilst introducing new materials to create a fresh 'new-old' dialogue (pp. 68–69).

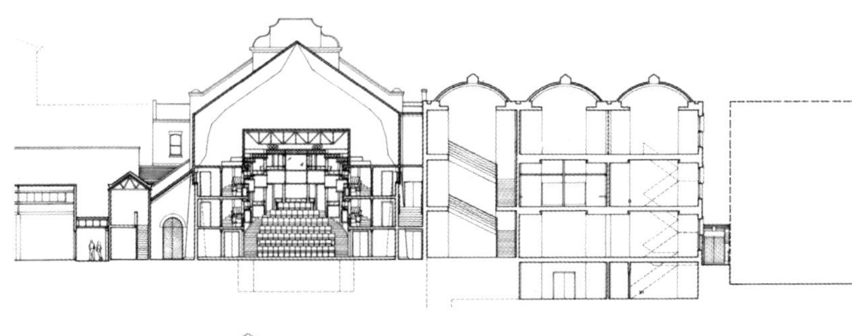

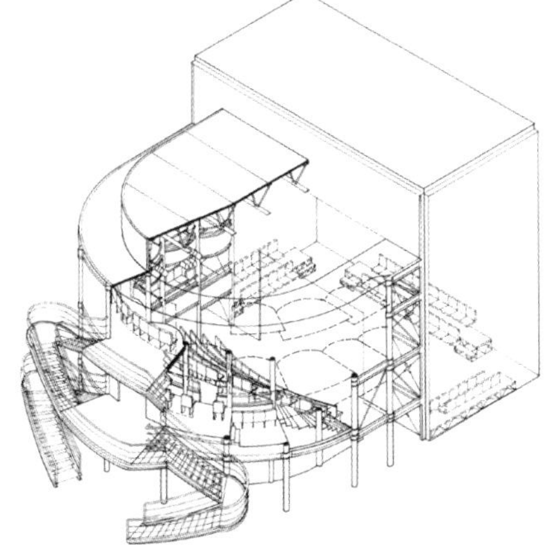

1987–1989
RADA; Second Project; Hoxton Square, London

Before finally committing to their existing site in Bloomsbury, RADA looked at numerous alternatives across London. The most promising was the old incinerator building in Hoxton Square. A full design was commissioned and planning permission obtained but despite the best efforts of HRH Princess Diana; Lord Attenborough; Gielgud and the RADA alumni, in those pre-lottery days, it proved impossible to raise the funds.

Shown above is the main performance space that would have sat within the industrial incinerator shed, much in the manner of the Royal Exchange Theatre in Manchester. It was steep raked with side boxes but the semi-circular plan pre-figures the eventual Jerwood Vanbrugh plan (pp. 108–111).

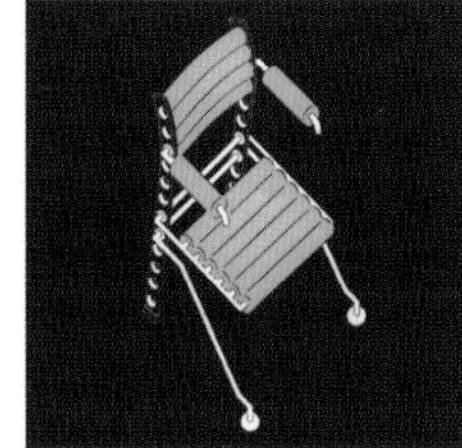

1987–1989
Plywood and Metal Chair

The chair was based on a sturdy pierced plywood backbone onto which different legs, seats and armrests could be attached to create a family of chairs, suitable for all sizes and purposes (pp. 82–83).

1987–1989
The Cellular Sedan

Cars consist of just three basic elements: a body cell, a front end and a rear end. Thus if the body cell could be standardised the front and rear ends could be separately sourced, allowing a far greater customising potential.

The front ends could have an economic city runabout engine during the week and a powerful motorway unit at the weekend and the rear end could be boot or hatchback; estate or van; flat back or even dicky-seated. (pp. 80–81 and Scenic Saloon p. 168).

1988
European Patent office HQ; Hague; Holland

The vast ridge-and-furrow glasshouses of Holland's horticultural conglomerates have become almost a local vernacular across much of the Netherlands. Their repetitive crystalline linearity, punctuated periodically by tall boiler flues, has contributed a bold new form to the landscape, as powerful in its evocation of place as the flat expanse of the polders or the sunken network of water-filled dykes. It was into this landscape that the new building, with its glazed roof and very large evaporative cooling tunnels was to be set (pp. 64–65).

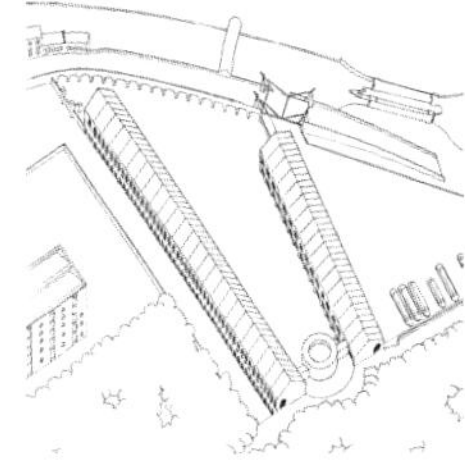

1988
RADA; Third project; King's Cross, London

In its search for alternatives in re-developing the Bloomsbury site, RADA commissioned this study of the 'Coal-Drop' buildings at King's Cross.It proved capable of providing a huge range of spaces but ultimately it took the Academy too far from its urban and theatrical roots in the West End.

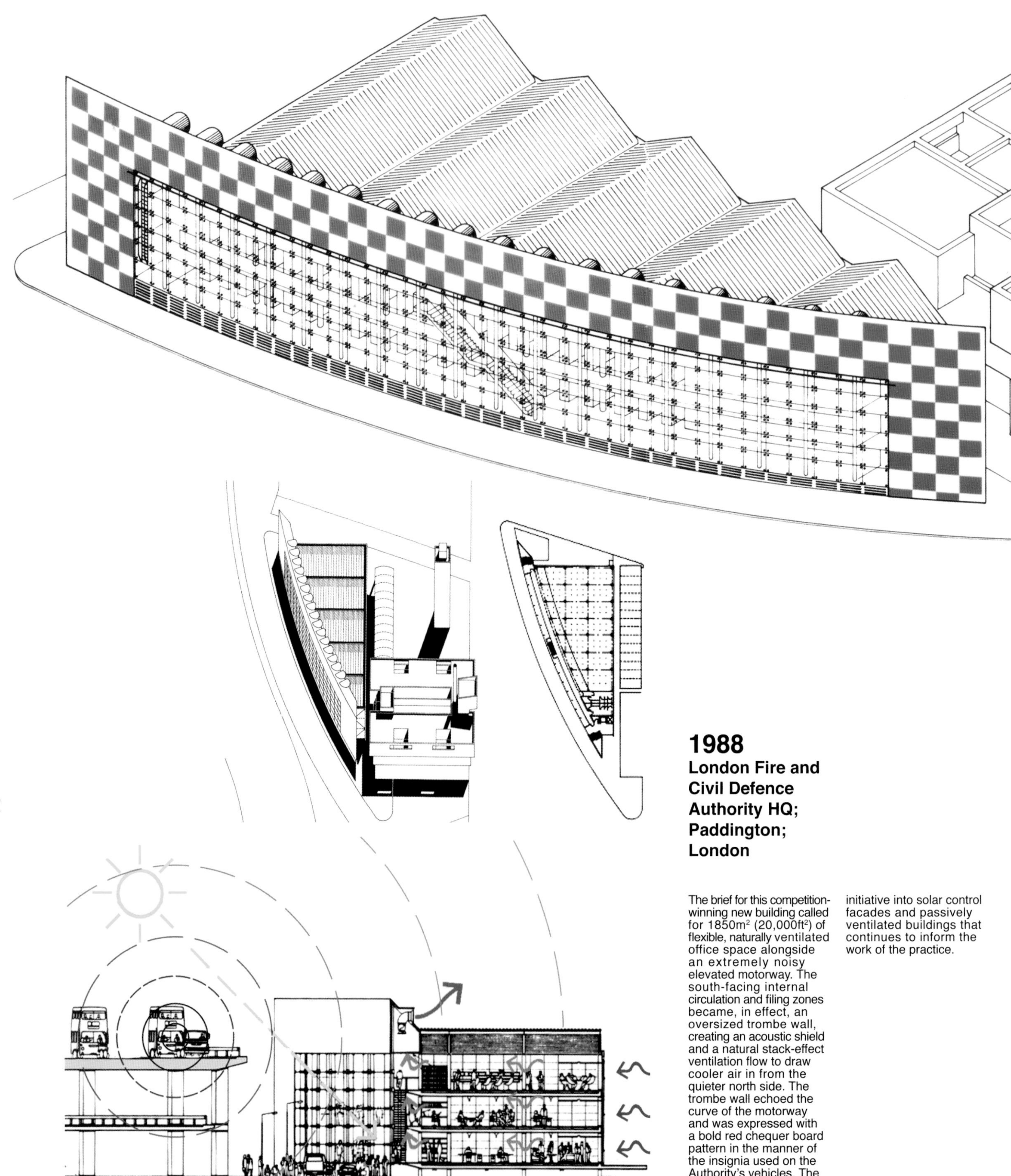

1988
London Fire and Civil Defence Authority HQ; Paddington; London

The brief for this competition-winning new building called for 1850m² (20,000ft²) of flexible, naturally ventilated office space alongside an extremely noisy elevated motorway. The south-facing internal circulation and filing zones became, in effect, an oversized trombe wall, creating an acoustic shield and a natural stack-effect ventilation flow to draw cooler air in from the quieter north side. The trombe wall echoed the curve of the motorway and was expressed with a bold red chequer board pattern in the manner of the insignia used on the Authority's vehicles. The project gave impetus to an on-going research initiative into solar control facades and passively ventilated buildings that continues to inform the work of the practice.

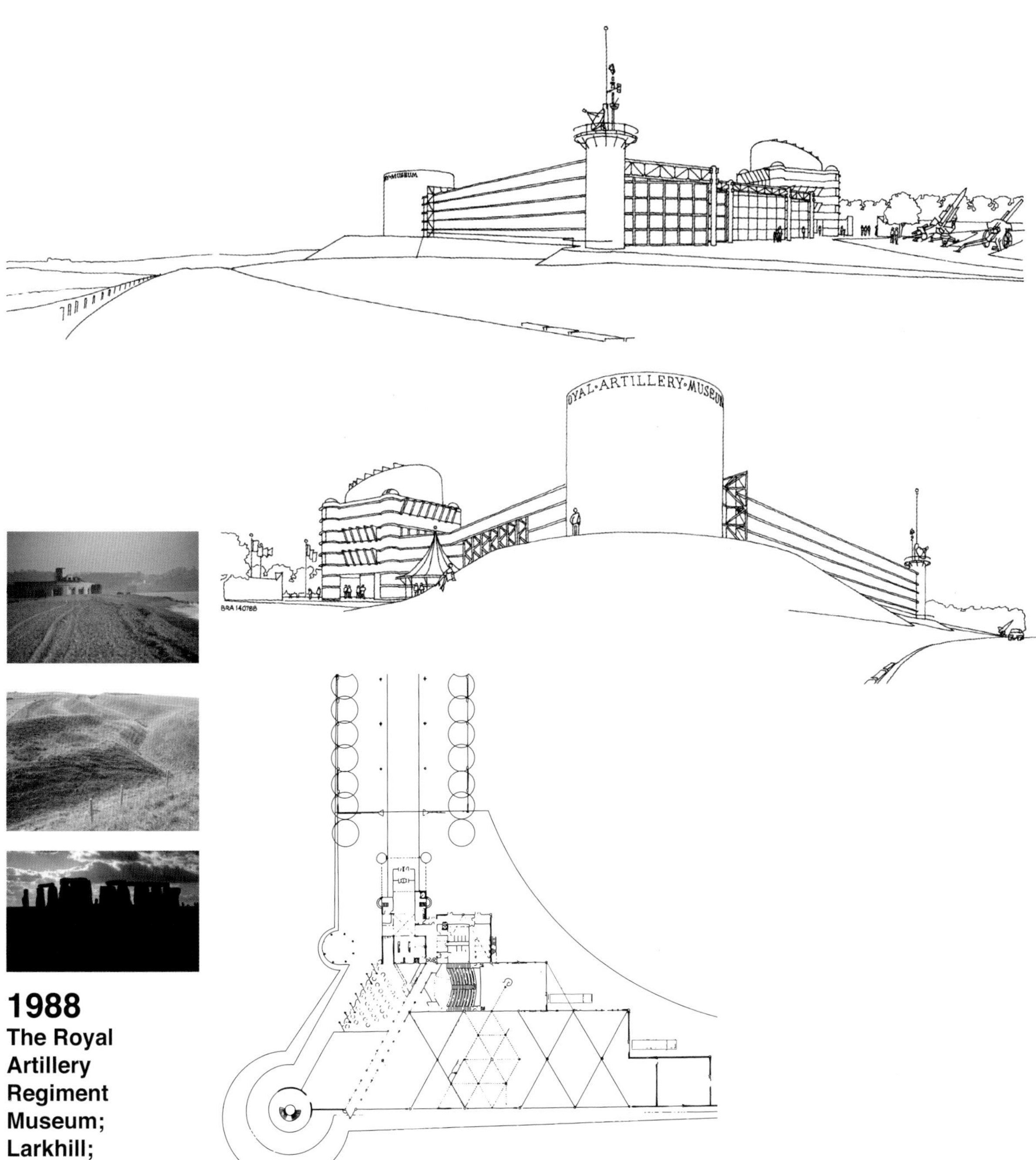

1988
The Royal Artillery Regiment Museum; Larkhill; Berkshire

Consider first the brief. Within a single building, space was to be created for a diverse range of needs—galleries in which to display priceless artefacts, (some small and lovingly crafted, others huge and brutally functional); a workshop (a no-nonsense oily environment echoing to the sound of mechanics at work); a library (a scholarly resource and irreplaceable archive of valuable manuscripts); a treasury (a repository for the regimental honours and silverware); a classroom (where the story of the regiment can be told); and finally, in some quiet corner, a chapel, a fitting memorial to those of the regiment who have given their all.

Consider then the new site and its surroundings: Larkhill, on Salisbury Plain, crisscrossed with tank tracks, its huge 'radome' ever vigilant and watchful still. The Plain itself, a rolling chalk downland of bleak sheep pastures. It may be quiet now but it resonates still with the memories of war.

Here, the Cold War troops of NATO were exercised and, before them, the allied armies that would liberate Europe. Nearby, too, Alfred fought the Vikings to a halt and made these the borderlands of his Saxon kingdom. Even earlier, the hillsides had been banked and bermed to protect the ancients. Durrington Walls, a 3,500 year old remnant of an Avebury-style Neolithic stone circle, abuts the site and just over the ridge, little more than a mile away, stands the bleak, brooding presence of Stonehenge itself.

The result of a competition win, the new design eschewed a single monumental form and sought instead to incorporate and resolve these many meanings within a metal and glass structure which would be both cohesive and elegant in itself and responsive to the particular contiguities and contents that the genius loci revealed.

Images: Above (top) View from the West, showing the electronics tower (centre); the regimental chapel (left) and the workshop, outdoor displays and library (right). Above (middle) View from the eastern approach road showing the chapel (centre); the workshops (right) and the library and treasury (left); The small tented structure is a reference to the existing museum in Woolwich—a giant 'field-tent' designed by John Nash to celebrate the Grand Meeting of Allied Sovereigns at St James's Park in 1814. Above (bottom) Ground floor plan.

Photos left (top) Hurst Castle; New Forest. (middle)Maiden Castle Hill-fort; Dorset. (bottom) Stonehenge.

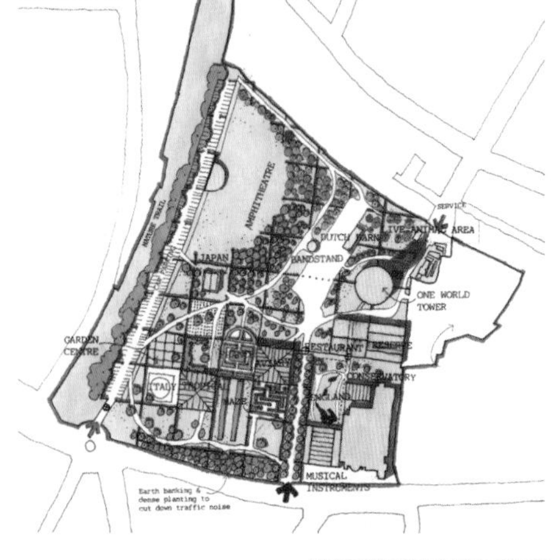

1989
Charterhouse Mews; City of London

For Hewitt Associates' new London base, the space was very limited—a single room, awkwardly shaped and with a ceiling height of just 2.45m. The design owes much to Soane. It uses a visually detached, secondary structure to articulate the main space off which four small 'poches' have been extended. The mirrors, polished lacquered surfaces and concealed lighting create a complex illusion of depth and the resultant space has an intimacy, and grandeur, that belies its size (pp. 66–67).

1989
The Horniman Museum; Forest Hill; London

The plan proposed the re-routing of the main entrance from the road to the garden-side to resolve the museum's access and internal circulation problems and to free up the frontage for a new music building. A new parking area was created alongside the disbanded railway line to the West, bringing people through a sequence of 'walled gardens', thus opening up the full 6.9ha (17 acres) to be a part of the museum's collection. The walled garden galleries would create a labyrinth of 'rooms within rooms', each a microcosm of a national garden typology.

At the end of the labyrinth, on the crown of the hill and with commanding views over the whole of London, a new 80-metre high steel and glass viewing tower was proposed in the manner of the pagoda at Kew. This was intended to raise the museum's profile and to house a new gallery that would raise an awareness of the environmental issues of our times. Above (top) the 'pagoda'; Above (middle, right) the masterplan; Above (middle left) the avenue up to the pagoda: (bottom) the existing museum by CR Townsend.

1990
Channel 4 HQ; Westminster; London

In 1990, Channel 4 was the youngest of the four national television companies and was required by its charter to have a cultured and innovative approach to programme making. This short-listed design sought to challenge the orthodoxy of centre-corridor office planning, with all its inherent problems of poor interdepartmental communications and identity, and to establish instead a new, more dynamic planning arrangement in which the various departments could be openly and flexibly arranged as autonomous but interconnected communities. This was termed a 'social focus' approach (pp. 12–13).

1990–1993
RADA; Fourth Project; Chenies Street

Following the failure of the fundraising to secure the Hoxton Square and King's Cross sites, the Academy decided to purchase a property in Chenies Street, very close to their main building. This very elegant high-ceilinged factory building for Jaeger provided the ideal shell for a phased conversion to workshops, rehearsal rooms, library and student refectory. It was to prove a crucial factor in securing RADA's long-term future as it could provide a permanent base whilst sometime later the main building was under re-construction.

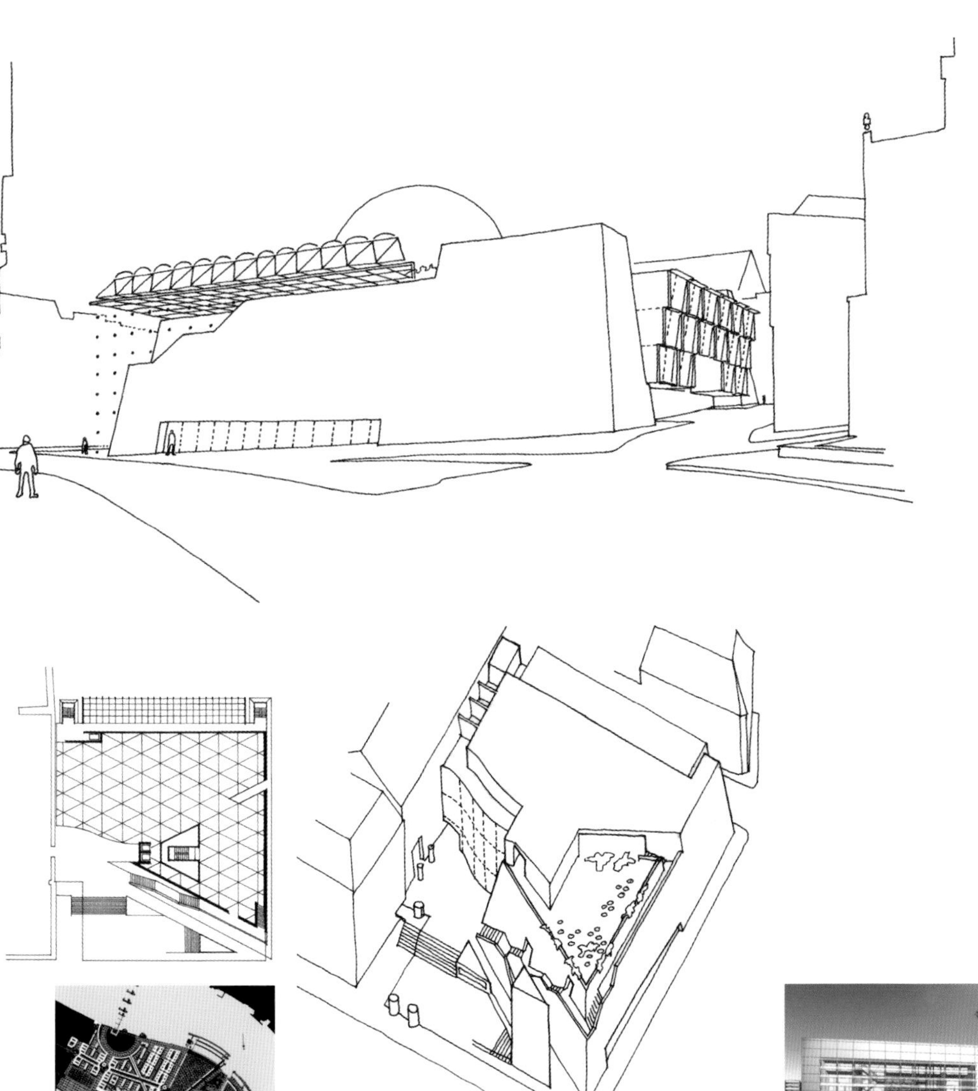

1990–1992
Silvertown; London Docklands

See drawings and text pp. 38–39.

1991
National Museum of Scotland; Edinburgh

The museum's purpose is to tell the story of Scotland —its land, its people and its culture.

The design used the metaphor of a rocky crag to create a stone-work mountainscape into which galleries were tunnelled and over which visitors were invited to scramble.

The galleries used a 60 degree diagrid concrete floor structure, a reference to Louise Kahn's Yale University Art Gallery, and the foyer had a glazed roof and a very deep multi-layered space frame ceiling structure to create a diaphanous cloud-like form within the space.

The entrance lifts were contained in a triangular stone stack, a reference to the Old Man of Hoy.

Above (top) view from George IV Bridge;
Above (bottom) block axonometric;
Above (left) upper gallery floor plan.

1991
Rank Xerox UK HQ; Welwyn Garden City; Hertfordshire

Commissioned as part of a major restructuring programme, the development comprised five buildings totalling 18,580m^2 (200,000ft^2) of office and laboratory space, a further 3,716m^2 (40,000ft^2) for 'special purposes', and parking for 1,000 cars.

The new buildings are aligned to defer to an earlier building on the site by Nicholas Grimshaw, (building far right of main perspective p. 64) thereby embracing it within the new corporate fold. Elements of aesthetic commonality have then been introduced to effect a resonance between the two (p. 18).

1991
Waste-to-Energy Facility; Portsmouth, Hampshire

In replacing an elderly incinerator to generate electricity from the waste, it allowed what was an un-heroic, even embarrassing, monument to the profligacies of our culture to become far more useful. Whereas such structures were usually designed to be no more than vast metal clad sheds with great chimneys attached, the very symbol of an alienating industrialism, here was an opportunity to design a modern, public utility building so useful it could be celebrated.

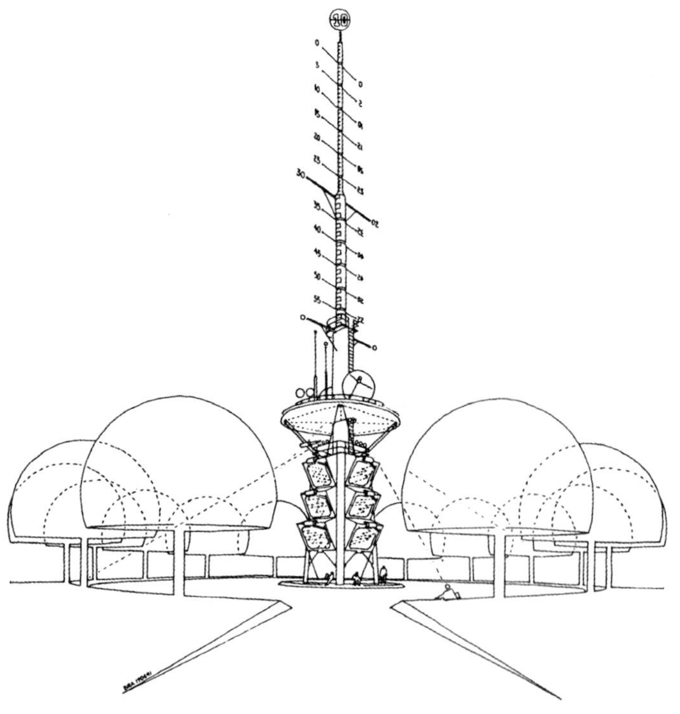

1991
Portsmouth School of Architecture Tower

The Tower was designed to commemorate the accession of the School of Architecture to University status and reflected its aim to become the centre of a global-networking initiative.

A solid base, nine metres high, contained high-definition electrographic displays of student projects and information about the city. The upper part supported communications antennae and an oildraulic-powered telescopic mast that would rise and fall to 60 metres every hour, on the hour, visible throughout the city. (above HMS Warrior—Portsmouth Harbour).

1991–1999
The British Film Institute; London IMAX Cinema

See pp. 8, 56–57, 118–125.

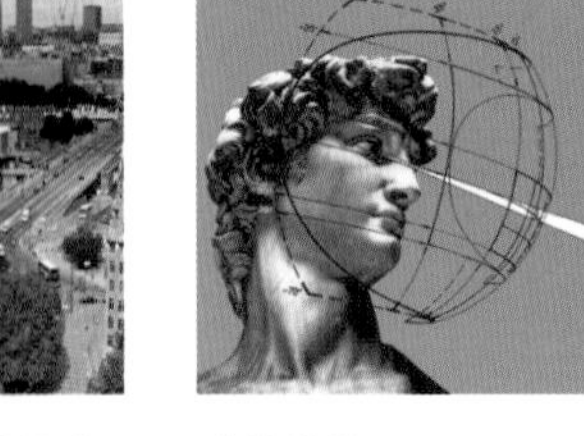

1992
Article; "Beauty is in the Eye of the Beholder"

Chapter 6. pp. 96–101.

1992–1993
National Film Theatre; Bookshop and Foyers

The new bookshop (pp. 112–113) was proportioned in 1:1 & 2:1 ratios and co-ordinated with the shelving and counter designs to create a new space of 'allusive illusion'—just 7'4" (2.25m) high.

The second phase involved restructuring the public areas to create larger foyers, new lavatories and new control and projection facilities for the main auditorium. A new display and information system was also introduced; the signage itself—reinforced here by large computer-generated film images—being a development of the 'line-of-sight' method first used at Plantation House (pp. 68–69, 140).

1993
RADA; Fifth Project; Chenies Street; New Rooftop Rehearsal Room

As part of the refurbishment and restructuring of this property, planning permission was obtained for a new roof top extension to create a much needed column-free studio theatre and rehearsal space. The roof was of advanced stressed skin plywood construction, spanning the full length of the site and it supported frameless sliding glass screens and plant covered trellises for solar shading.

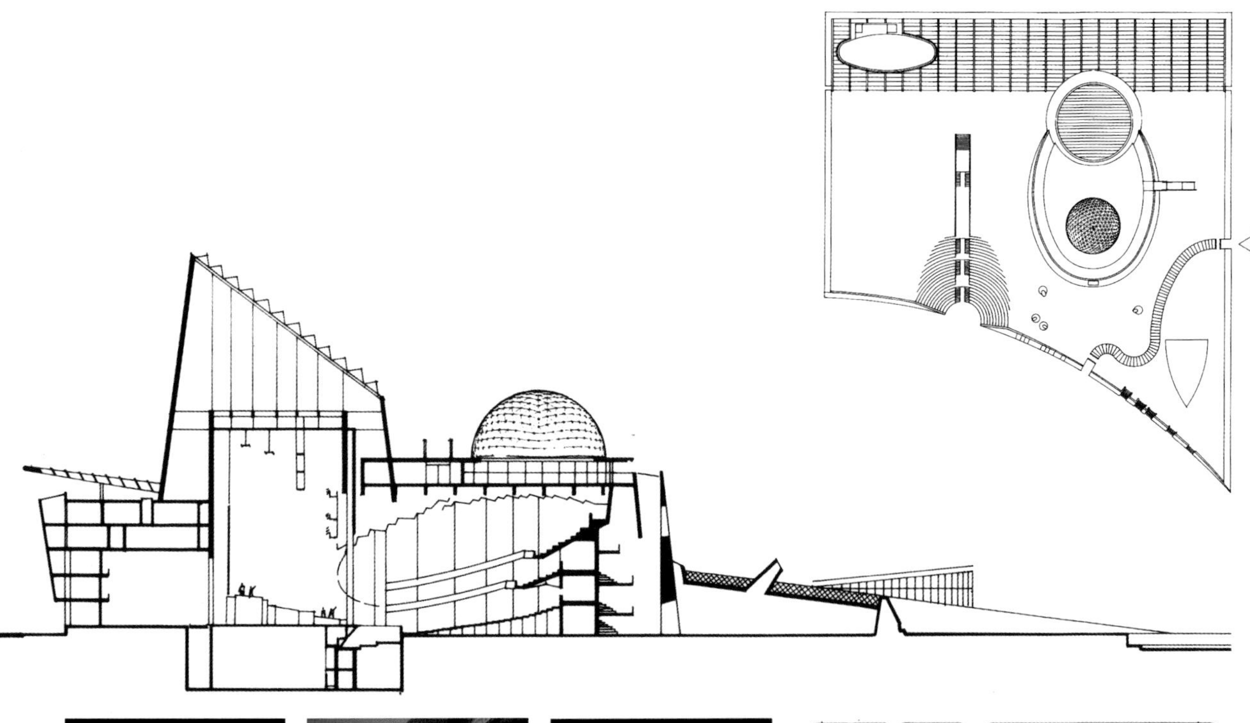

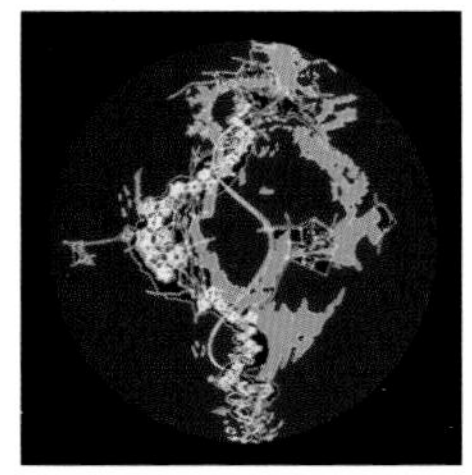

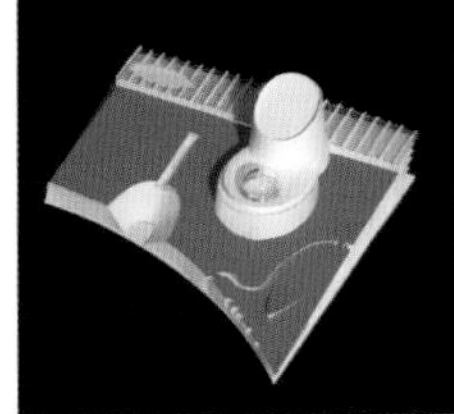

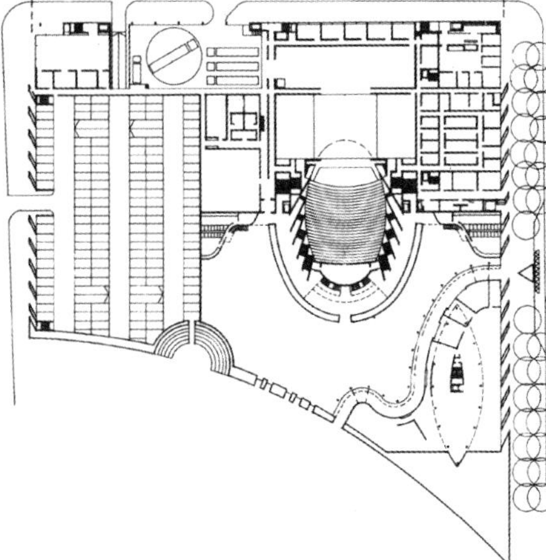

1993
Wilderness City; The Helsinki-Tampere (Finland) Project

Wilderness City is a critical assessment of the symbiotic relationship that exists between the city and the countryside. It proposes to reinforce the values of both by constraining the city to make it more truly urban thereby freeing the countryside to revert to its pre-industrial condition as a rural idyll. In this project the entire population of Finland could be housed in an environmentally sustainable city, thereby leaving the rest of the country to revert back to it's natural wilderness (pp. 4, 20, 56–7, 80, 131).

1994–1996
No. 1 Neathouse Place; Victoria; London

The main challenge was that the floor-to-floor heights were well below the standard required for modern air-conditioned offices. However, by reconfiguring the core and creating small 'on floor' plant rooms in pods hung from the structure at each end of the building, it was not only possible to bring the building up to the high specification standards demanded in today's market but also to win the UK's top award for commercial buildings—the BCO Award. (pp. 14–15, 48, 70–77 89–92, 131).

1994
The Opera House Competition; Cardiff

Conceptually, this was not so much a design for a building, as the definition of a place.

The aim was to subsume the three principal elements—the Opera House, the Welsh National Opera Company, and the car park, all within a cohesive and poetic environment—a place specific to its site.

Environmentally, the building was shielded from the prevailing winds by stonework 'cliffs'. Above the cliffs, the huge landscaped roof garden operated as a thermal store and thick insulating blanket, its slope automatically generating a 'stack effect' natural ventilation system within.

The model for this was a landscaped 'wedge' facing the harbour, a metaphor for the coastal landscape of South Wales, representing in microcosm both its natural and man-made features with sheltered arbours and clefts whose meaning was rooted in its locale (p. 17). Above (left) Model; Above (right) Ground floor plan; Top (left) Section; Top (right) Roof plan.

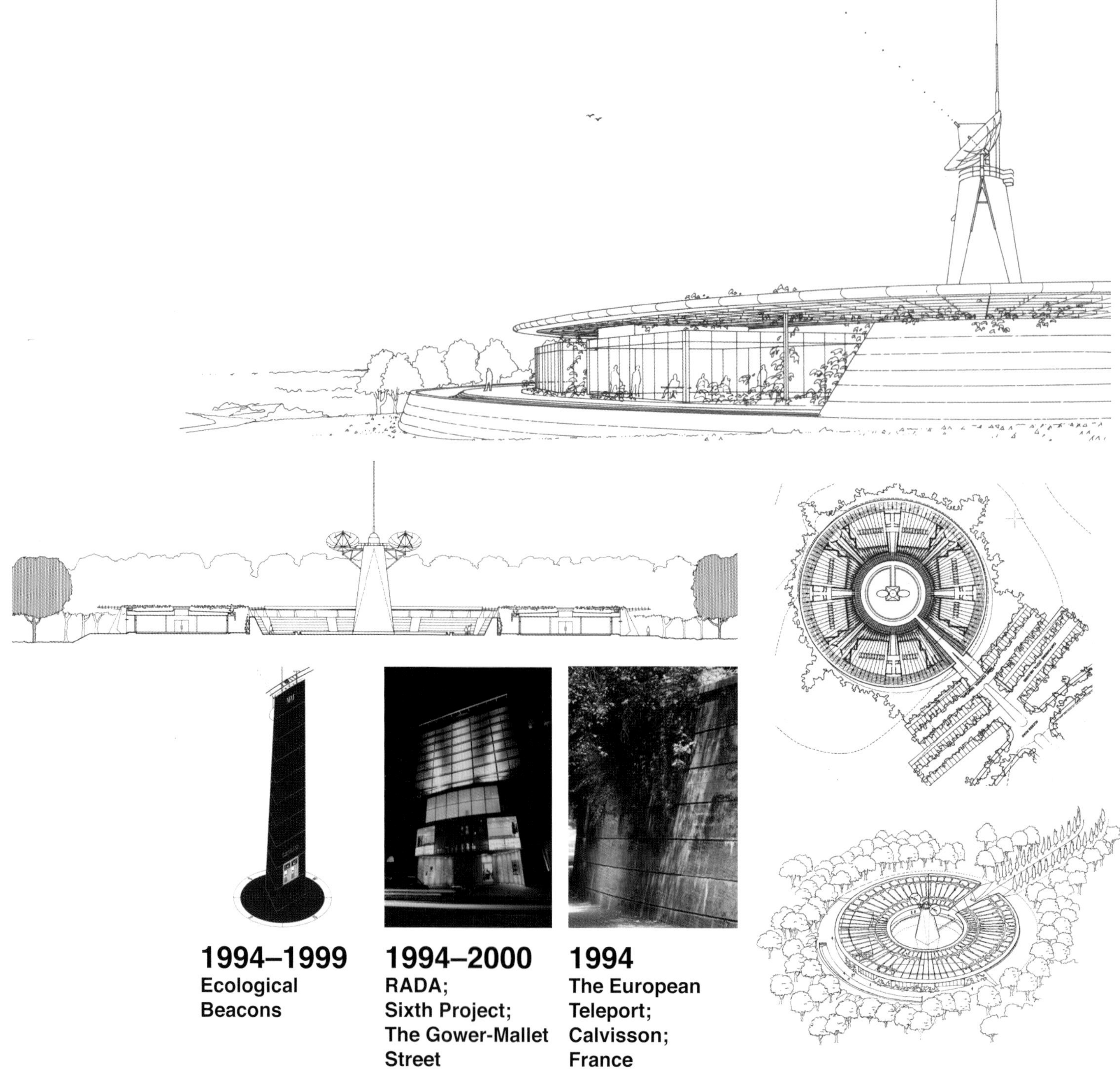

148

1994–1999
Ecological Beacons

The project was a collaborative project with Richard Weston. It proposed a national network of interactive monumental landmarks to promote public awareness of ecological issues. Each beacon has electronic sensors on a rack at the top which measure local environmental conditions and these are displayed on touch-screens at the base. (pp. 17, 61, 86–87).

1994–2000
RADA; Sixth Project; The Gower-Mallet Street Re-development

RADA celebrated its first century in 2004. Bedded almost invisibly into the terraced fabric of Gower Street on the edge of London's West End theatre district, it is probably the world's most famous drama school. Its alumni list reads like a role-call of many of the most famous British actors and actresses of the twentieth and twenty-first centuries. It includes Lord Attenborough, Sir John Gielgud, Dame Judi Dench, Dame Diana Rigg, Sir Anthony Hopkins, Alan Rickman, Juliet Stephenson, John Thaw… to name just a very few. (pp. 10, 104–111).

1994
The European Teleport; Calvisson; France

The Teleport project for La Vaunage-Calvisson, was intended to act both as a symbol and a prototype for Europe's first privately owned, satellite-based business and telecommunications community. Circular in plan, it was to be sited within a 142-hectare, ecologically planned development on a wooded hill-top, close to the city of Nimes.

In the first proposal, the two 7-metre diameter antennae that provide the community's satellite links were mounted on a polished aluminium pylon like a giant megalith. To heighten the effect, the megalith was placed in a circular reflective pool within a surrounding stone collonade in the manner of the Island Pavilion (Teatro Maritimo) at Hadrian's Villa (pp. 9, 92).

The building itself was made up of several independent, single storey office 'cabins', all naturally ventilated and warmed by heat pumps. These were protected from both the cold winter winds and hot summer sun by a radiating vine-covered pergola which spanned between the massive stone walls surrounding the pool and earth berm that encircled the development. Originally planned to provide 600 square metres of office space and parking for 60 cars, the design was expanded to provide 2700 square metres of offices with detached parking for 162 cars.

Above (left) Striated concrete wall in Coulsden. Surrey; above (right) the first proposal; above (middle, left, right and top) the second proposal (p. 61).

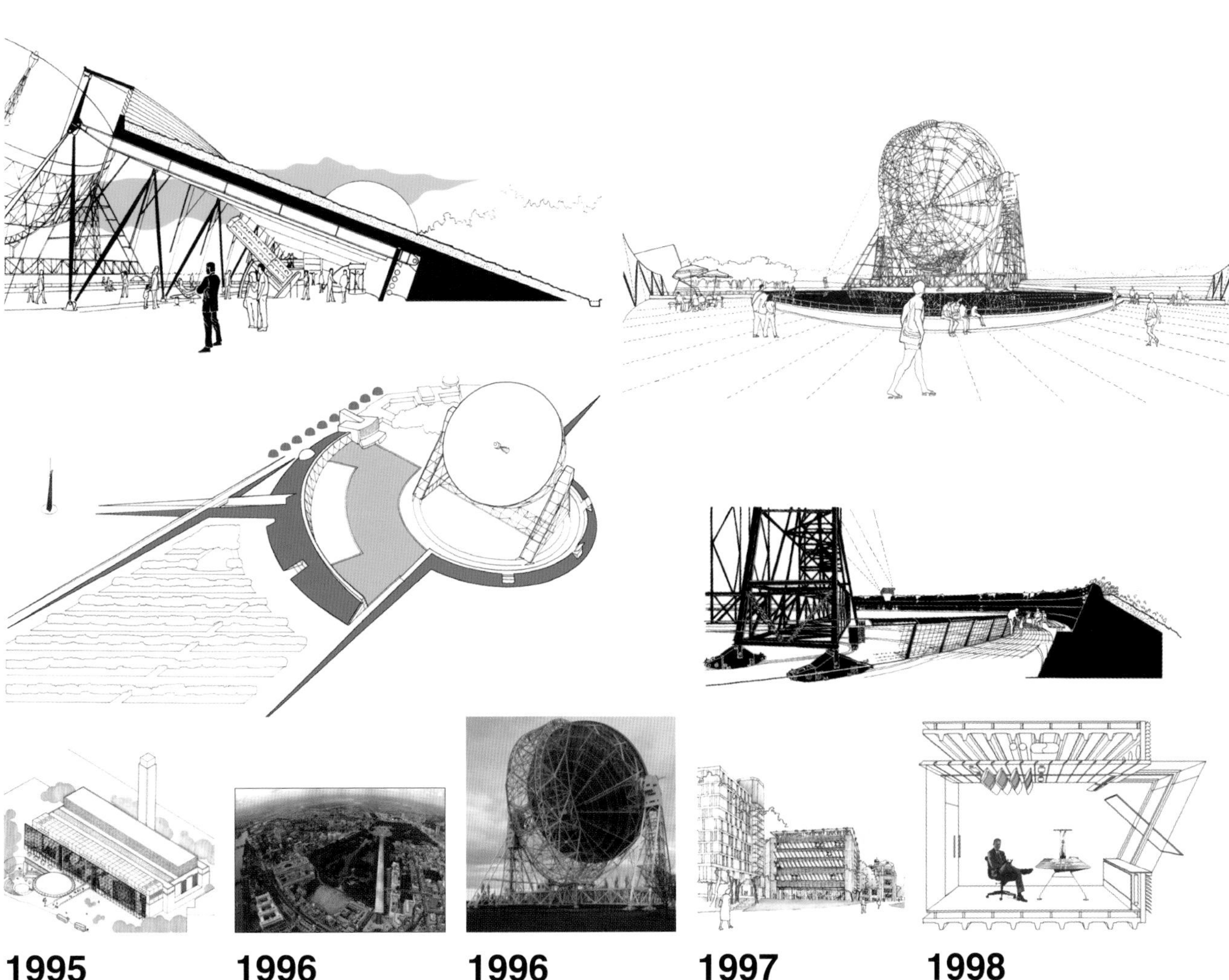

1995
The British Film Institute; Tate Modern; London

Shortly before construction commenced on the BFI London IMAX a number of feasibility studies were undertaken to relocate the entire BFI complex to Tate Modern, using the (then) unused rear structure and underground oil tanks as the basis for a new National Film centre combining the NFT, MOMI, IMAX and the BFI (p. 117).

1996
The Mall; London

At the heart of the scheme lay a proposal to pedestrianise the Mall to link St James's with Green Park and to cover the Mall with a translucent glass canopy. Ceremonial and other events could thus be staged, and viewed, in all weathers from gently sloping terraces lined with kiosks and public facilities which would transform the civic life of London and provide a new social focus for the nation. (pp. 52–53, 61).

1996
Visitor Centre Jodrell Bank; Cheshire

The visitor centre was designed as a gently curving, grass-banked structure that melded invisibly into the university's arboretum. A pool serves as a foreground for photos and as an unobtrusive barrier to keep the active research areas secure. To keep the visitors safe when the telescope moves, a raised walkway in the form of an ampitheatre, with seats and lighting, encircles the dish. It is here, under the stars with sound and light, that the giant structure and its story would come alive.

1997
James Went Building; De Montfort University Leicester

The aim was to replace one half of an existing laboratories block with a more efficient deeper plan building that would also repair and re-vitalise the civic space beside the old art college building.

The new building thus defers in scale to the art college but its south facade uses the sun's heat within a double walled glazed cavity to drive a stack-effect ventilation system to draw cool, fresh air in from the north facade—much in the manner of the earlier LFCDA project (p. 142).

1998
CORUS Low Energy Office Project

Developed from the LFCDA project (p. 142), this composite steel and concrete system for the UK steel company CORUS provides thermal mass and allows the diurnal heating and cooling cycle to operate through the perimeter office and into the deep-plan spaces beyond.

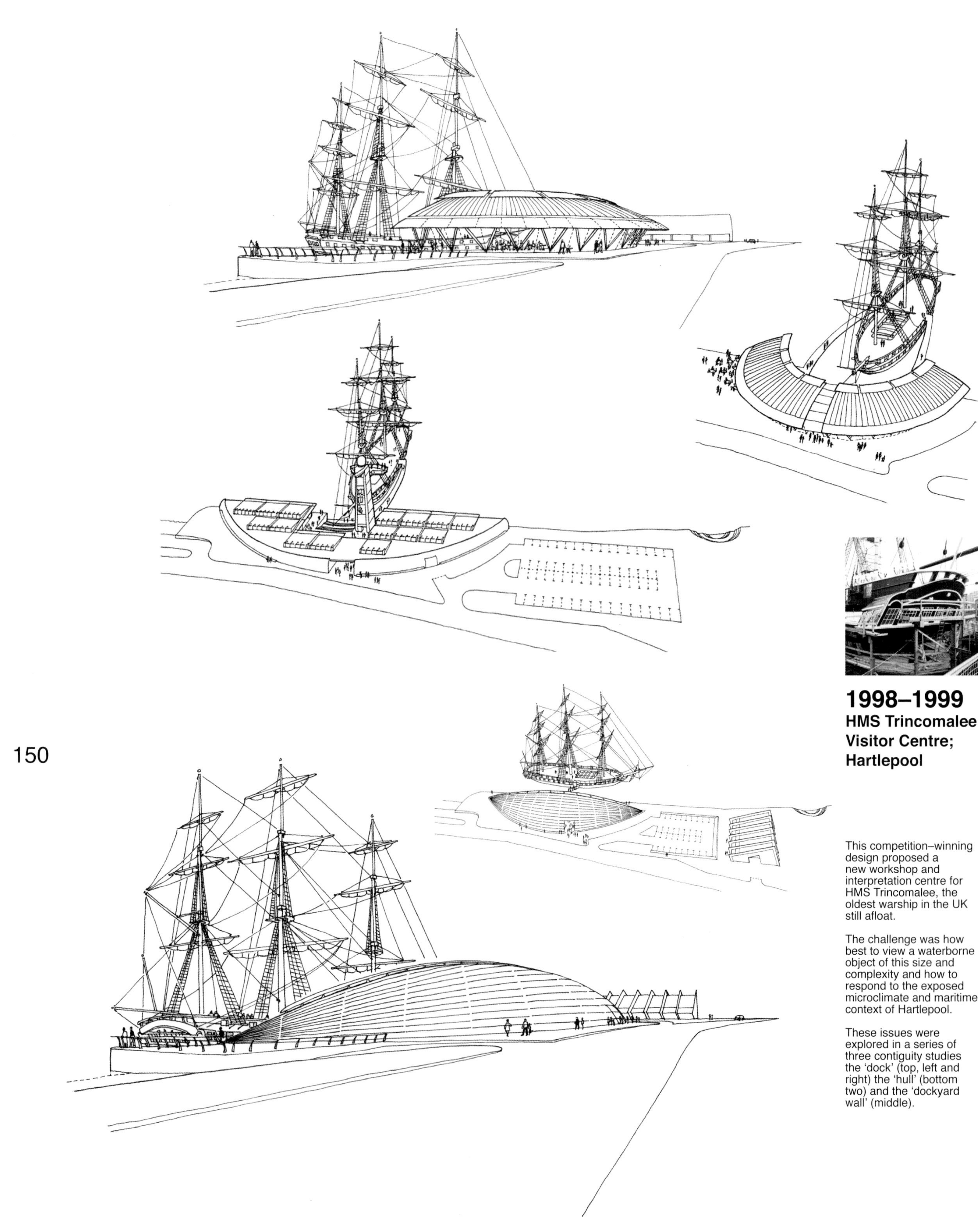

1998–1999

HMS Trincomalee Visitor Centre; Hartlepool

This competition–winning design proposed a new workshop and interpretation centre for HMS Trincomalee, the oldest warship in the UK still afloat.

The challenge was how best to view a waterborne object of this size and complexity and how to respond to the exposed microclimate and maritime context of Hartlepool.

These issues were explored in a series of three contiguity studies the 'dock' (top, left and right) the 'hull' (bottom two) and the 'dockyard wall' (middle).

1999
The Sketches Museum; Lund; Sweden

The Sketches Museum is devoted to the study of the conceptual stages of artists' works—the process whereby initial thoughts are explored and crystallised into the finished art-work.

The white glass facade of the entrance was seen as a page from a sketchbook, a 'golden rectangle' upon which ethereal images could be projected to appear and disappear—like an artist's thoughts on a work in progress.

1999
St Martin's Court; London

The narrow alleyways behind the Albery and Wyndham's theatres in London's West End were the site for this interactive guide to London's theatre culture. The plan was to have a real-time link to each theatre to show what was being played there and the facility then to research upcoming productions and ultimately to book seats.

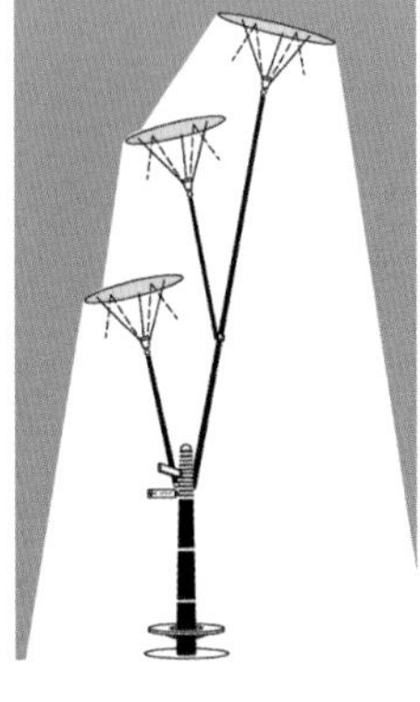

1999
Pavement Post

The multi-functional 'pavement post' (1999) was inspired by plants like Cow Parsley and comprises a cast metal base to which direction signs, notices, seats, etc, could be attached. The aim was to have one post to provide the support for all the attachments that currently litter the streets. The lighting was by fibre optics through the stems from a light source accessible within the body of the post (pp. 84–85).

1999
Meridian Mount; London

A spiral promenade in the manner of Le Notre was the centrepiece of this waterside park. It rose to 130m (426ft) and enveloped a vast end-of-the millenium exhibition space (p. 8).

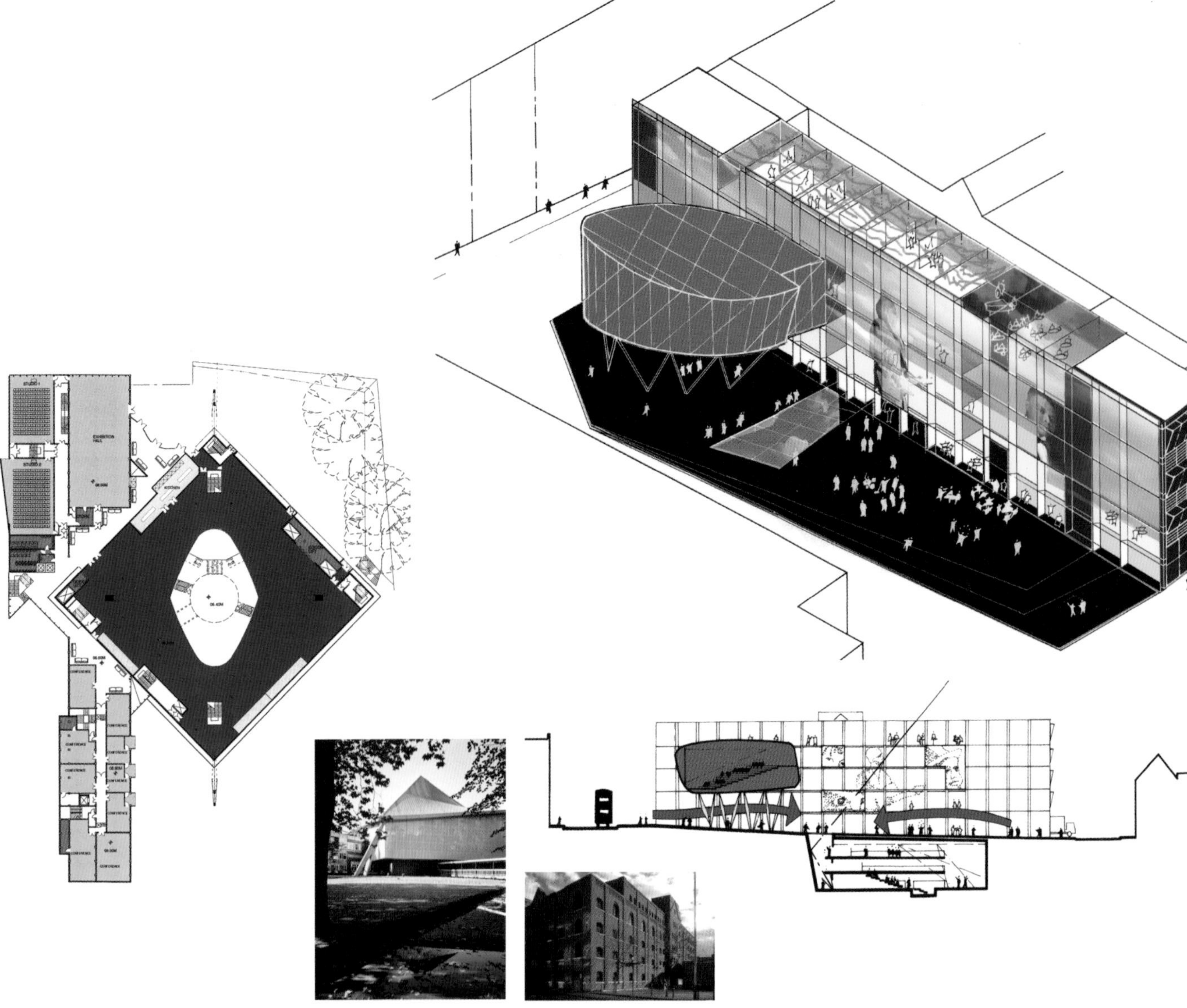

1999–2003
The Commonwealth Institute; Kensington, London; First Project

The aim of the first project—a competition winning proposal—was to greatly increase the capacity of the building for conference, exhibition and performance use. The key to this was separating the conference visitors from those attending the exhibitions or performances and this was achieved by creating a new access route at the front and a new service area at the rear with a terrace overlooking Holland Park (above, above left, and p. 127).

1999
Phoenix Theatre; Leicester

The large flexible theatre space was put below ground and the foyer, café, small cinema, gallery space, offices and the 'get in' were all planned into a long single aspect block that cloaked a multi- storey car park. This not only released a considerable part of the site at ground level for new civic purposes, but allowed the audience to enter the building very conveniently from every level of the car park (above, existing car park, above middle; cross-section and above top, isometric view).

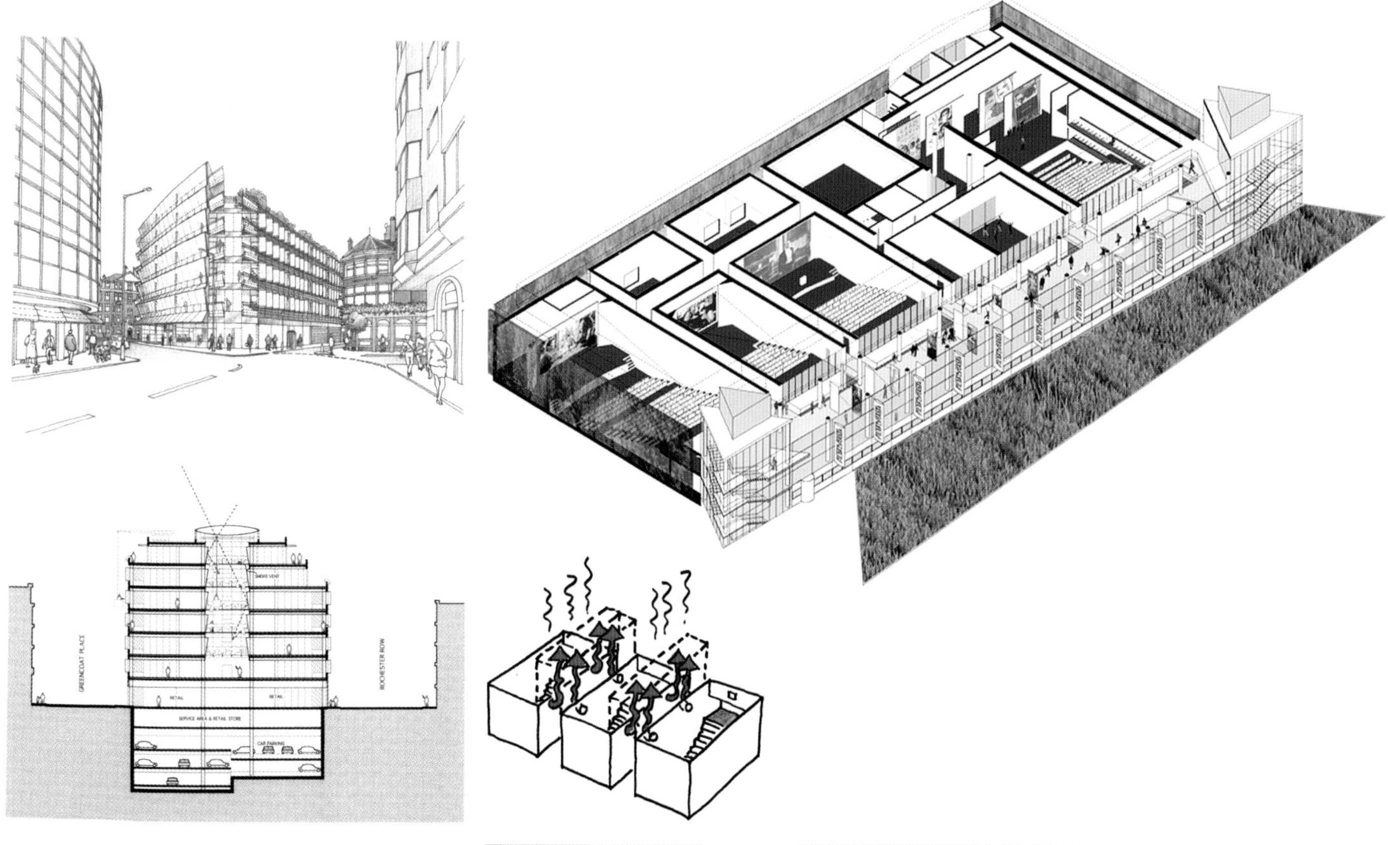

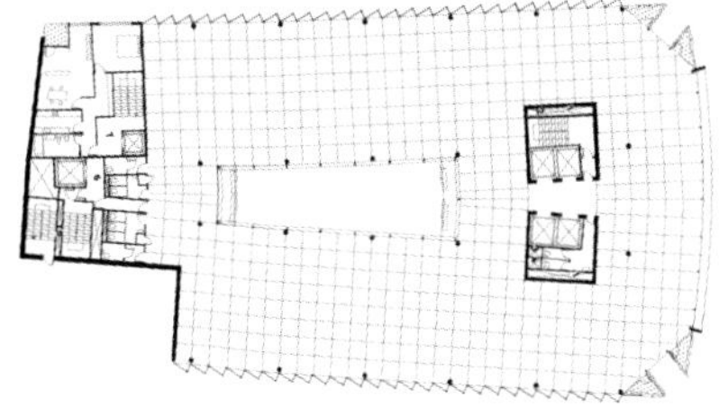

1999
Office Development; Rochester Row; London

Located not far from the Neathouse Place project (pp. 14–15, 70–77, 89–92, 147) the design released valuable development potential by relocating an existing multi-storey car park below ground. It used similar formal elements to Neathouse Place too but responded more overtly to the different contextual circumstances of the three facades.

1999
The National Centre for Film and Drama; University College; Dublin

University College is justly renowned for having produced many of Ireland's most distinguished novelists, poets, performers, dramatists, screenwriters, filmmakers, directors and producers:

The essence of the design was that all the spaces, be they cinemas, multipurpose performance spaces, lecture theatres, rehearsal rooms or the foyer—should be treated as workshops providing an opportunity for anything to happen; spaces which could be configured and re-configured as needed, and all visible and accessible from a new public exhibition space—the new heart of the campus.

This gave rise to an unusually efficient and compact plan and because the lightweight construction required that an acoustically attenuating void be provided between the various performance spaces, it also allowed a very simple passive ventilation system to be used.

To express this externally, the vegetation covered wall found on the campus (above) suggested that the new building could also have a similar 'green' aspect—a green wall—similar in principle to the one created a the Bfi London IMAX (1991–1999) (pp. 8, 56–57, 118–125) and proposed on several projects subsequently (Goldsmiths College p. 157; Full Picture Company Film Studios p. 161; Wood Green Library p. 161; Newcasle College p. 162; HQ for IDS p. 175; Pimlico School p. 175).

LEICESTER
SQUARE
WC2
HOUSES

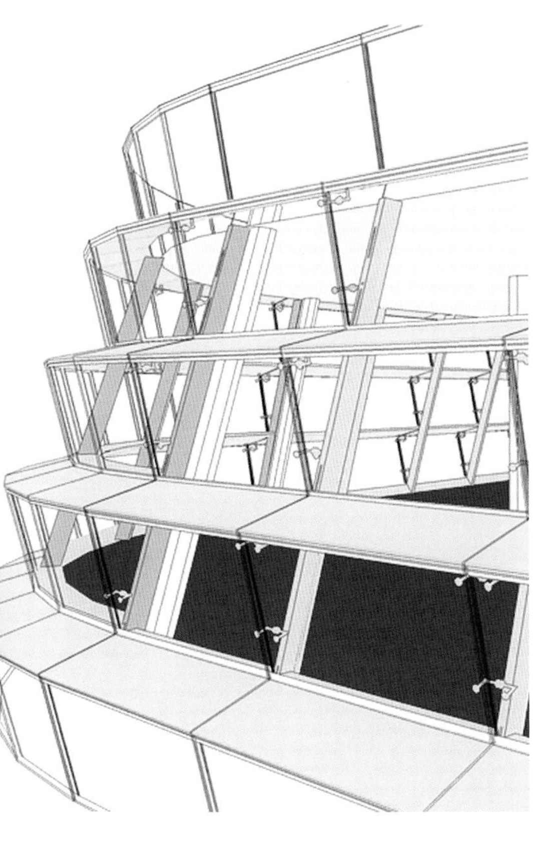

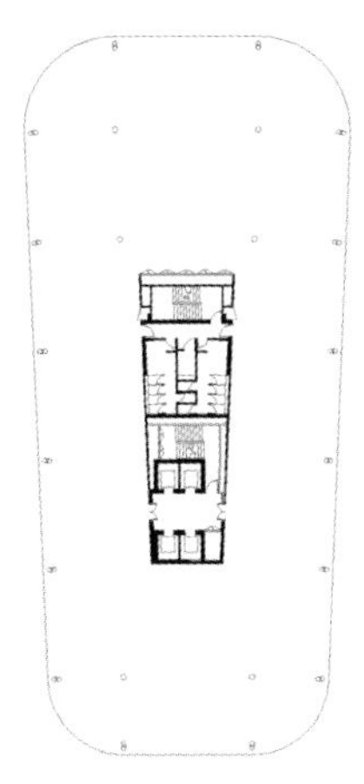

2000–2004

The Swiss Centre; Leicester Square; London

This design for a mixed-use development on the Swiss Centre site was designed to bring the glitz and glamour of 'going up west' back to the architecture of Leicester Square. Commissioned by the British Land Co. plc it consisted of 13,935m^2 (150,000ft^2) retail, office, restaurant and cinema uses. The tapered profile of the building was developed to maximise the gross floor area whilst maintaining the rights of light and daylight/sunlight requirements of adjacent properties.

The innovative energy saving facade is developed from a long lineage of earlier projects—Rochester Row (1999) p. 153; The CORUS project (1998) p. 149; the James Went Building (1997) p. 149; No. 1 Neathouse Place (1994) p. 147; Rank Xerox (1991) p. 145; Channel 4 (1990) p. 144; Royal Artillery Museum (1988) p. 143; the ATH Projects (1984–1985) p. 140; NFT Riverside (1982–1983) p. 139; Royal Military College (1981) p. 137; Dubai Airport (1975–1976) p. 135; Heathrow offices (1972–1975) p. 62 and ultimately right back to the Sailing Club project of (1964–1965) p. 7.

It consists here of prefabricated raked glazing modules, with almost a 50/50 solid/glazed ratio.

Research of the earlier projects had shown that raking the glass to increase its coefficient of heat absorption, and its angle relative to the sun to increase its reflectivity, can reduce the heat gain very significantly.

This, together with the photovoltaic arrays on the top surface, which generate electrical energy, and the reflectivity of the under-surface, which directs day-light deep into the interior to save on artificial lighting, resulted in a truly integrated environmental facade design.

It also created a facade that responded to the occupants' desire to see down to the activities on the street and when viewed from the street the building's glazing would not just reflect the sky, but the activities on the street too, resulting in an active, ever-changing kaleidoscope of movement and colour.

REFLECTED SUNLIGHT RESULTING IN INCREASED AMBIENT LIGHT LEVELS INTERNALLY

SOLAR SHADING PROVIDED BY ALUMINIUM PANELS

VERY GOOD LEVELS OF NATURAL DAYLIGHT WITH REDUCED SOLAR HEAT GAIN

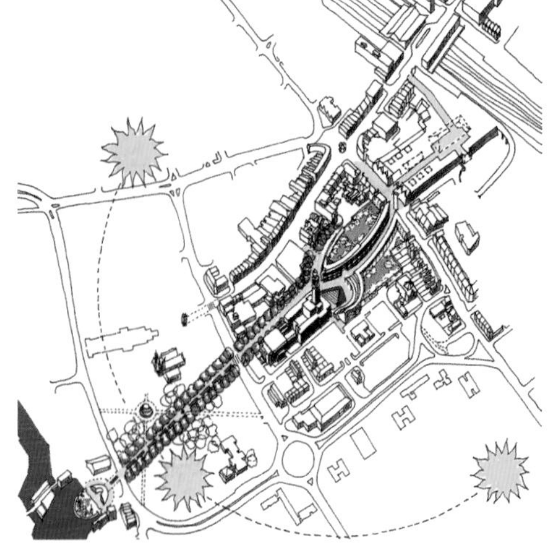

2000–2002
The Curzon Cinema; Pimlico; London

The 'Tachbrook Triangle' is a significant site in the heart of Pimlico. It had been compulsorily purchased by Westminster City Council for a road-widening scheme that never happened. The local residents' associations came together and agreed that a mixed development with flats, shops, restaurants, a medical centre and an art-house cinema run by the Curzon Group, should be sited there. Designs were duly prepared but were refused Planning Permission on the grounds that the cinema would attract undesirable elements (people) to Pimlico.

2000–2003
Barking Town Masterplan

Won in competition together with Urban Catalyst (developers), Gustafson Porter (landscape) and Shelagh Wakely (artist) the proposal aimed to regenerate the town centre by creating a new mixed-use development and performance-based square in front of the town hall and a new 'ceremonial avenue' out to Barking Creek.

Above, one of the may development options, this one comprising 16,370m^2 (176.000ft^2) of shops, office and residential uses.

2001
Barking Town Library

A key component in this competition winning design for the regeneration of Barking Town Square, was the provision of a new Central Library. Its entrance was via a bookshop and café and once inside, escalators would take people up through an unusual key-hole shaped atrium to a public exhibition space and roof terrace with magnificent views back down Clockhouse Avenue to the Creek.

Above, bottom left and right: the Town Hall and one of Shelagh Wakely's community arts events;

Above, top: section through the library showing the lightweight PTFE pneumatic roof and the 'panoptican' effect of the multi-level key-hole plan.

Opposite page, top: plan of the library and the central area; Middle: first floor plan; Bottom: top floor plan.

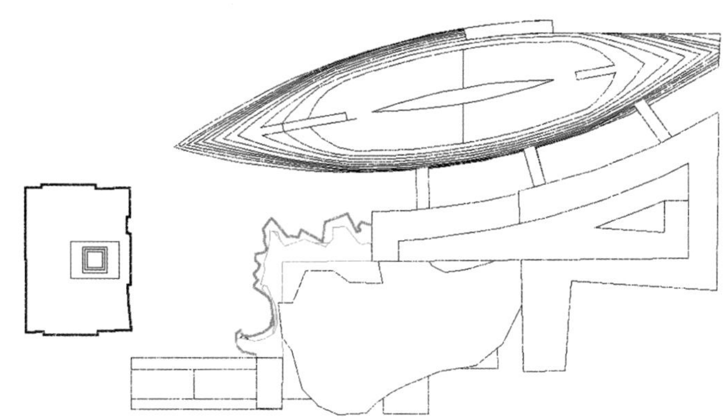

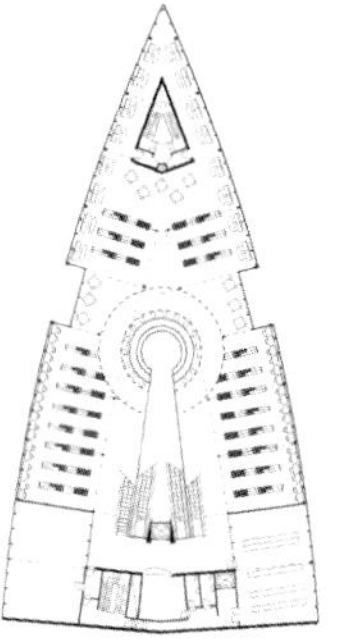

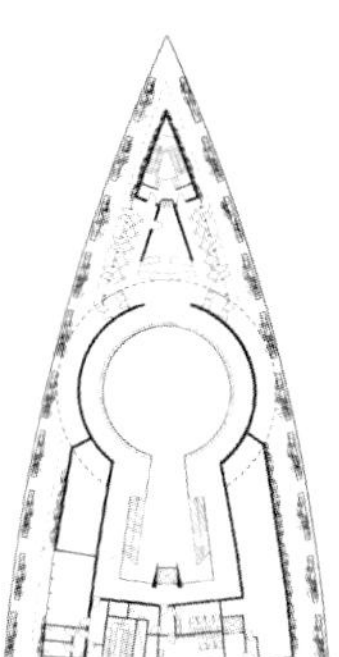

2001–2007
London Transport Museum; Covent Garden

Won in competition in 2001, the museum occupied an 1872 iron and glass Grade II listed flower market building in Covent Garden. Into this a substantial new gallery has been inserted at high level and a new lecture theatre has been excavated out from under what had once been the off-loading canopy. This has enabled a new entrance to be built with a bookshop and café on the Covent Garden piazza. The building is largely passively ventilated and has one of London's largest arrays of photovoltaics to generate power (pp. 127–130).

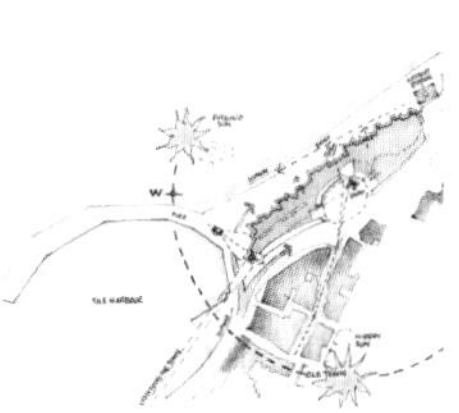

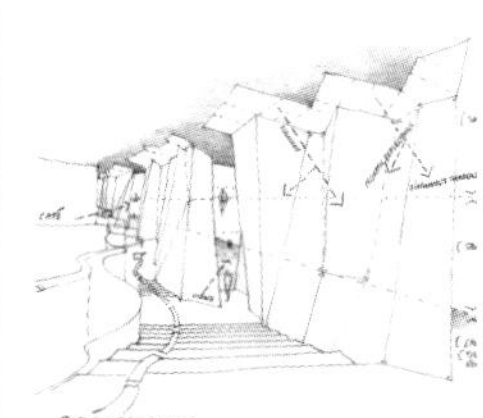

2001
Turner Gallery; Margate; Kent

This design for a landmark gallery to house works by JMW Turner took its inspiration from the form of the white chalk cliffs that had stood on the site in Turner's time. By day, it would form a dramatic glazed promenade like a cliff-walk with an ever-changing play of light reflected from the sea below, and by night, it would become a shimmering translucent skin, a beacon across the bay.

Above, top, sketch plan: bottom, the internal cliff path linking the galleries (p. 12).

2001-2004
Commonwealth Institute; Second Project

After having set up an architectural competition in 1999 (p. 152) to increase the building's capacity for conference, exhibition and performance use, the Institute then secured its independence from the Government, and this plan was abandoned. Instead, a restoration programme was undertaken involving the complete replacement of the roof and cladding, preparatory to putting the building up for sale (p. 127).

2001
Goldsmith's Art College; New Cross, London

The building was conceived as a 'warehouse of creativity', a series of robust, top-lit studios all in ratios of the golden rectangle in plan and section, and stacked up into a kind of 'rocky mount', covered in natural vegetation.

This man/nature dialogue in which the mathematically proportioned studios were counter-pointed by the robust growth of the natural vegetation is a feature of many projects—but here it suffused the whole three-dimensional form.

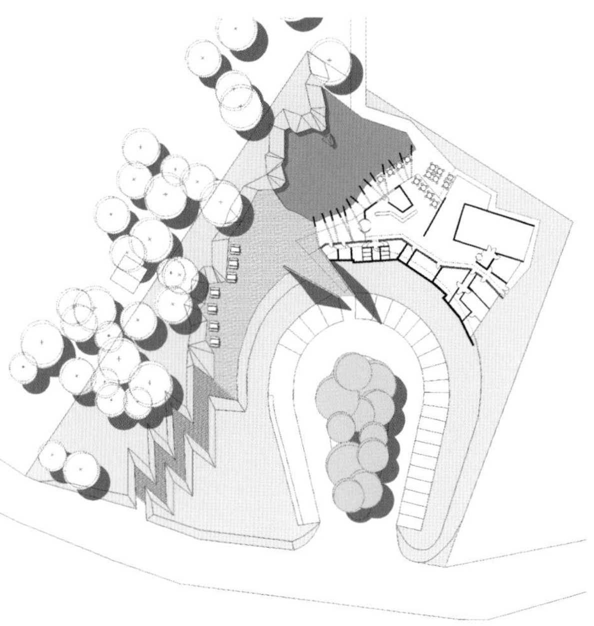

2001
Thiepval Memorial Visitor Centre; The Somme; France

The Thiepval Memorial, designed by Lutyens, commemorates the 74,000 British and Commonwealth soldiers who died during the First World War at the battle of the Somme—but whose bodies were never found.

The design of the visitor centre was intended as an allegory of the conflict, its forms deriving from a narrative of the experience of the young soldiers who had to cross the channel and face the trenches.

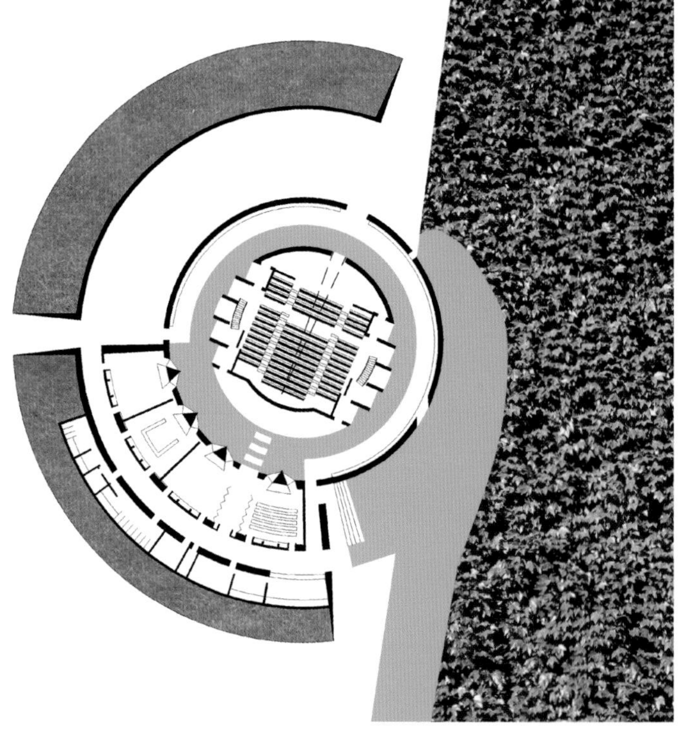

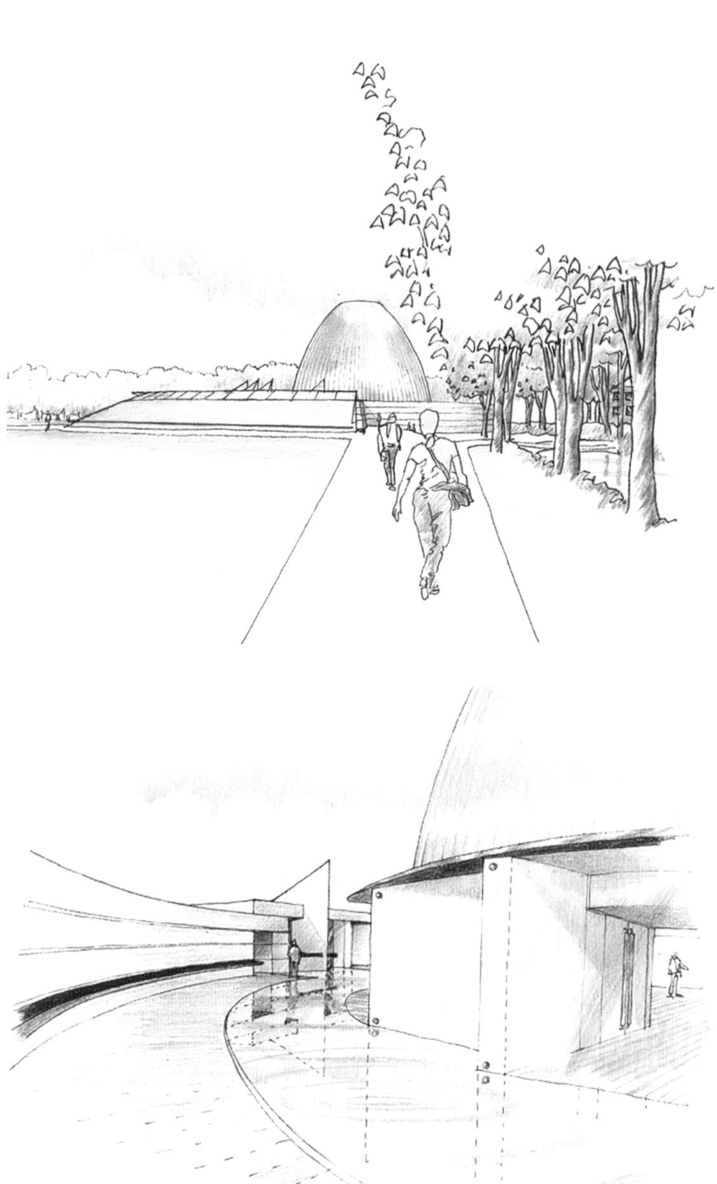

2001–2002
Oakham School; The Jerwood Innovation Centre

Won in competition, the Oakham School Jerwood Innovation Centre was an expression of a new educational model, a partnership between the school and the workplace pioneered by the headmaster. The Innovation Centre was a multi-purpose performance laboratory/ teaching and events space with break-out classrooms and lecture/ seminar rooms.

The site was a very sensitive one between an old canal and the school's playing fields (above). A protective earth berm circles the Centre and a continuous stone seat at its base provides a vantage point from which to watch the sporting activities. Within the berm, the canal has been extended to envelope the main space in another re-interpretation of the Island Pavilion at Hadrians' Villa, this time using a stone walled ambulatory to create a sense of mystery and contemplative calm (p. 9).

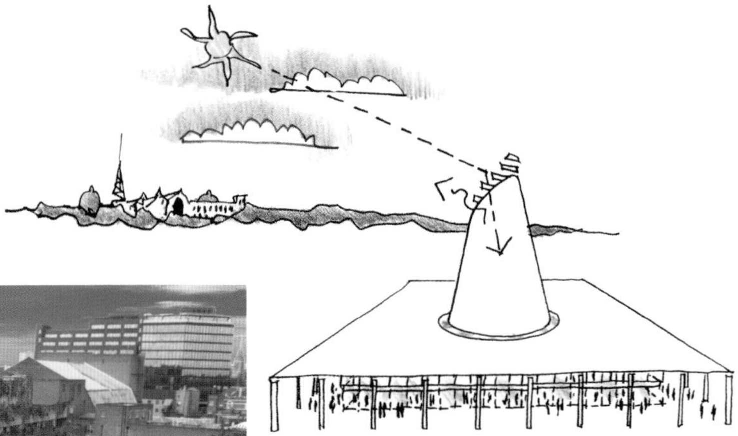

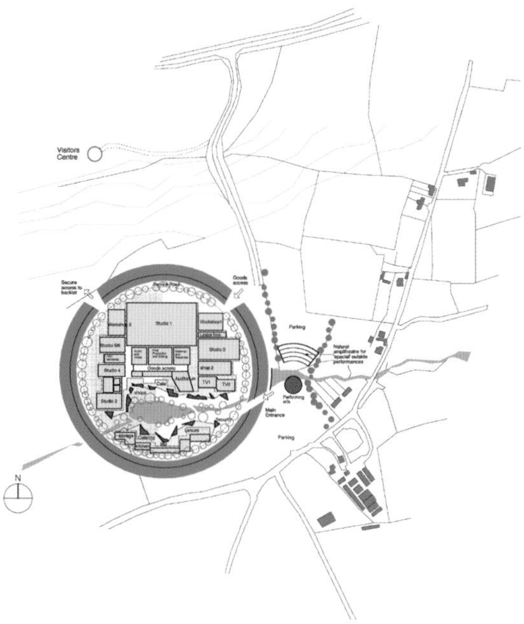

2002
Full Picture Company Film Studios; Nr Exeter; Devon

The challenge was to find an economical but elegant way of inserting a series of very large and very pragmatic studio spaces, workshops, auditoria and production suites, into a sensitive rural setting. Following the thoughts developed for the Oakham Project (preceding page), the solution proposed was a loose-fitting circular tree-lined grassed berm in the manner of an ancient downland hill-fort inside which a studio 'settlement' could be formed complete with a lake formed by damming a small stream. The public performance spaces have been placed outside the walls like the early Elizabethan theatres, to keep the studios secure.

2002–2003
Wood Green Library; London

As a result of a feasibility study won in competition together with AEA Consulting, a number of studies were undertaken to test the viability of either retaining the existing library or relocating it.

In the first study (above, centre left) the existing building was retained and extended at the front with three bold new Corten steel 'stacks' housing a public café and shop. The bleak concrete library block behind was then overclad with vegetation to soften its character and help endear it more to its users.

In the second study (top right) the library was relocated to a new redevelopment site and a distinctive form was developed for it derived from notions of the panoptican and the stack-effect ventilation potential of Le Corbusier's Assembly building in Chandigarh, India.

2002
Bascule Bridge; Poole; Dorset

The concept of the bridge was to provide a sheltered walkway with viewing places in order to encourage people to want to cross the harbour.

The two central spans were to be openable to allow tall masted yachts to pass through and the mechanism for this took the form of a central bascule with weights within the high sail-like form which would drop to move the two roadways upward.

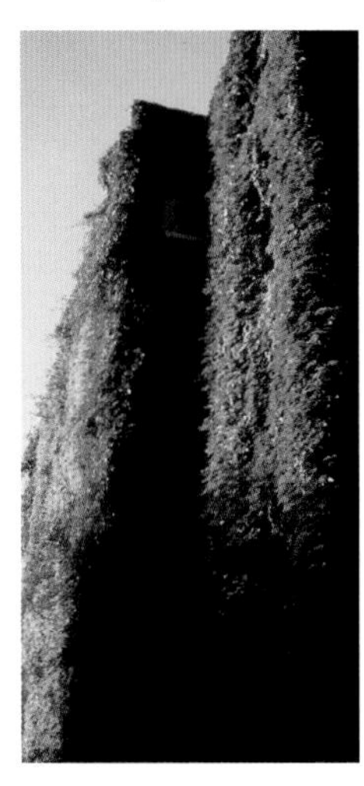

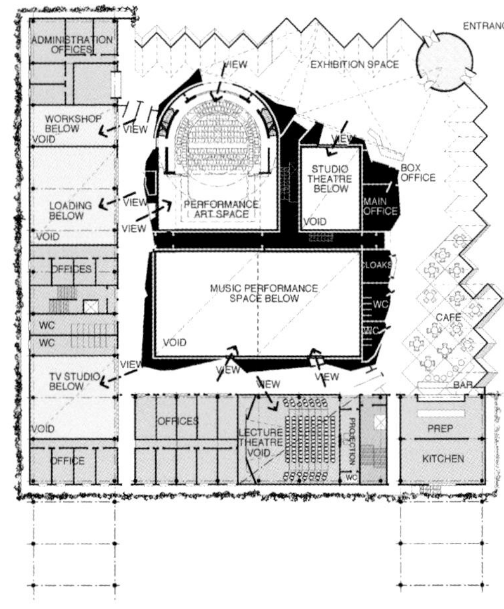

2002
Newcastle College; Performing Arts Centre

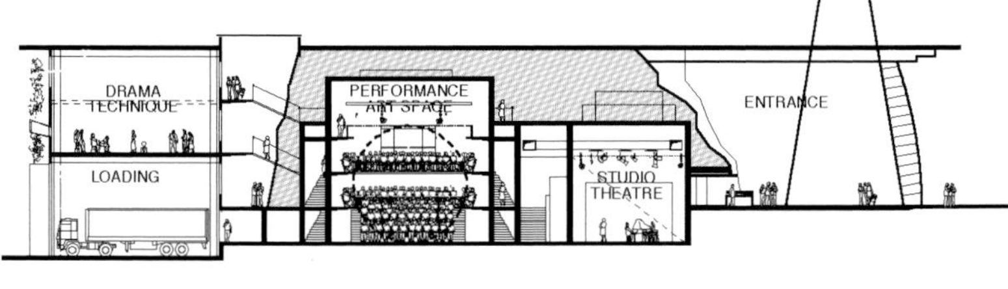

The Centre was intended to help nurture the creative talents of both the young and those who, for whatever reason, might otherwise have missed the normal opportunities for further education in the arts.

The building was conceived and organised to express a series of counterpoints: public/private; rational/intuitive; physical/cerebral etc, which were then subsumed within a single envelope which itself expressed further dualities of solid/void: back/front; organic/inorganic etc.

Top: The South and West facades were covered entirely in vegetation through which large colourful splayed window reveals were punched like the Alpine buildings that so inspired Le Corbusier (pp. 6–7; The Shanghai Expo project p. 21 and the IDS project p. 175).

Above middle left: A green wall in Wandsworth; London: Above middle; the public foyer with a shiny, coal-black wall to the performance space at left; Above right: ground floor plan. The auditorium geometry is a development of that used at RADA (p. 110).

Above: Cross-section. Note the change of level that allows back-stage servicing below the public levels and for large scenery, the ceiling/ floor here lifts up.

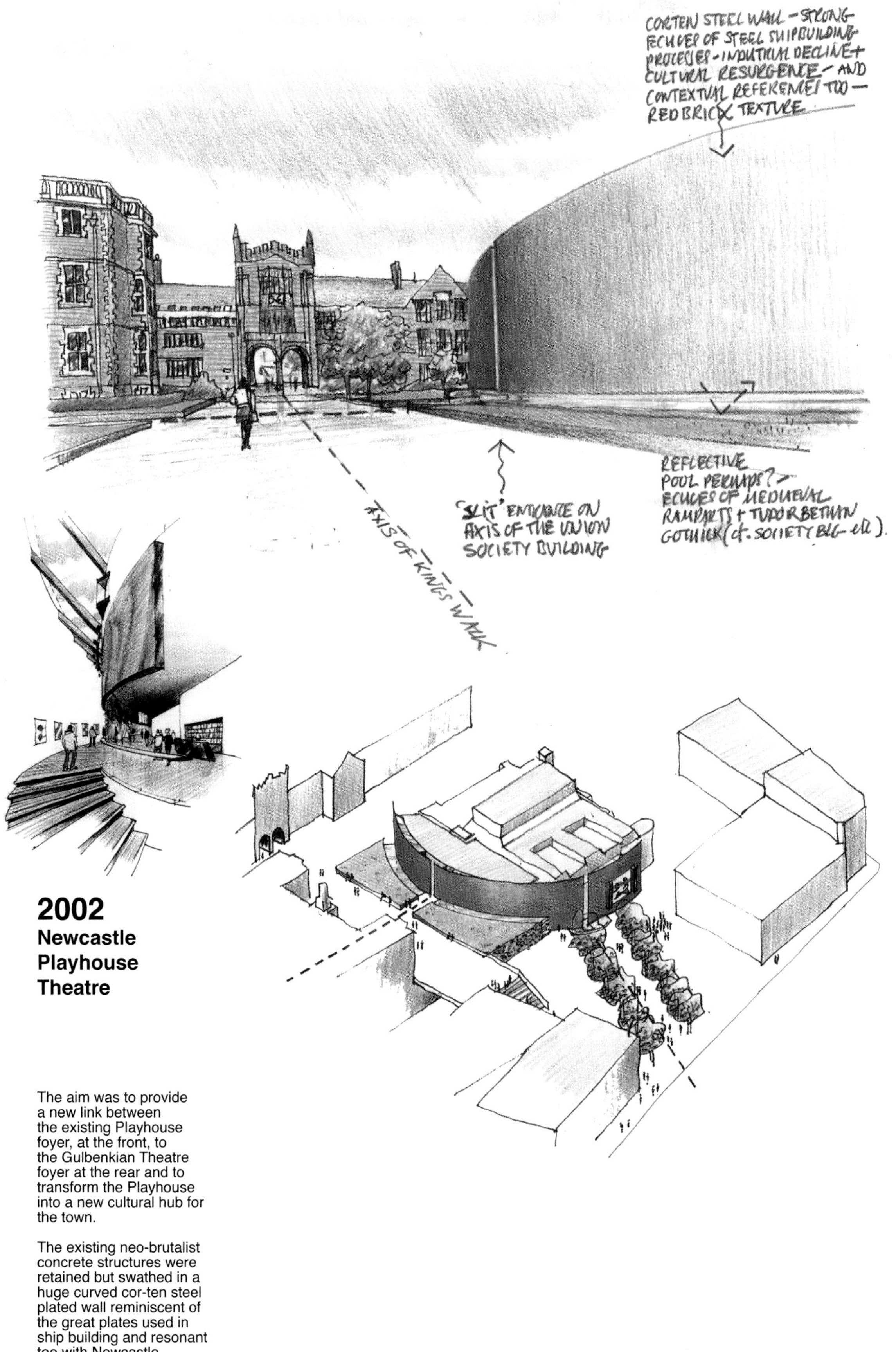

2002
Newcastle Playhouse Theatre

The aim was to provide a new link between the existing Playhouse foyer, at the front, to the Gulbenkian Theatre foyer at the rear and to transform the Playhouse into a new cultural hub for the town.

The existing neo-brutalist concrete structures were retained but swathed in a huge curved cor-ten steel plated wall reminiscent of the great plates used in ship building and resonant too with Newcastle University—a red brick university—wherein the theatre sits.

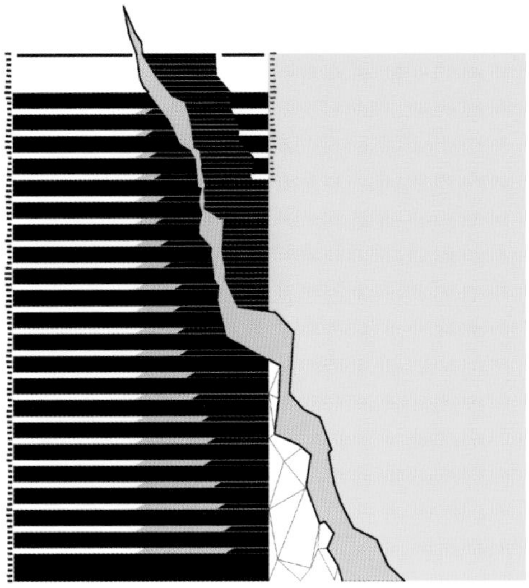

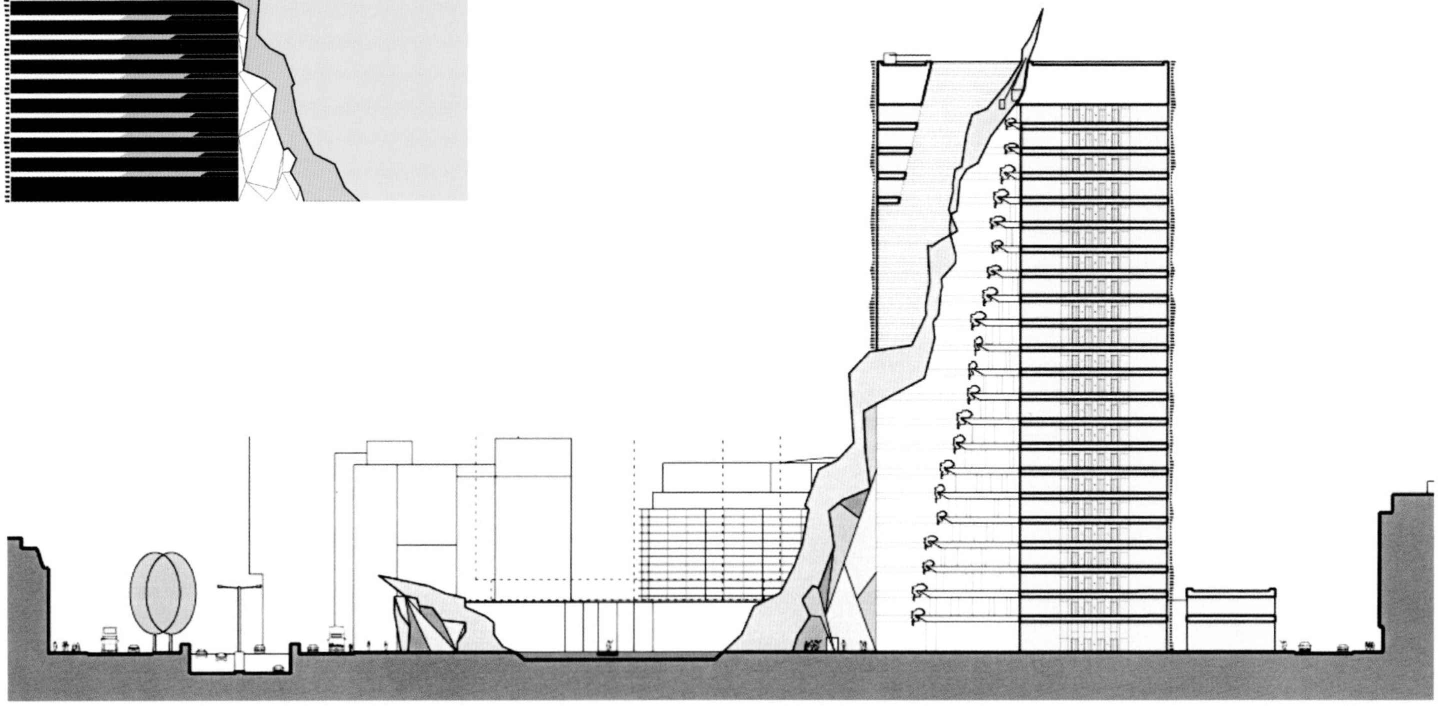

2003
Office Tower;
Regents Place;
London

This design for a 20-storey office building of 33,444m² (360,000ft²) formed part of the British Land plc's Regents Place development. The plan form is a simple square with an offset service core to make a double-cube block. The block is clad with a random cut stone brise-soleil made to appear solid when viewed from below like a stratified rock monolith. A fissure has been cut through the monolith to form an atrium from which a cascade of glass crystals pours like quartz into a black, reflective pool in the square below (pp. 16–17).

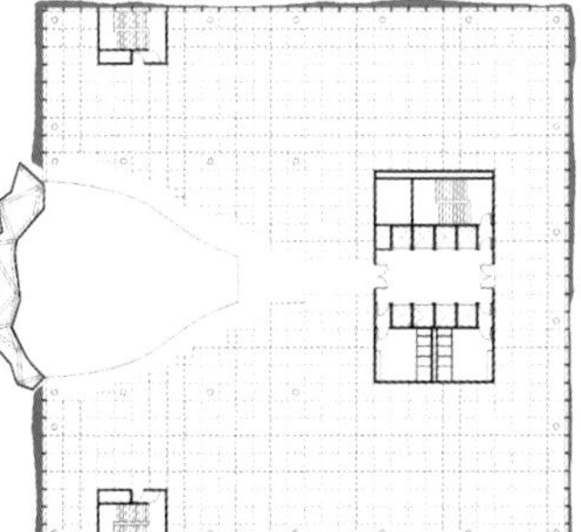

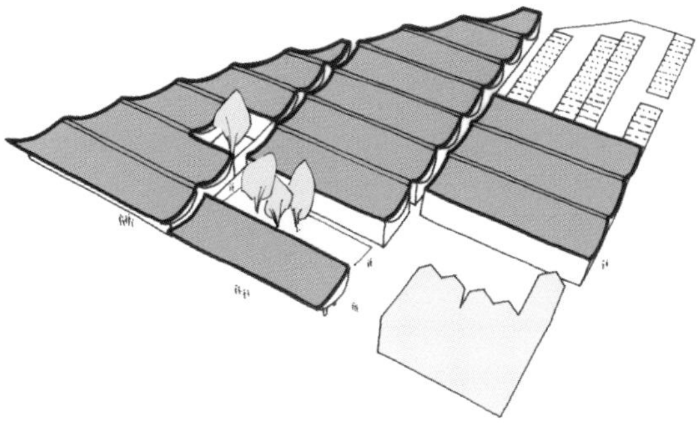

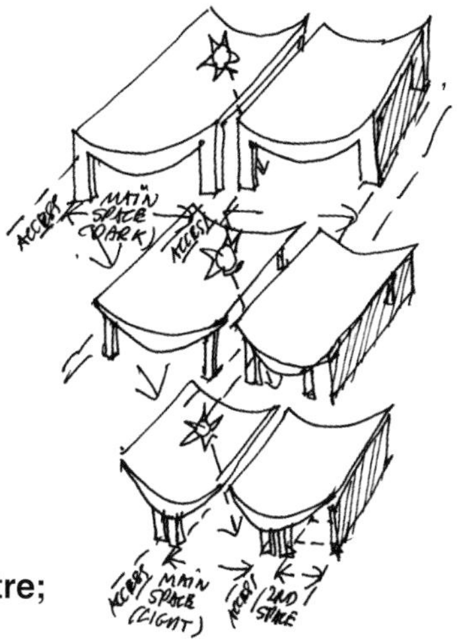

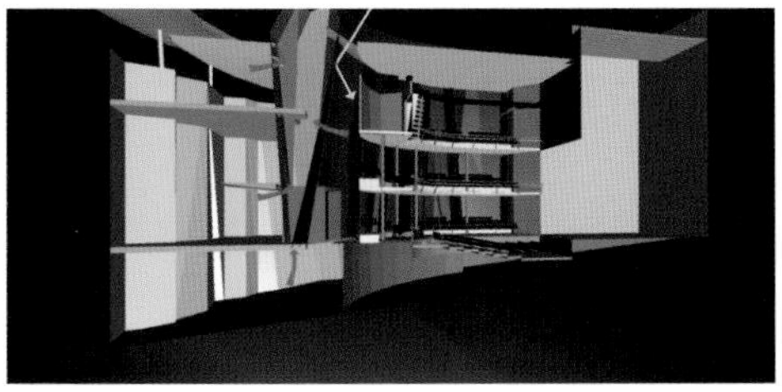

2003
Lyric Theatre; Belfast; Northern Ireland

This new state-of-the-art 400 seat theatre on the banks of the river Lagan was intended to mark the 50th anniversary of the Lyric Theatre.

The Theatre has an unexpected and unusual location at the end of a tiny nineteenth century street of red brick terraced housing, giving it a powerfully evocative expression of the Theatre's roots in its community.

Nor can it be ignored that the dark days of Belfast's recent past will have influenced the city's culture, and perhaps the new building should speak a little of this, too.

The design has a glistening black cave-like internal ambulatory wrapped around the theatre with a fissured and fractured white opalescent glass facade to frame the views down across the river.

2004–2006
Cheltenham Town Hall

It was after seeing Jamie Callum perform in the Hall in the Spring of 2004 that the idea began to germinate that the Hall was a very much underused asset and one with a very valuable but hitherto hidden potential.

The thought was that if the existing back-of-house facilities overlooking Imperial Gardens could be demolished and replaced by an extension with dressing rooms, toilets, management offices, and most crucially, a new café and bar, this re-orientation towards the gardens might then become the principal public entrance.

2004
Archive Centre; Hull

This design owes its genesis a visit to Louis Kahn's Kimbell Museum in Fort Worth, Texas where it was apparent that this stunning work had in turn been influenced by Le Corbusier's house for Sarabhai in Ahmedabad. Thus the design here uses the same repetitive long-span vaulted rhythms to create internal spatial oppositions between the axial and cross-axial dynamics but it differs from the Kimbell in that the vault has been inverted in a cross-section reminiscent of the pages of an open book. This refers back to Corbusier's school of Architecture at Chandigarh, India, with its wonderfully saggy beams and creates an intriguing wave-like form externally and a 'hull'-like form internally.

This long trail that George Kubler so eloquently writes of in 'The Shape of Time' is how architecture evolves.

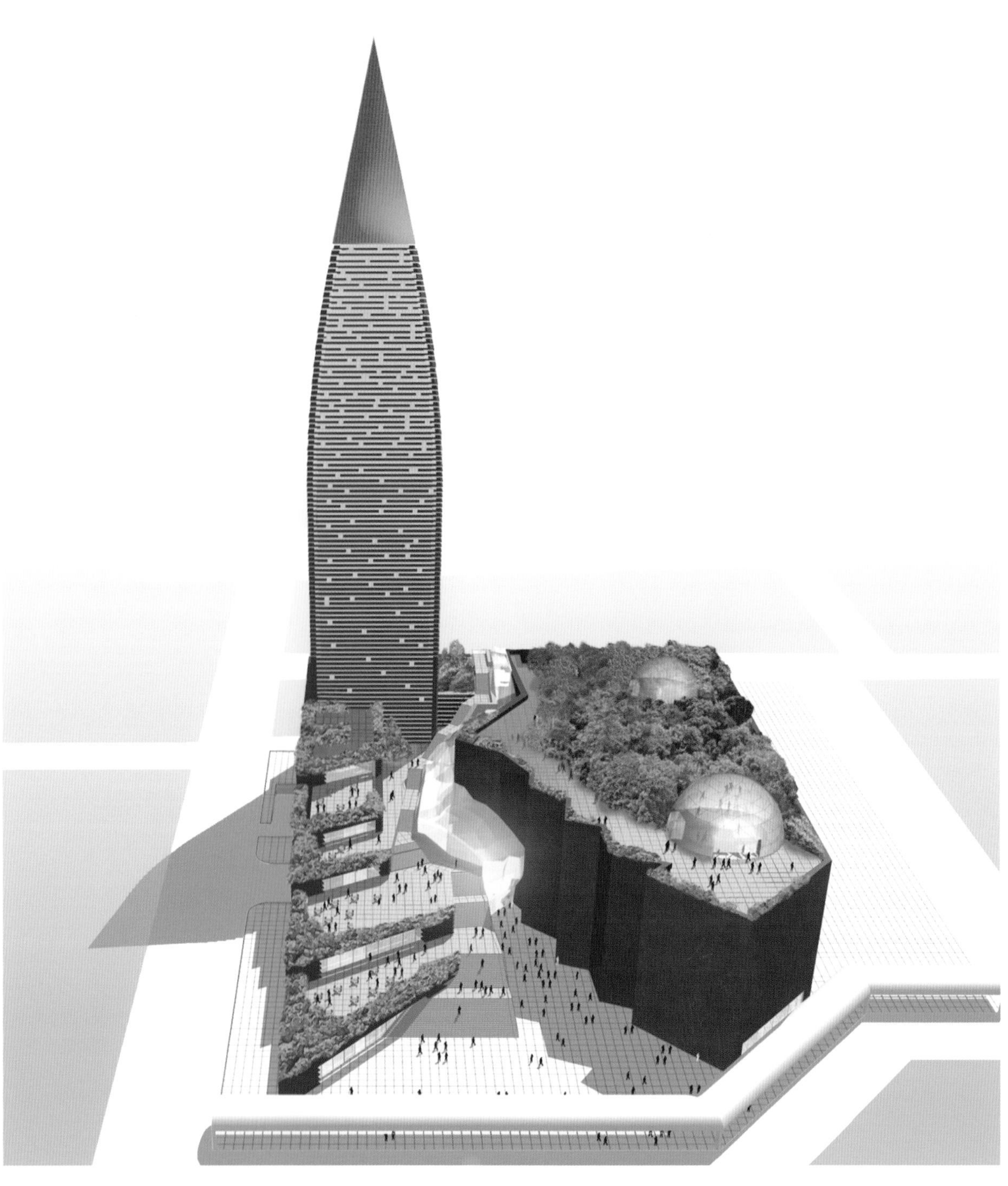

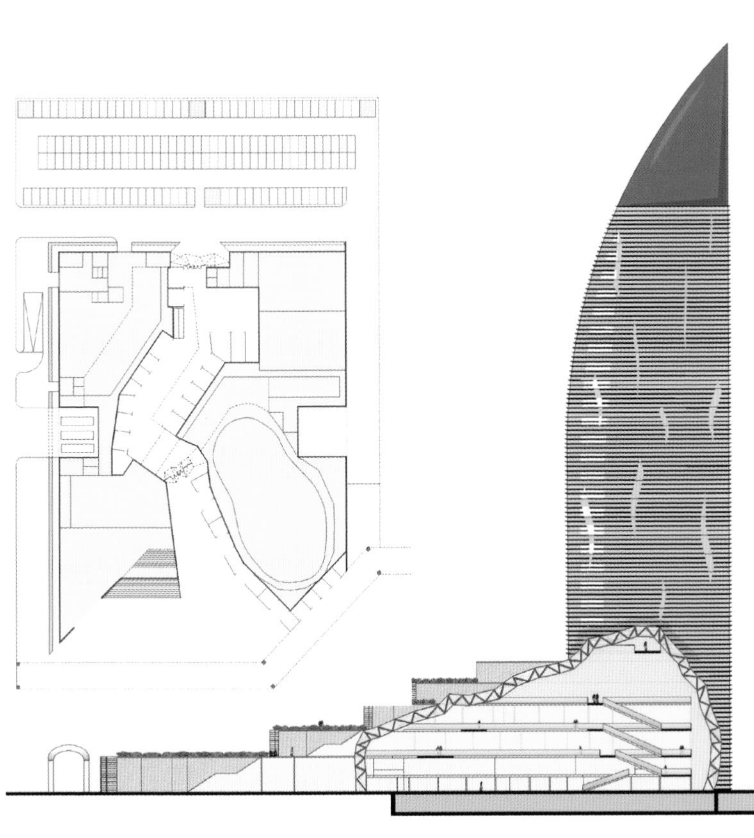

2004–2005
Kolkata New Town; India

Kolkata is a city of 10 million people, and growing. To help absorb this enormous expansion a New Town has been established on the perimeter of the city with a target population of 1 million.

At its centre, a new development was commissioned comprising 52,000m² (560,000ft²) of mixed-uses including one hundred shops, offices, a fitness centre, ice-skating rink, swimming pool, two cinemas, a banqueting suite, several restaurants and a range of apartments in a 30-storey tower.

The form has been structured as a metaphor of the West Bengal landscape. It represents the topographical transitions from the flat floodplains of the Ganges delta around Kolkata up to the tea terraces of Darjeeling and beyond to the glaciers of the Himalayas and the great peak of Kanchendzonga, the highest mountain in India (p. 17).

2005
Bridge across the Quay; Lymington; Hampshire

The bridge is formed of two graceful shallow arched spans following the curve of the river.

The first arch has a 40m clear span, the second 24m, like the trajectory of a pebble thrown across the water, the second skip being shorter than the first.

Between the two, where the 'pebble' would bounce first is a small artificial island which incorporates a miniature bascule bridge to provide access to the pontoon docks beyond and to create another perfect place for the town's children to go crab-fishing.

2005
Fibre-Bike; Bicycle Design

A design for a light-weight carbon-fibre bicycle with integral storage space (p. 83).

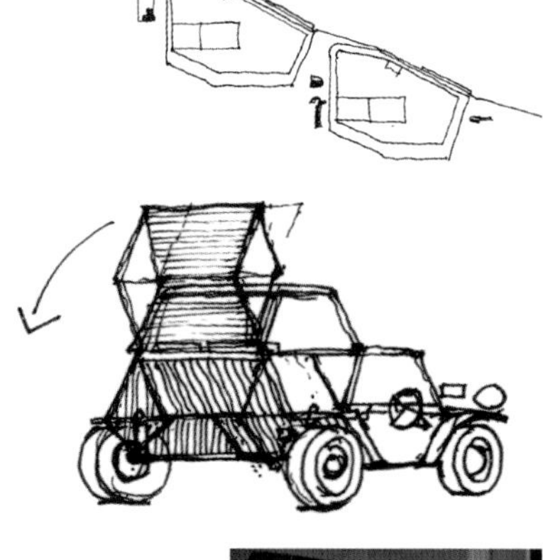

2005
Scenic Saloon

Developed from the dicky-seat model in the Cellular Sedan range, the Scenic Saloon was intended as a small all-terrain utility car offering unusually capacious storage space and, for its rear-seat passengers whose noses now press upon the head restraints of the seats in front, an unusually privileged view—returning the rear seats to the special status that they had enjoyed at the start of the motoring era (p. 81).

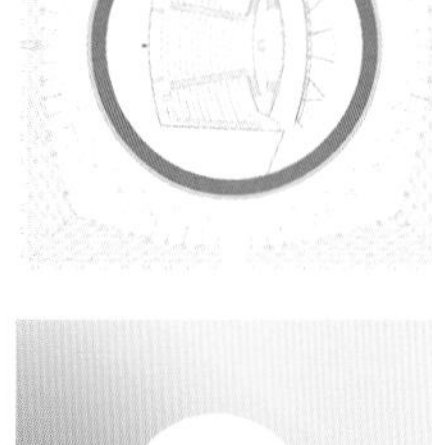

2005
IMAX; Dubai

This IMAX was intended purely to show a specially commissioned film on the origins and development of Dubai. The building could therefore develop in a more overtly, expressive language—of Ledoux—the oasis and desert dunes—a response to the extraordinary genius loci that is Dubai.

The concept of the circular watercourse and island refers again to the Island Pavillion at Hadrian's Villa. The 'bridge' to the island here was equally emotive—it comprised an open metal grid that would disappear back beneath the water after the audience had crossed into the auditorium (p. 9).

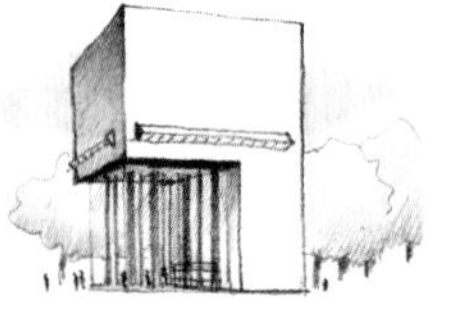

2005
Tontine Street Theatre; Folkestone; Kent

Three lines of thought developed from the contiguity studies of the site and context.

The first derived from the white chalk cliffs of this part of the coast, continuing an exploration begun with the Margate Project (pp. 12, 157); the second referred to the local black tar-painted fishermen's houses; and the third (above) created a miniature forest to integrate with a re-planted public park behind the site (p. 12).

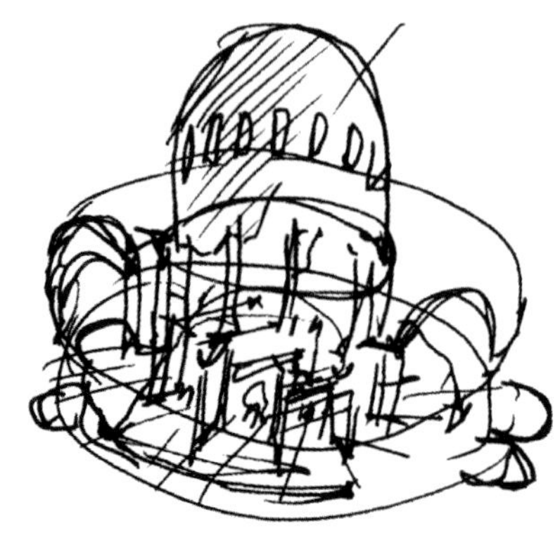

2005–2007
Oakham School Concert Hall; Rutland

The Concert Hall was the second project at Oakham and was commissioned by a new headmaster.

The intention was to expand the school's existing music department (the 'U'-shaped courtyard building at top left in the plan opposite) by creating a new extension to the south in the form of a brick cloister that opened through a concealed passage and flight of steps into the Headmaster's garden. The new Concert Hall was sited at the East end of this cloister abutting a road and a listed public house to give greater public prominence to the school's music programme. The Buttercross in the market Square at Oakham (above, bottom) was an early inspiration for the design. It represented the place where the local community could come together as a social group. So too was the School's Chapel—another significant 'coming together' space and much used by the school for choral music (above, middle, left).

These ideas of 'coming together' and 'ritual' implied the need for a complex space that would have the character of both an experimental performance space like the Manchester Royal Exchange Theatre and sacred spaces like Santa Constaza in Rome (sketch top).

The result (sketch above, bottom right) was a low dark cave-like stone

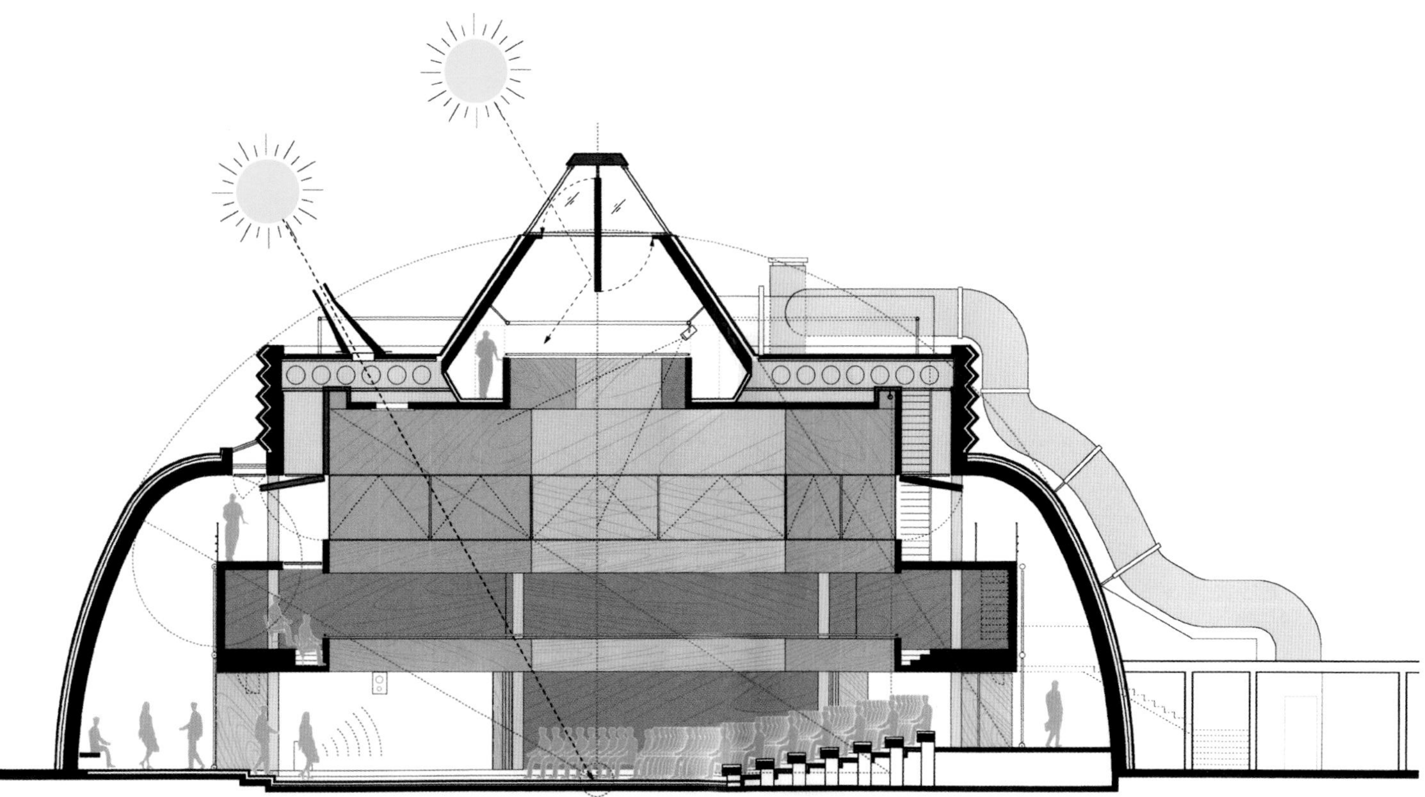

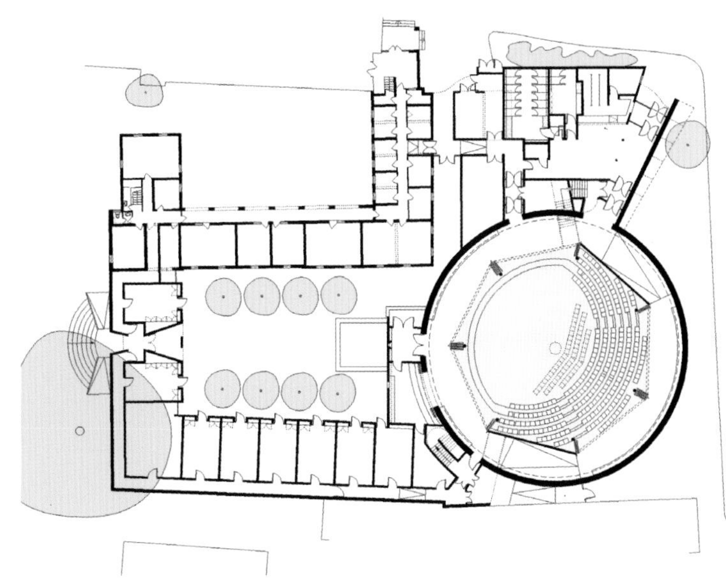

ambulatory surrounding a tall light-timbered inner drum. The drum admits daylight through an occulus that can be opened and closed by rotating a diaphragm. The upper wall panels of the drum open and close too in order to vary the rooms' volume, and thus its reverberation time, as the music requires.

The external expression of the hall was driven by the idea that the hall was in itself an instrument for making music. The black stone ambulatory was expressed as a resonating chamber, like a blackened gourd, and the other elements were treated like the finely made silver valves and fittings that make musical instruments such very tactile objects.

Versailles.

2005–2006
The Princess Alexandra Hall; Royal Overseas League; St. James; London

The ambition for the hall was to improve its acoustics, increase the capacity of the stage, and create a flexible, state-of-the-art multi-purpose concert venue.

The existing gallery and stage (photo above, bottom, right) were stripped out and replaced by an interior of mirrors and polished lacquered panels that alluded to the 30s stream-form of this wing of the building. This enabled the asymmetric window/wall rhythm on one side of the hall to be balanced by a reciprocal mirror/wall rhythm on the other in the manner of the Salle des Glaces at Versailles (sketch opposite, top). This not only brought an elegant proportion and symmetry to the space but it improved the acoustics immeasurably too. However, as the walls of the hall were also made non-parallel for acoustic reasons, the mirrors, being parallel with the window wall (photo above, bottom, left) concealed this fact yet were able to create that same spatial illusion as at the IMAX, that from the public's perspective at the entry, the hall appears impressively large, whereas from the musicians' perspective from the stage, the hall appears reassuringly intimate.

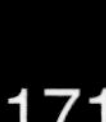

2006–2009
Offices; Old Bailey; City of London

This 75,000 ft² (6,968 m²) nett new office building in the City of London sits within a sensitive conservation area close to St Paul's Cathedral. The back of the property abuts the Roman Wall and Amen Court, a quiet ecclesiastical enclosure with private landscaped gardens. The front of the property abuts the Old Bailey, the most famous courthouse in England.

The design responds to these issues by keeping the height at the back to the minimum and cladding the facade with vegetation so that it will, in time, appear as a green backdrop to the Roman Wall. The windows here are proportioned as golden rectangles and are provided with a 'ruff-like' stainless steel picture frame to project out through the vegetation (above bottom middle and left).

At the front, the design takes its cue from the Old Bailey and uses similar materials and massing to create a round topped casket of Portland stone through which the office windows have been punched like the 'juliet balconies' of a theatre wherein to view the nefarious comings and goings next door.

To offset the loss of floorspace that a conventional vertical atrium would have caused in a building that tapers so markedly to the roof, the atrium here has been turned into a curve to channel morning sunlight right down into the entrance lobby. This has also the effect of creating a periscopic image of St Paul's, visible from within the lobby (above bottom middle and far right) (pp. 14–15).

The building was designed in association with Sidell Gibson Architects.

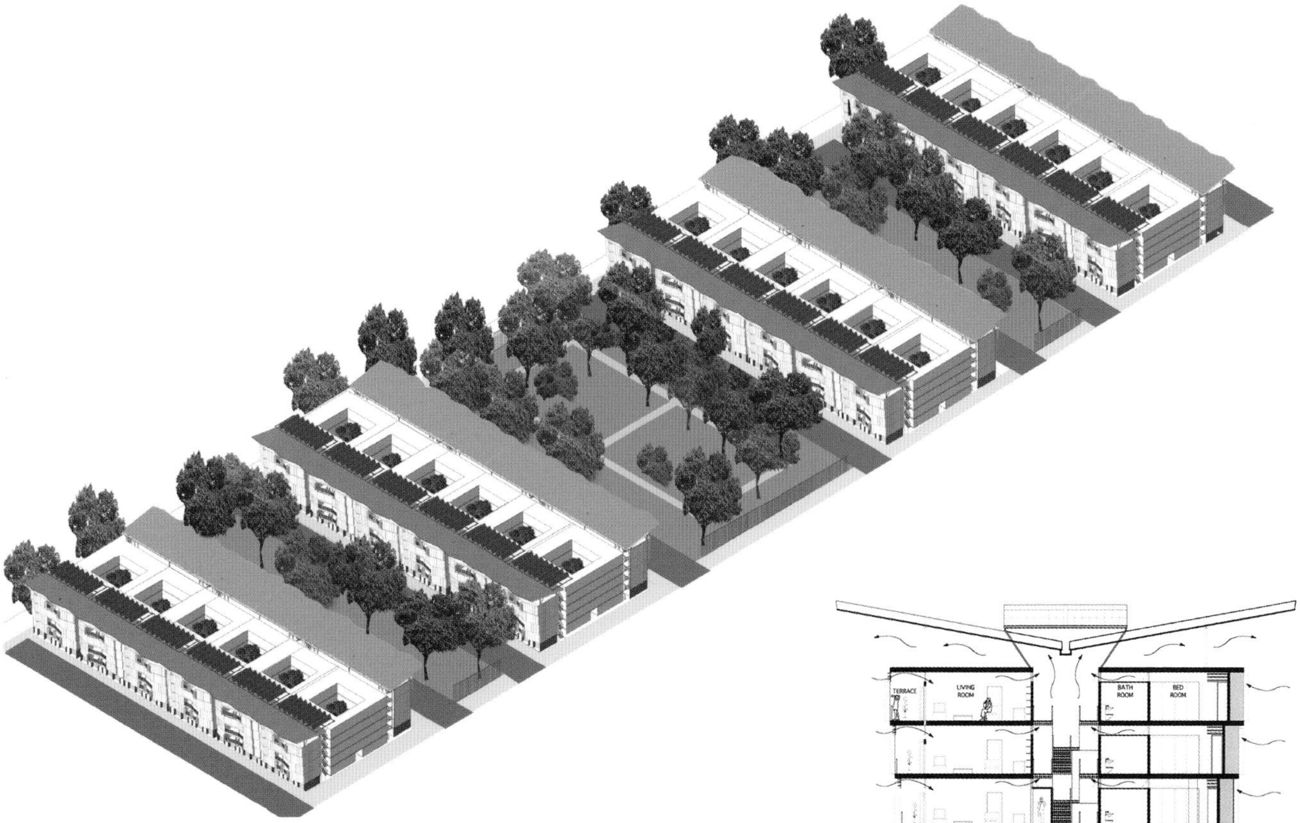

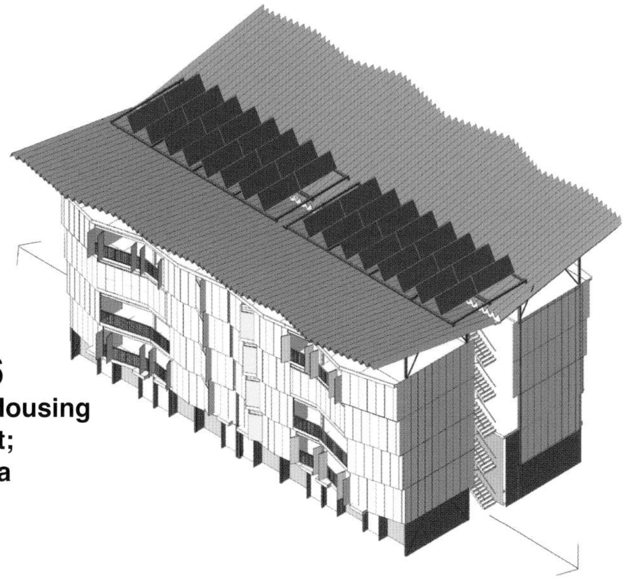

2006
Steel Housing Project; Kolkata

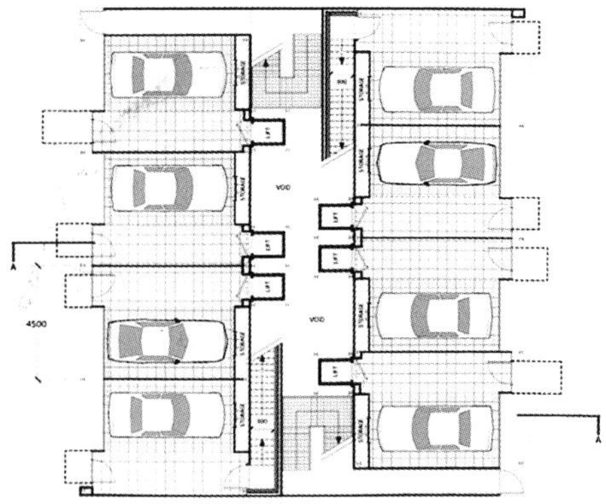

This project pulls together many of the themes developed in the earlier ATH housing projects (pp. 38, 54–57, 140) and relates it to the specific issue of the climate and culture of Kolkata.

Thus, in this archetypal ex-colonial city the tradition of breezy, tree-cooled garden squares is re-introduced, lined with mixed-use back-to-back housing and live-work units.

The units use the lift access principle, developed originally for the european situation of a demographically ageing population, but used here to explore the possibility of providing a secure and private ground level entrance with lift access to each flat above the first floor.

The wide service void thus formed is used to create through-ventilation for the flats and to provide also a means of upgrading the technical services to each flat without disturbing the occupants.

Clockwise from above: Isometric back-to-back; isometric back-to-back with commercial developments and garden squares; cross-section; ground floor plan, upper floor plans.

2006
Theatre for the Onassis Centre; Athens; Greece

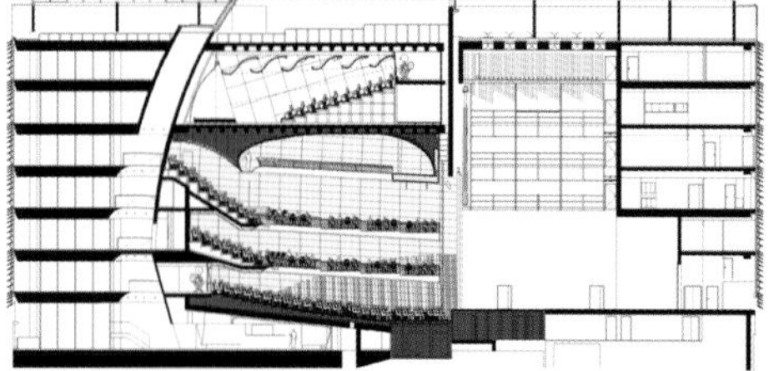

The Onassis Foundation were in the process of building a new cultural centre in Athens and required it to have two new performance spaces—a multi-format theatre and concert hall seating 1080, and a new lecture and film theatre seating 170.

The intention for the main space was to create a resonance with the Onassis Foundation through the use of a shipping metaphor. The interior therefore has been shaped to a timber hull-like form; the balconies have a breaking wave-like leading edge and the ceiling is sculpted in back-lit shimmering green glass layers—like looking up from underwater at the rippled surface of the sea above.

The detailed cross-section (bottom, right) shows an alternative proposal for the building's external cladding. The intention had been to clad it with a grillage of horizontal stone louvres but as this would have presented severe maintenance and cleaning problems and would have obscured views into the building from the street, this alternative design was developed based on the cladding design for the earlier Swiss Centre project. This design used photovoltaics on the top surface to generate electricity as in the Swiss centre project and would not only be transparent to views 'in' but fully shaded against the sun too. (pp. 154–155 and the DMU project p. 178).

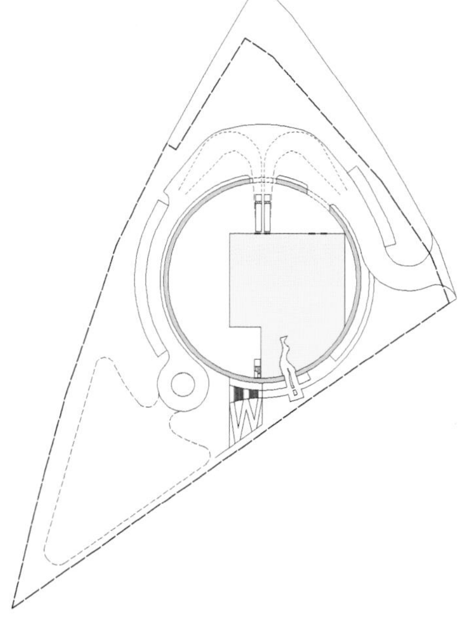

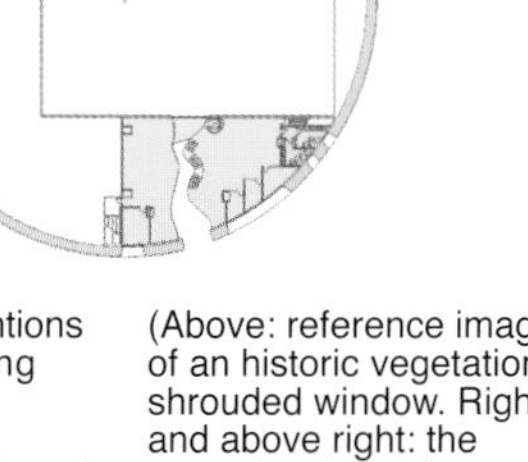

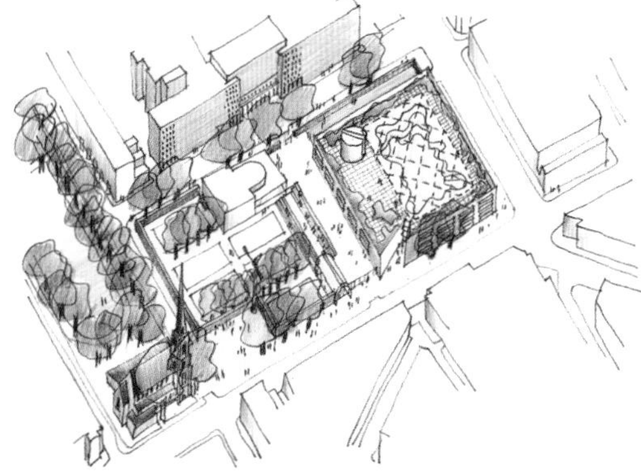

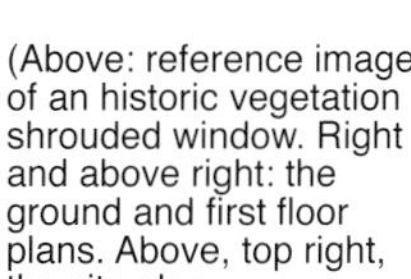

2006–2007
HQ For international Dance Supplies; Devon

2006–2007
Schools for the Future Programme; Pimlico School; London

Having outgrown its existing warehouse and offices, the company wanted to create a new headquarters that would not only be an exemplar of the highest environmental standards and a pleasurable place for its staff, but would also celebrate its business and passion—dance.

The building was set within a wooded area beside a busy dual carriageway in South Devon. It was designed to have the smallest volumetric envelope to conserve energy and was surrounded by a ring of sheltering vegetation that allowed the building within to expand and to change and adapt over time without the need for additional expensive architectural interventions and lengthy planning applications.

The offices peek out through the vegetation, with colourful reveals, in a similar manner to the projects for the Old Bailey (p. 172), Newcastle College (p. 162) and Shanghai (p. 177).

The entry is seen as a "slice" into the building, revealing its contents, but the slice is not a regular cut, it wriggles as if with male and female curves, dancing.

(Above: reference image of an historic vegetation shrouded window. Right and above right: the ground and first floor plans. Above, top right, the site plan.

The design was commissioned by the local community to provide a template for a new 1,200 pupil school.

The plan incorporates two community-focused buildings, a library and a performing arts centre, plus a high density highly sustainable new school building in a block plan that re-establishes the'Pimlico Grid' as set out originally by the architect-builder Cubitt.

These are contained and defined by a new interpretation of the traditional green 'hedge'—a visual continuation of St Georges Square adjacent.

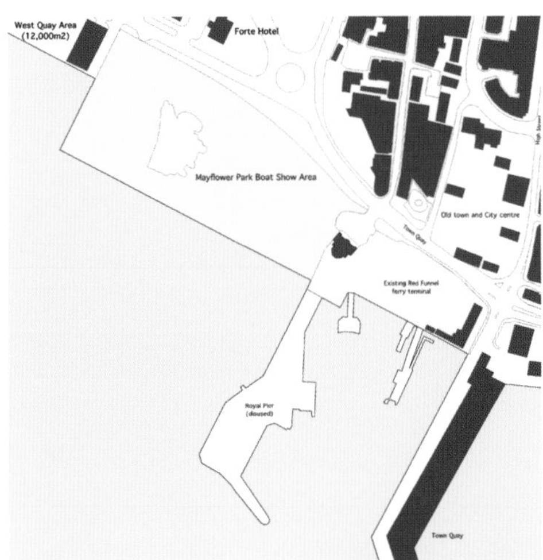

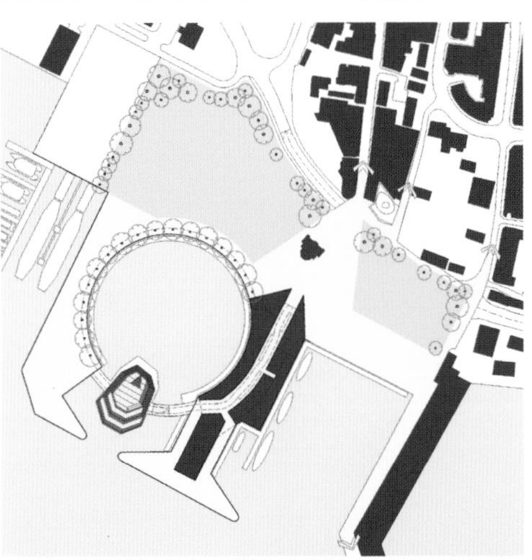

2006–2008
Waterfront Masterplan and New Museums for Southampton

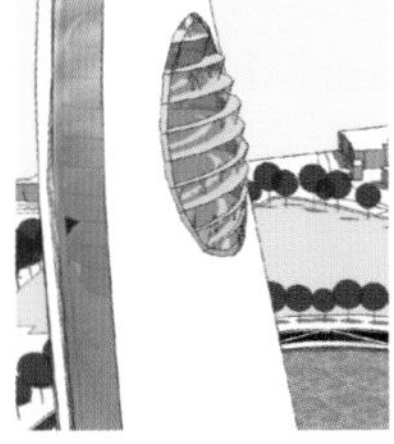

The project was commissioned by the Southampton Heritage Federation to explore the potential of Mayflower Park, the only significant waterside site in the city, for building a new maritime and aeronautical museum.

The proposal recommended the relocation of the Isle of Wight ferry terminal, currently between the town Quay and Royal Pier, to the Western end of the site, in a land-swap that would put Mayflower Park into a pivotal position linking the city centre with its two public piers (the two 'before' and 'after' plans above right). This connection could be additionally strengthened in time by the sinking of the very busy Town Quay Road into an underpass to create a pedestrianised public realm all the way from the city centre to the waterfront.

It also recommended that the currently derelict Royal Pier be re-built and extended to include new retail, leisure, cultural and hotel uses and that a new 'Town Quay' and 'Round Pond' be created that would be used not only by the Boatshow for its moorings, but also by the town for water-borne recreational activities and events.

The new museum was placed at the head of the Round Pond with the Heritage Collection arranged in a spiral so that people could promenade up and down and celebrate the arrivals and departures of the big ships that visit the port.

In a subsequent iteration (bottom left and right), the museum incorporated a capsule ride taking people to a height a little over that of the London Eye (pp. 126–127). It contained 4,132m^2 (41,500ft^2) of display space to trace the development of the city with particular reference to its marine and aerospace traditions. Thus it would include an underwater aquarium, an oceanography and diving display, and features on the Pilgrim Fathers and the great ocean liners—of which the Titanic, whose final voyage started from here and whose seamen were largely from this area, was arguably the most famous.

The galleries above would tell the story of the region's amazing aerospace heritage, the D-Day landings, the Empire and Princess Flying Boats, the Schneider Trophy Seaplanes, the Black Knight rockets, the Hovercraft and of course the Spitfire, the wing shape of which is the inspiration behind the design (pp. 126–127).

Clockwise from top right: Mayflower Park as existing: as proposed; the Spitfire Wing; close-up of the viewing galleries of the spitfire wing; shell sketch; the spiral museum.

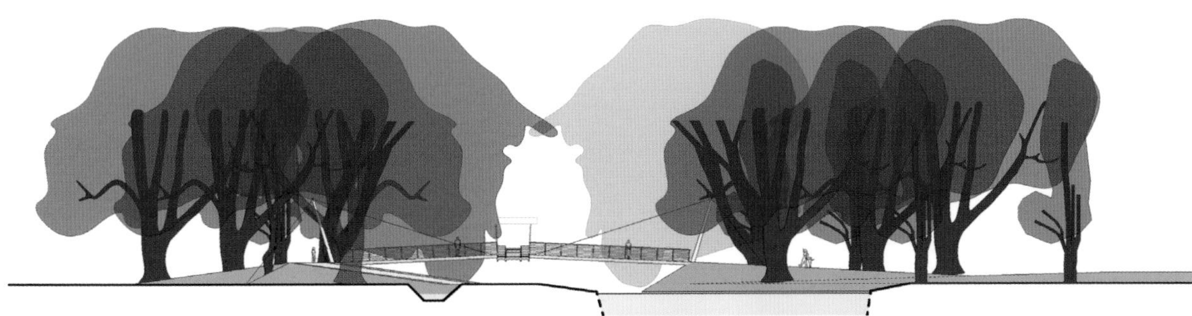

2007–2009
**Theatre;
Repton School;
Derbyshire**

2007–2008
**British Pavilion
for Expo 2010;
Shanghai;
China**

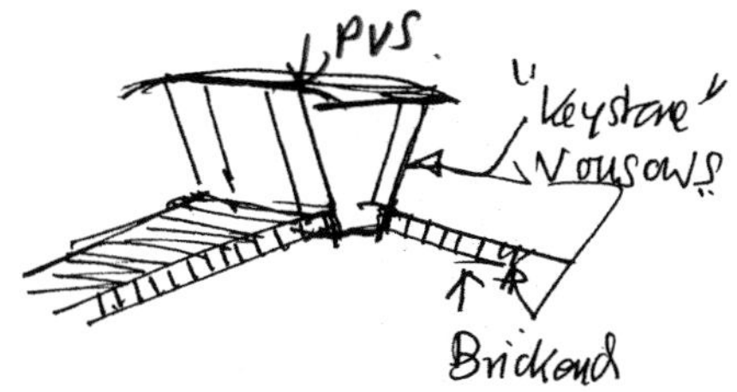

2007–2008
**Footbridge;
Christ Church
college;
Oxford**

A competition win; the school's existing theatre is a significant landmark so the new theatre has been placed inside it. It has a capacity of 310 seats on two levels using a very intimate geometry, similar to the Vanbrugh Auditorium at RADA (pp. 108–111).

The new foyer (above) uses a diagrid to counterpoint the axial symmetry of the existing theatre and inflects both the picturesque irregularity of the site and the important diagonal line-of-sight that links the Hall to the school's Chapel.

Construction commenced in 2010.

One of six practices short-listed for the commission; the design responded to the Expo theme of "better city, better life", by evoking the principles of Wilderness City.

Britain was the first to industrialise so it was also the first to confront the issues of urban alienation. In so doing, it pioneered what is arguably the most successful new model for modern urban development—that cities work best when they address the human need for a small scale local identity and a rapprochement with the natural world (pp. 20–21).

The new footbridge was designed to replace a disused ferry and thereby re-connect the college with the Liddell Building and playing fields on the opposite bank of the Cherwell.

The genius loci here must include, of course, the beautiful setting, but it must include too the fact of Oxford and Christ Church and the classical context.

It cannot ignore either that the bridge is to be used by students, hugely talented young people who will come here to Christ Church Meadow, perhaps prosaically just to cross the river, but who might also come to reflect in solitude, or join with friends, or even to pursue a romantic dalliance.

The bridge, then, is more than just a crossing, it is a place. To celebrate this special place there are some seats at the centre of the span, like a theatre 'box' and over them, a laminated white glass canopy to provide shade and shelter. Embedded within the canopy are photovoltaic cells to generate electricity for a dramatic illumination of the bridge at night.

In this way the Bridge has every potential to become a small but very significant new landmark and a practical but exciting new addition to the life of the college.

(Above, bottom: the meadow; above, bottom right: concept sketch; above, middle left and right: views of model; above top: elevation).

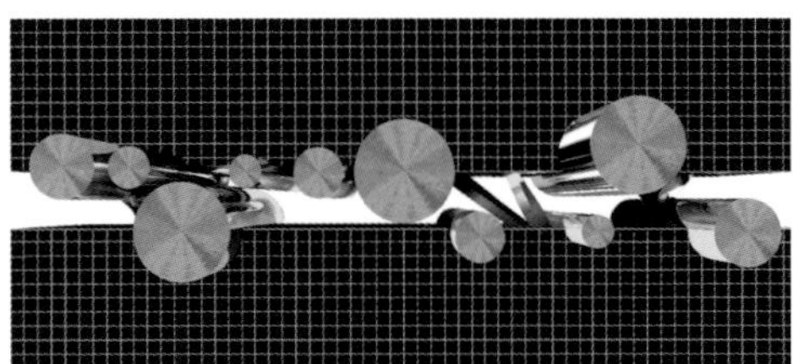

2008–2009

Faculty of Art and Design; De Montfort University; Leicester

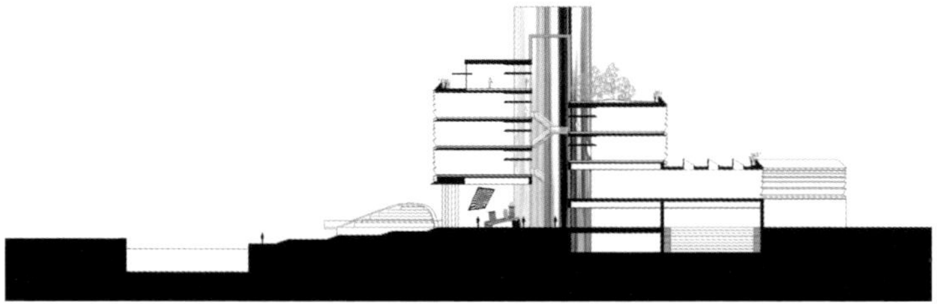

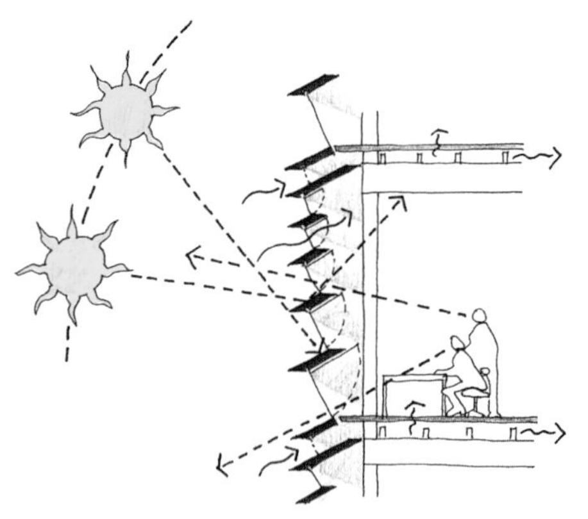

The aim was to form a memorable new gateway to the University by turning the new Art and Design (and Architecture) building away from the river to face the bridge and thereby create a generous south-facing, fan-shaped riverside terrace for use by the students and public alike.

The building has a spacious double-height ground floor for the public display of the students' work and above, the floors are arranged in pairs, each a standard very flexible floor plate 82.5m x 15m, but separated in plan by a 6m wide atrium and in section by a half-storey change of level.

The effect of this is to create a system of interlocking floor plates in the manner of the Spiral Office Project (p. 63), which offers a huge variety of potential space options for the faculty's departments to expand or contract into over time.

In addition, by placing all of the building's services within the atrium and by using a stack-effect chimney ventilation system, it not only frees up the floor plates but creates a labyrinthine spatial quality that enables departments to express their individualities and to share them with everyone using the building.

In generating the external form, the primary references are the adjacent engineering building with its ventilation towers; the precision-machined stainless steel bobbins that powered Leicester's fabric industry, and the warp and weft of the fabric as it was built up on the looms—echoed here in the photovoltaic powered solar control facade pioneered in many of the practice's other projects, e.g. the Onassis Foundation (p. 174), the Swiss Centre (pp.154–155) and No. 1 Neathouse Place (pp. 14–15, 48, 70–77, 89–92, 147).

Bottom left; section through the external wall. Middle, left;the floor plate concept. Middle right; cross-section through the site. Top; panoramic view across the canal.

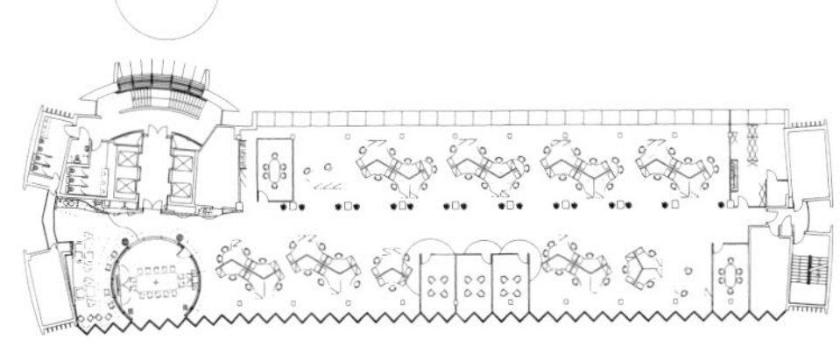

2009
Interior at No. 1 Neathouse Place

2009
Museum; Southend-on-Sea; Essex

No. 1 Neathouse Place was completed in 1996 (p. 147).

The new brief called for the design of break-out spaces, kitchens and conference rooms to be built on each of the seven operational floors plus a new boardroom suite on the top floor.

The design has a cylindrical conference room placed at the entrance to each of the operational floors to echo the drum that marks the entrance to the building (plan above top).

This powerful architectural form is intended to define the spaces around it as four connected but individual areas; an open plan office area, a break-out space (perspective above), an entrance area and a kitchen.

The new Board Room on the top floor uses a curvilinear organic form to symbolise the company's mining and minerals interests and to create a sensuous space for dining and receiving visitors with stunning views over central London (pp. 74–75).

The museum is intended to bring together several of the town's existing collections plus a new one in celebration of the recent discovery of the burial treasures of an Anglo-Saxon prince.

The site is a splendid cliff-side location within sight of the town's famous pier, reputedly the longest pleasure pier in the world.

This provided an opportunity to demonstrate the practice's philosophy that engaging the spirit of 'place' with the spirit of 'thing' can generate huge expressive potentials.

Three generic approaches were explored. The first was to create a new route from the top to the bottom of the cliff and to bed this into the site contours.

This created the opportunity for an external (public) route to zig-zag down the cliff face and to cross at intervals through the museum via terraces in the manner of those at the temple of Hatshepsut at Thebes (above) and at Sanssoucci in Potsdam (overleaf, bottom). It also crossed a second (private) route that ran down in a giant cascade of steps intended as a social meeting space in the manner of the Spanish Steps in Rome. The steps taper to the bottom to create a visual foreshortening and sun-warmed, cloud-like panels suspended below the roof glazing power the stack-effect ventilation system for the whole building (overleaf, middle two illustrations).

The second approach was to express this route more dynamically by detaching the museum from its landscape and creating thereby a singular form connected only tenuously to the cliff top by a glass 'pier' (opposite).

The museum is structured as a white glass cube and double-walled for solar powered ventilation. Its proportions are 3:4 and square on plan and the bridge pierces the building at the golden mean (0.618 of the width). This defines the major and minor spaces and is marked by a spiral staircase much like that at the Bexhill on Sea Pavilion by Mendelsohn and Chermayeff.

The third approach (top, this page) was to take this a stage further and, as the coast here is extremely shallow and waves do not form a significant threat, to relocate the museum to the water's edge. The impetus for this was that once disengaged from the issues of the cliff, the principal influence was the estuary.

Southend is at the mouth of the Thames estuary and the Anglo-Saxons were not alone in using it as an easy way to invade the country. For this reason it has long been heavily defended and in similar such places, the Solent approaches to Southampton and Portsmouth for example, the mouths of such estuaries have long been guarded by forts.

The museum may be seen therefore as a sentinel, put there to guard the environment of the estuary and to keep safe its precious character.

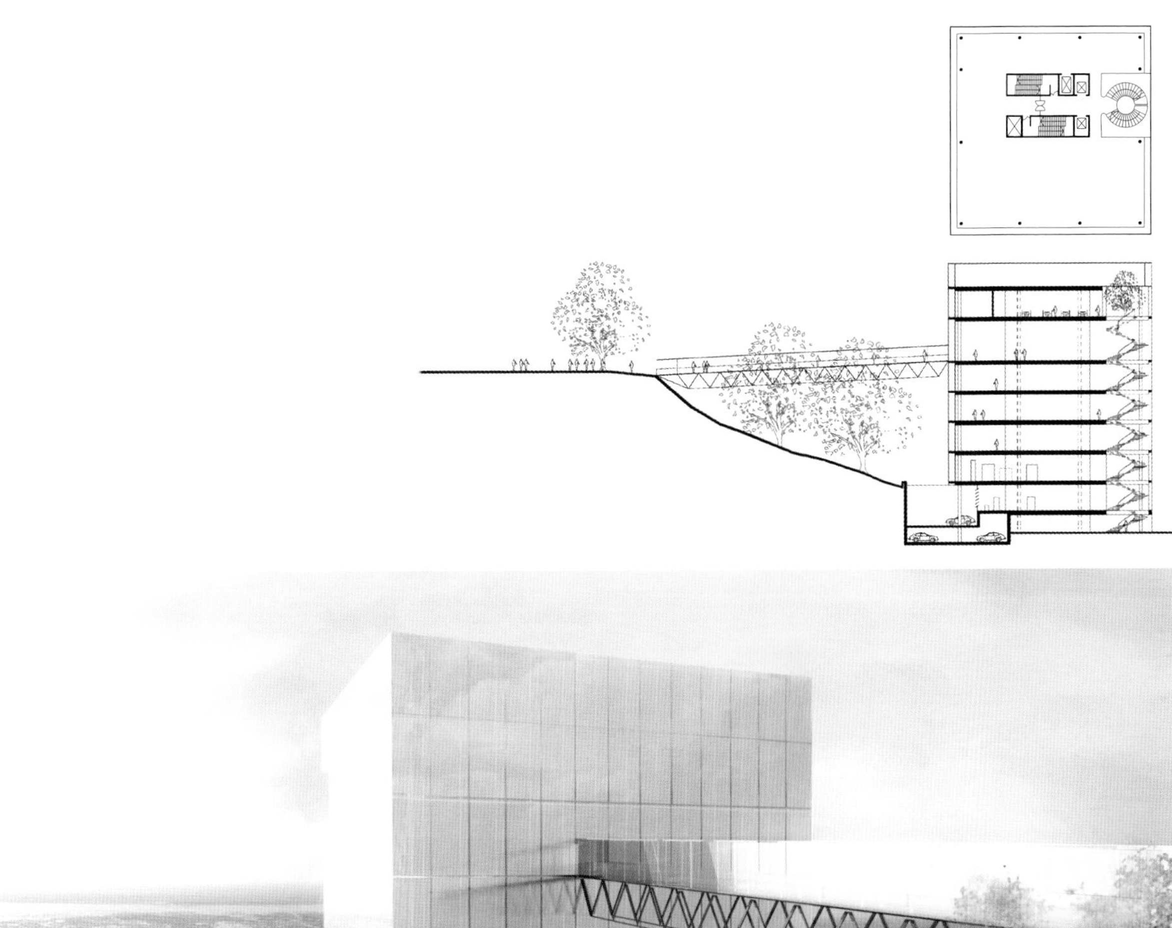

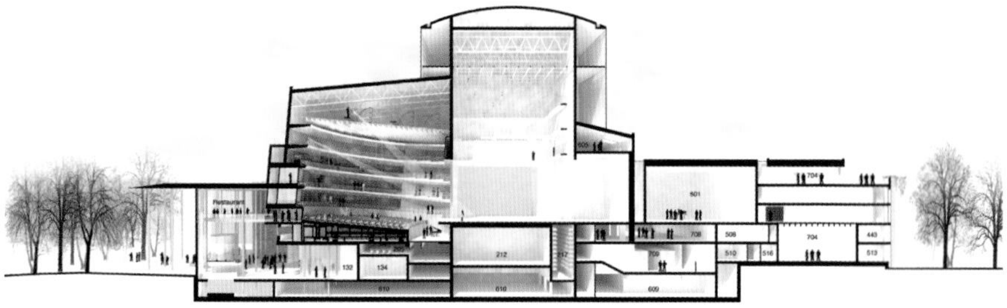

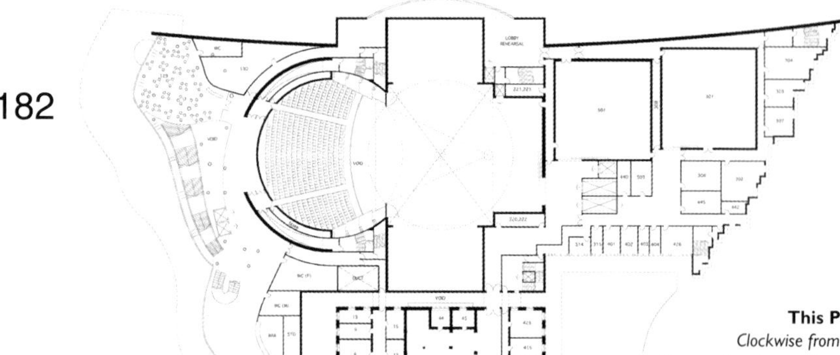

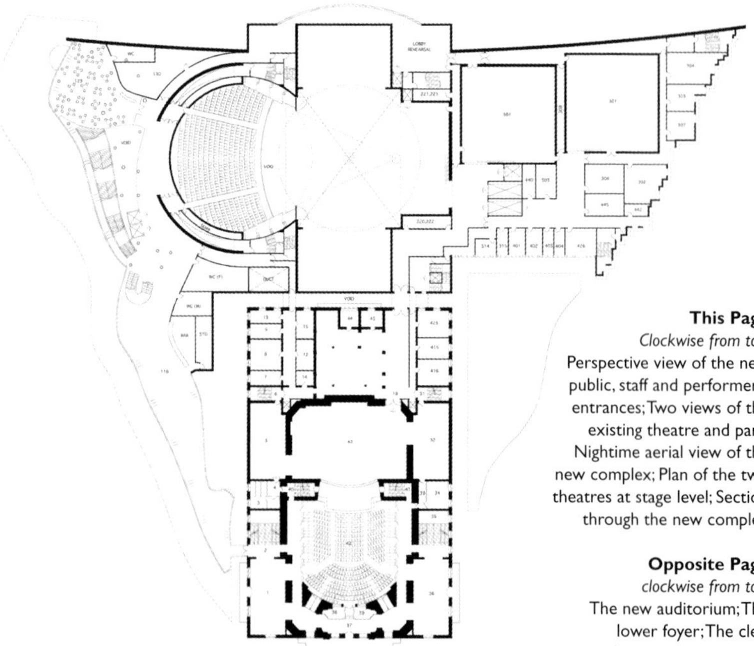

This Page
Clockwise from top: Perspective view of the new public, staff and performers' entrances; Two views of the existing theatre and park; Nighttime aerial view of the new complex; Plan of the two theatres at stage level; Section through the new complex

Opposite Page
clockwise from top: The new auditorium; The lower foyer; The cleft between the new and existing theatres; The foyer connecting new and old; The Eastern facade

2009–2010
The Tchaikovsky Ballet and Opera Theatre; Perm; Russia

The philosophy of the design is twofold; firstly to celebrate the powerful Russian spirit of 'oneness with nature' as immortalised by so many great Russian artists, and secondly to create a world-class arts complex in a dynamic and harmonious relationship with the much loved Tchaikovsky Opera and Ballet Theatre.

This new-old dialogue begins in deference to the existing theatre by placing the very much larger new building behind it at the northern (rear) end of the park. There the two flytowers, the most dominant elements on the city skyline, can be aligned on axis, the one melding with, and partially concealing, the other. There too, the form and massing of the existing theatre can be continued into the new structure, creating a visual continuity between the two.

The placing of the two theatres back-to-back in this way means that not only can the front-of-house facilities be shared most effectively and efficiently, but it enables the vehicular access for the "get-in" and the staff and performers' entrance to be grouped together in a single, secure and easily monitored position.

The new auditorium has 1100 seats arranged generously with 550 mm seat widths and 1000 mm wide rows. It is incredibly versatile, providing for opera, ballet, dance, orchestral works and for civic use, conferences, receptions, fashion shows, etc..

The new/old dialogue is nowhere better expressed than here. In the purity of its geometry it refers both to the great baroque theatres of the past that continue still to create such an exciting sense of occasion and to the double-sphere geometry of the Jerwood Vanbrugh Auditorium at RADA (pp. 108–111)

The East (technical) side is cliff-like in appearance, the walls here being made of irregularly faceted clear and white opalescent glass sheathing a thick thermally insulating masonry wall.

The glass can be back-lit at night such that the walls shimmer and glow white through the silver birches like ice-cliffs in winter. The west (public) side is, by contrast, more organic, the curvaceous forms of the foyers being expressive of the ballet and the thousands of sinewy rivers and streams of the Perm region.

The axiality of the existing theatre is reinforced by a cascade of reflective pools either side of which secret forest paths meander amongst the trees leading, as pleasurable surprises, to statuary commemorating the famous Russian artists and intellectuals associated with Perm.

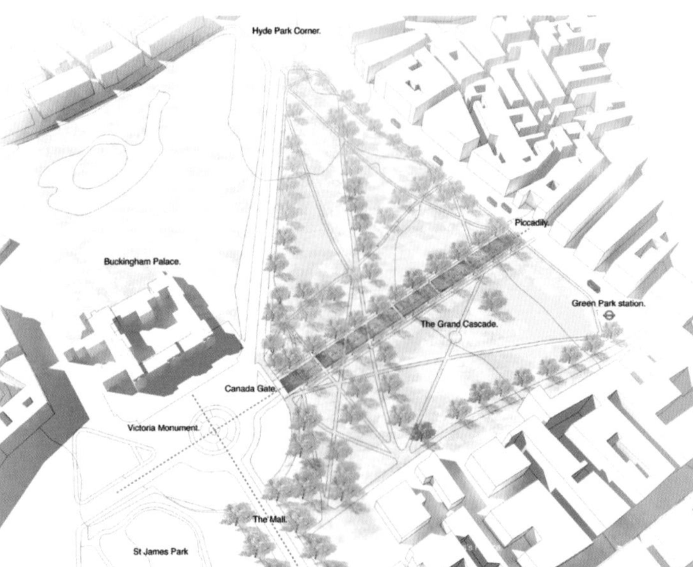

2009–2010
The Grand Cascade; Green Park; London

Green Park is the Cinderella of London's Royal Parks. Despite it being the most central, the closest to the West End, and having, uniquely, an underground station within its boundaries, it still remains the least memorable and least visited of all the parks.

In part this is because it sits between two more glamorous neighbours, St James's and Hyde Park, but in part too it is because it has no defining feature. There is no attractive circumambulation as there is in the other parks, no "walk around the lake and back" and hence few stroll there.

Furthermore, apart from two wonderful avenues of London plane trees, there is little to occupy the eye, no long vistas or features whereby to sit and muse, and there is insufficient distance from the noise of Piccadilly to make such a place tranquil.

The park has thus gradually been relegated into the pragmatic service of providing as short a route as possible for commuters and tourists between Green Park Underground and Buckingham Palace—and as a recreation ground at lunchtime and after work for nearby office workers.

To correct this, the proposal is to create a sequence of reflective pools that will cascade down the 10m (33ft) fall between the two avenues. The pools will be shallow enough to be safe and the fall of water will generate a delightful background noise to drown out the traffic.

At intervals during the day, a mist will be created over the pools like the mists over the Thames and then, as the mists clear, a series of multiple water cannons will project huge cascades of water over the pathways, ascending up the slope like a shoal of salmon leaping. At the top, when the last leap has been made, a row of spectacular fountains will erupt like geysers—like old faithful in Yosemite National Park.

Such will be the delight of this that Green Park may attain a new and unique character of it's own and people, instead of passing through it, may come to enjoy it, to circum-ambulate around it, and to embrace it as one of the most dramatic and compelling of London's sights.

This Page
Above, bottom left: plan of Green Park with the Grand Cascade; *above, bottom right:* The salmon leap beginning; *above, top right:* The mist forming; above, *top left:* The reflective pools viewed from the top.

Opposite Page
Top: the reflective pools viewed from below;
Bottom, far left: one of the grand avenues of Plane trees;
Middle left: the central space looking down towards The Victoria Monument;
middle right: the Victoria Monument behind Canada Gates;
Far right: Buckingham palace.

Footnotes to Chapter 8
The Museum of the Moving Image (MOMI) 1984–1988

This world famous museum (MOMI) was built under a fast-track 'design, manage and construct' contract with a timetable from first instruction to submission for planning of twelve weeks. Almost uniquely for a project of this size, the funding came entirely from private donations, just sufficient at commencement for a simply serviced shell covering 40,000ft^2. (3,716m^2). As nobody was sure how successful the fund-raising would be, the design had to have the flexibility to grow incrementally during the construction process. So successful was it, that it eventually grew to encompass a fully air-conditioned building covering 55,000ft^2 (5,110m^2.) with an additional undercroft, a small experimental cinema (The Image Workshop) and a temporary exhibitions gallery.

The 'Image Workshop' was technically a very difficult design challenge. The cinema had to be completely silent yet there was a huge amount of traffic on the bridge just overhead and the ceiling had to be demountable—and waterproof too. It was arguably the most innovative and successful of the NFT auditoria. It had a motorised screen gantry to alter the focal length of the image and four screens of different specifications so that films from different periods could be matched more accurately. It also had a glass wall to the colonnade so that films could be seen from the street outside at night.

The intention had been to operate the museum in synergy with the IMAX thereby sharing audiences, but just as the IMAX opened, the museum was unaccountably closed. (pp. 2–3, 61, 84–85, 112–117)

The BFI London IMAX Cinema 1991–1999

This 500 seat large screen IMAX cinema was built for the British Film Institute (BFI) and opened in May 1999. It is by far the largest screen in Britain and, at 67ft high (20.4m) by 90ft 7in (27.6m) wide, it is also one of the largest in the world.

The first design used a standard Imax prefabricated metal enclosure, mounted on a platform and simply overclad. With its circular plan reflecting the roundabout, it was covered entirely in vegetation with a metalwork structure that spiralled to support a hydroponics watering system and automatic leaf trimmers.

The aim was to 'green' this part of the South Bank's urban jungle with Japanese honeysuckle, a hardy evergreen which bears tiny white flowers and has a delicate and delightful fragrance.

However, visitor research indicated that the project not only needed a dramatic form to be viable but if a form could be created that also gave clues to the building content, rather then one that was purely abstract, it would generate an extra 200,000 visitors a year. This led to gradual pruning back of the vegetation to reveal more of the structure behind.

The pruning back eventually led to a 'butte' like scheme with a fabric-filled frame that rose from a 'scree' of vegetation. However, whilst the giant back-projected images expressed the Imax function well at night, it remained unanimated by day.

The penultimate stage model shows the vegetation pruned back even further and the introduction of a glazed gallery to create a contiguity with MOMI, the image wall here being wrapped around the building in a manner of a colonnaded rotunda. This not only resolved the night/day identity issue but made it possible to express, through the building's form, the meaning of the IMAX.

Thus the shallow domed roof was used to express the large public volume within, in the manner of the Pantheon, and the rotunda-form made reference both to classical structures like Bramante's Tempietto in S. Pietro in Montorio, Rome, as well as to filmic structures like cycloramas and the panoramic nature of the Imax format. Similarly, by suspending the external glazing from huge brackets at the top it was possible to allude both to the triglyphs of a temple entablature and to the slots in a "zoetrope" (one of the earliest rotary filmic experiments from which the film strip was eventually derived).

This rotary motion is also implied in both film making and film showing, and in such devices as the rotary image projector and carousel—a term that alludes also to the 'merry-go-round' and thus to entertainment—the essence, in effect, of the Imax experience. The word "carousel" in English also means "roundabout" (a traffic circle): a particularly apt form here, as the building does not rotate, but the observer and thus the image, does.

In the fifth and final scheme these references are all explored and developed further in a language that also expressed the advanced technological nature of the Imax system. The building thus has the necessary stature to command the urban space surrounding it and has, as a result, already become a key catalyst in the social and economic regeneration of the area.

The public spaces around the base of the building were no less important. The aim was to counterpoint the bleak concrete fastnesses of the South Bank with a new garden 'oasis', like Xanadu, a fabulously planted space at the end of the labyrinth of tunnels.

Five Artists were commissioned, one per tunnel, to explore the theme of Eurydice (Orpheus and the underworld) and the last remaining artwork, a poem by Sue Hubbard, lasted until September 2009 before it was painted over.

The huge mural by Sir Howard Hodgin that originally adorned the building and was intended as the first of an annual commission to encourage new urban-scale artists, was eventually taken down in 2006 and replaced by commercial advertising. (pp. 8, 56–57, 118–125, 146)

Project Awards:

7–10 Old Bailey

Chicago Athenaeum International Architecture Award: Judged as one of the 95 most significant new buildings in the world 2010.
Civic Trust Commendation 2010

London Transport Museum

Museums & Heritage Awards Winner; "Best New Permanent Gallery" 2008

RADA

RIBA Award 2001
Camden Design Award 2001
Camden Building Quality Awards 2003- for Excellence in Inclusive Design
The ADAPT Trust Access Award 2001
USITT Award 2003–United States Institute of Theatre Technicians
BIAT Award 2002 British Institute of Architectural Technologists open award for Technical Excellence in Achitectural Technology 2002
Civic Trust Commendation 2002
FX International Interior Design awards 2002

IMAX

Designated Landmark status by Westminster City Council 2010
British Construction Industry Award 1999
Comedia Creative City Award for Urban Innovation, May 2000
Civic Trust Award 2000
Millennium Products Award 1999
FX International Interior Design Award 1999
National Drywall Award 2001

Neathouse Place

Designated Landmark status by Westminster City Council 2010
British Council for Offices Award: Winner of best "Urban Workplace Building", May 1998
Westminster Society's Award 1997
Glassex Award, winner of "Best Building" category 1997
Millennium Products Award 1999
British Institute of Architectural Technologists Award 1999
Civic Trust Commendation 1998
The National Lighting Design Award 1997/98
Aluminium Imagination Architectural Award, winner of "The Shapemakers Award" 1997
British Construction Industry Award, "high commendation" 1997
Nominee MIPIM Awards 1998

National Film Theatre

Minerva Award 1994

Plantation House

City Heritage Award 1992

Museum of the Moving Image

Civic Trust Award 1989
PA Award for Innovation – Public Buildings category; for innovation in building design and construction 1988

Advanced Technology Housing

UNESCO Award 1985

Credits: Photographs:

Chapter (1)
p.011 RADA: Main image: Mark Tupper.

Chapter (2)
p.036 Africars: unattributable.
p.037 Pre-war labyrinthe: unattributable.

Chapter (4)
p.066 Charterhouse Mews: Martin Charles.
p.067 Charterhouse Mews: Martin Charles.
p.068 Plantation House: 3 photos: Peter Cook.
p.069 Plantation House: 8 photos: Peter Cook.
p.073 No. 1 Neathouse Place: 2 photos: Peter Cook.
p.074 No. 1 Neathouse Place: 1 photo: Peter Cook.
Chapter (5)
p.085 Plantation house: Fire point photo: Peter Cook.
p.090 No. 1 Neathouse Place: photo bottom left: Peter Cook.
p.092 No. 1 Neathouse Place: 2 photos bottom right and left: Peter Cook.

Chapter (7)
p.104 RADA: Mark Tupper.
p.106 RADA: top left photo: unattributable. Photo right and 2 at bottom left: Mark Tupper.
p.107 RADA: 3 photos (top two right and bottom): Mark Tupper.
p.108 RADA: main photo and bottom left photo (balcony) by Mark Tupper.
p.109 RADA: main picture: Mark Tupper.
p.110 RADA: Mark Tupper.
p.112 NFT: Foyer: Peter Cook.
p.113 NFT: Bookshop: Peter Cook.
p.119 IMAX: left, second from bottom: Tim Stallion.

Chapter (8)
p.140 Plantation House: Peter Cook.
p.144 Charterhouse Mews: Martin Charles.
p.144 RADA: Peter Cook.
p.146 NFT Foyer: Peter Cook.
p.146 RADA: Peter Cook.
p.148 RADA: Mark Tupper.
p.170 Royal Overseas League (all except the existing photo bottom right): Tim Stallion.

All other photographs are by Bryan Avery.

Credits: Paintings and Sketches

All paintings and sketches are by Bryan Avery. The remainder of the drawings, diagrams and illustrations are by Bryan Avery and the staff of Avery Associates.

Acknowledgements for the projects illustrated:

No work of architecture is achieved alone. A vast number of people are involved; manufacturers and suppliers, craftsmen and contractors, statutory bodies, consultants – a veritable army from all across the globe – and whilst it would be impossible to list them all, there are some who do deserve special recognition for their contribution to this body of work.

Clients:

(for the built works illustrated here only and, in view of which, they should probably be more accurately called Patrons):

The British Carpet Trade Centre: in particular Sir Tatton and Michael Brinton and Brian Shepherd.

The British Film Institute: in particular Lord Richard Attenborough; Anthony Smith; Leslie Hardcastle; Michael Prescott, Ian Temple and Paul Collard.

The British Land Co Ltd: in particular John Ritblat; Steven Kalman; Nigel Webb and Adrian Penfold.

Chesterfield Properties: in particular Roger Wingate, whose confidence in our design for No. 1 Neathouse Place was of critical importance in the practice's development; Rob Cossey; David Henderson-Williams; Guy Middleton and John Gamble.
The Commonwealth Institute: in particular David French and Paul Kennedy.

The Jerwood Foundation: in particular Alan Grieves.

The London Transport Museum: in particular Sam Mullins; Rob Lansdowne; Belinda Betts; Robert Millar; Oliver Green; Claire Ingham; Michael Walton and Liz Collins.

7-10 Old Bailey: Sidell Gibson, in particular Ron Sidell and Giles Downes.

The Royal Academy of Dramatic Art: in particular Lord Richard Attenborough, (without question the finest client the practice ever had the privilege to work with and without who's patronage there would have been very little built); Dr Oliver Neville; Nicholas Barter; Alan Rickman, Ellis Jones, Pat Myers and Giles Favell.

The Royal Overseas League: in particular Robert Newell and Roderick Lakin.

Contractors:

Bovis Construction
Du Boulay
Farrow Construction Ltd
Herbert Construction
John Laing
John Lelliot
Myton
MACE Ltd
Wates Construction Ltd

Structural Engineers:

Adams Kara Taylor
Anthony Hunt Associates (now SKM Anthony Hunt)
Baldock Quick
Buro Happold
Ove Arup and Partners

Services Engineers:

Cadogan Tietz
David Kutt and Partners
Fulcrum
Greatorex
Hall and Kay
John Brady Associates
Max Fordham
Ove Arup and Partners
Oscar Faber
R W Gregory
Roger Preston and Partners
Voce Case and Partners
YRM(E)/TME Engineering

Quantity Surveyors:

Davis Langdon
E C Harris
Gleeds
Leonard Stace
Northcrofts
Victor P Cockett
Walfords

Project Management:

Bovis DMC
Buro Four
Epsilon Management Services Ltd
Farrow Construction
MACE
Myton
Peter Finney Associates
Stanhope

Acoustics Consultants:

Applied Acoustic Design
Arup Associates
Bickerdike Alan
Paul Gillieron Acoustic Design
Museum Designers
Conran
Neil Potter
Ralph Appelbaum
Theatre Consultants
Charcoalblue
Iain Mackintosh
Theatre Projects
Landscape Consultants
John Medhurst

Access Consultants

All Clear Design
Andrew Walker

Lighting Consultants

DHA Design Services

Staff and Contributors to Projects (1976–2010)

Simon Adeyinka: John Ahern: Eze Angelo: Alain Bacon: Pedro Barreto: Bruno Berchi: Stephen Best: David Blanco: Chris Boddington: Maurice Brennan: Louise Broderick: Alan Camp: Anthony Carlile: Matt Cartwright: Michael Chadwick: Marie Clayton: Philip Coffey: Rob Cole: Arthur Collin: May Corrigan: John Dawson: Callum Davis: Ashanti Derby: Barry Edwards: Martin Edwards: Simon Ewings: Adam Firth: Gabriele Friedrich-Steen: Robin Gill: Adriana Gotowiecka: Simon Grout: Mark Gruenberg: Greg Hall: Mike Haste: Tim Healy: Amanda Henderson: Tom Hewitt: David Hines: John Howard: Julia Hwang: Guiseppi Intini: Redmond Ivie: Ian Kendall: Paul Kerr-Hislop: Andrew King: Matthew King: Marcus Kirk: Paula Kirkpatrick: Saskia Koopmann: Myriam Lengline: Yuon Fei Leow: Rennie Liffen: Sandra Loschka: John McDougall: Nancy Moorcroft: Louise Moore: Ellen Morgan: Lee Morris; Brian Murphy: Antoinette Nassopoulos: Michael Neale: Judith Newby: Jon Neville-Jones: Julian Odile: Karin Pahl: Louise Potter: John Randle: Gary Reading: Emma Reale: Thiery Reinhardt: Garry Reynolds: Delia Richardson: Ruth Rigler: Paul Scott: Louise Spearing: Wes Spees: Mary Stutter: Paul Summerlin: Lucy Thompson: Tim Thompson: Simon Toussaint: Tim Uden: Lindsay Urquhart: Chiara Vittucci: Mike Walter: Ian West: Mark Whiteley: Geoff Whittaker: Warren Whyte: Louise Williams: Debbie Willmore: Marcus Wilshere: Brian Wilson: Jennie Witchell: Peter Witham: Steve Wright.

Acknowledgements for the Book:

It will come as no surprise to those who have published before to hear that the compilation of this book has proved to be unexpectedly demanding, and without help of the highest calibre, it is doubtful whether it would ever have been published at all. The person who should be thanked above all others is Duncan McCorquodale of Black Dog Publishing. His good humoured patience in the face of protracted procrastination is beyond all understanding.

Others without whom this book would never have happened are Gabriele Friedrich-Steen and Jenny Witchell, whose enthusiasm and painstaking researches provided the essential backbone to the story, and Anthony Carlile, a brilliant young post-graduate architect who took the manuscripts, layouts and images and, armed only with an Apple Mac, page grid and unwavering energy, transformed them all into the book that you see before you.

Index:

Printed in China by Everbest Printing Co.Ltd

British Library Cataloguing-in-Publication Data. A CIP record for this book is available from the British Library.

ISBN 978 1 904772 58 3